Chefs of the Mountains

JOHN F. BLAIR, PUBLISHER
Winston-Salem, North Carolina

Chefs of the
Mountains

Restaurants and Recipes from
Western North Carolina

JOHN E. BATCHELOR

JOHN F. BLAIR,

PUBLISHER
1406 Plaza Drive
Winston-Salem, North Carolina 27103
www.blairpub.com

COVER PHOTOGRAPH
  Pimientos de Piquillo by Chef Katie Button of Cúrate, Asheville / Photo by Peter Frank Edwards
FACING PAGE
  Lobster Ramen by Chef Nicholas Figel of Cyprus, Highlands / Photo by Clinton O'Brien, Fonck Films
Page x
  Photo from The Painted Fish, Banner Elk, by Heather Turner

PAGE ii, CLOCKWISE FROM TOP:
  Randall Isaacs of The 1861 Farmhouse, Valle Crucis; Patrick Bagbey of Louisiana Purchase, Banner Elk; Michael Barbato of Chetola Resort, Blowing Rock; Nicole Palazzo of Sorrento's Bistro, Banner Elk
PAGE iii AT TOP:
  Josh Emerline of Best Cellar, Blowing Rock; Sean Ruddy of High Hampton Inn and Country Club, Cashiers
PAGE iii AT BOTTOM, CLOCKWISE:
  Judd Lohof of Café Azalea, Asheville; Katie Button of Cúrate, Asheville; Damien Cavicchi of Biltmore, Asheville; James Welch of Green Park Inn, Blowing Rock

Library of Congress Cataloging-in-Publication Data

Batchelor, John E. , 1947- author.
  Chefs of the mountains : restaurants and recipes from Western North Carolina / by John E. Batchelor.
    pages   cm
  Includes indexes.
  ISBN 978-0-89587-581-5 (alk. paper) — ISBN 978-0-89587-582-2 (ebook) 1. Cooks—North Carolina, Western—Biography. 2. Restaurants—North Carolina, Western—Guidebooks. 3. North Carolina, Western—Guidebooks. 4. Cooking—North Carolina, Western. I. Title.
  TX649.A1B38 2012
  641.5092'2756—dc23

                    2012020466

10 9 8 7 6 5 4 3 2 1
Design by Debra Long Hampton

*For my wife,
who accompanies me
when I review restaurants and
eats my cooking at home*

Western North Carolina

Valle Crucis
Boone
Banner Elk
Blowing Rock
Spruce Pine
Linville
26
Hot Springs
Asheville
40
Waynesville
Hendersonville
Saluda
Cashiers
Flat Rock
Highlands

N

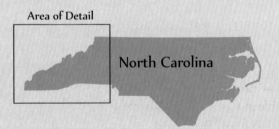

Area of Detail

North Carolina

Contents

Preface

I am not a chef. I do not want to be a chef. Chefs put in too many hours on their feet, labor too late at night, and in general just work too hard. But I appreciate what chefs do, and I very much enjoy the products of their work.

That is the subject of the first section of each profile in this book. What sparked such a strong interest in cooking? How did that interest lead to a career? How did they learn, how did they train, who influenced them along the way, how do they approach their craft, and how do they create recipes? Some fascinating stories come to light here, from a young man who escaped East Germany barely a week before the Wall went up; to a chef who met his wife when a waitress told a group of women that the best dessert was not on the menu but rather the new guy in the kitchen; and to a young lady who left a rarified academic track to spend time in kitchens that led her into some of the world's best restaurants.

The book is also about the restaurants where these chefs work—the concepts that underlie the establishments, the ambience they convey, what the menus offer, what is unique about the food. The mountains of North Carolina are home to some great restaurants, as well as some wonderful inns and hotels that serve excellent food. They are well represented in these pages.

Finally, although I do not want to be a chef, I would like to be able to cook like one on occasion for friends, for family, or maybe just for myself. That is what the rest of this book is about. The chefs have provided recipes characteristic of their restaurants, formatted for the home cook, with careful directions. The recipes range from the simple to the complex. Anyone can find something interesting and fun to cook in these pages. Ambitious cooks will have the means to replicate in their own homes dishes from some of the South's—indeed, some of the nation's—best restaurants. Careful attention is paid to presentation as well as preparation. These dishes will look professional on your table, in addition to having professional-quality taste. Chefs, restaurant owners and managers, and in some cases professional public-relations officers were given multiple opportunities to review relevant portions of my manuscript drafts and to check and recheck the content, especially the recipes. I often found that steps that are second nature to chefs need to be explicitly stated for home cooks. I hope readers find the directions logical and easy to follow.

In order to select chefs and restaurants for initial screening, I used participation in the Western North Carolina Chef's Challenge and the Fire on the Rock Chef's Challenge. The Western North Carolina Chef's Challenge includes the area in and around Asheville; information about the competition can be found at www.wncmagazine.com/wineandfood/tickets. Fire on the Rock focuses on restaurants in and around Blowing Rock and the High Country; information is available at www.fireontherock.com. I highly recommend these informative and entertaining events to anyone interested in food, cooking, and dining. My wife says my cooking improved noticeably after I started judging them. I also looked at chefs who have entered the Best Dish North Carolina competition (www.bestdishnc.com). Then I looked at several websites, including those of the Foodtopian Society, the Asheville Independent Restaurant Association, Carolina Epicurean, and Select Registry, as well as sites that rate restaurants, inns, and hotels. I also contacted restaurants recommended to me by friends, readers of my restaurant review columns, and other restaurant professionals. Of course, I also considered my own acquaintance with restaurants in the mountains.

A small number of restaurants I contacted said they were not interested. Some others never responded at all, in spite of repeated efforts to contact them. Of those that did respond, a few never got around to completing materials, participating in interviews, or writing up and submitting recipes. I nevertheless wound up with over 40 highly interesting restaurants and chefs who supplied some genuinely intriguing stories and recipes that I have enjoyed cooking. To those chefs who completed their homework, I would like to voice a strong thank-you. If you know someone who might be interested but did not participate, or if you represent a restaurant and would like to participate in the future, please contact me at john.e.batchelor@gmail.com.

No chef or restaurant paid anything to participate in this book. The information in the chef and restaurant profiles came from oral and written interviews, from restaurant websites, and in some cases from personal visits.

In the process of researching the book, I found a culture that is devoted to local foods. Given the rural nature of much of western North Carolina, that is understandable. But the chefs often revealed a passion for fresh ingredients grown or raised nearby that was stronger than I have encountered in other locations. It is fairly common to see "farm to table" off-menu specials prepared from local ingredients in restaurants throughout North Carolina and elsewhere. But in these pages, you will encounter restaurants that frequently organize their entire menus and core concepts around partnerships with local farms.

In addition to introducing the chefs and their restaurants, I use sidebars to describe 10 sample farms, cooperatives, and producers that I consider unique. I chose these particular operations either because chefs mentioned them by name or because I became familiar with them in the course of my research. I tried to include producers who sell directly to the public, from websites, at farmers' markets, or from retail outlets. Consider using their products when you prepare these recipes.

Communities in North Carolina benefit from chefs' orientations toward locally produced foods as farmers struggle to transition from a tobacco-dominated system to a much more diversified one that includes vegetables, fruits, grapes for wine, and pastured animals. Many farms operate in a manner now called "organic." But as farmers point out in the sidebars, what they are doing is what their families did a couple of generations back. I also discovered a generational phenomenon of family members moving off the farm, often going to college and starting careers, but eventually returning to the land and readopting a lifestyle and an approach to farming closely mirroring those from a hundred or more years ago.

I have been interested in North Carolina restaurants (as well as restaurants elsewhere) all my life. I have been writing about restaurants for 30 years. I have been the restaurant reviewer for both the *News and Record* of Greensboro and the *Winston-Salem Journal.* About a thousand of my articles on dining, food, and wine have been published in these newspapers as well as in regional and national magazines. My reviews have been selected for reprinting in a best-selling college composition textbook and in other instructional materials as models for expository writing. In addition, I have written occasional articles about travel, and I host groups on trips related to food and wine. See my blog, http://johnbatchelordiningandtravel. blogspot.com/, for more information.

But above all, I enjoy cooking and eating!

Chefs of the
Mountains

Blowing Rock

Josh Emerline

Josh Emerline
Photo by
John Batchelor

Best Cellar

203 Sunset Drive
Blowing Rock, N.C. 28605
828-295-9703
www.ragged-gardens.com

The Chef

Josh Emerline is a Raleigh native. While a student at Appalachian State University, he was recruited to the Best Cellar by his brother, who was already working for owners Rob Dyer and Lisa Stripling, who had bought the restaurant in 1997.

Josh washed dishes for two years. Eventually deciding he did not want to be "the last person out every night," he asked the chef to help him learn to work on the line. He started out cutting up vegetables, then made stocks and soups, then moved into sauces. After about five years, he was promoted to sous chef.

Being a sous chef generated an ambition to become a head chef. Josh's aunt lived in Florida, near a culinary school. He began making arrangements for formal training there. But when Best Cellar's chef departed, Rob and Lisa offered him the head chef position, and he decided to accept that role instead of going to school. "They are just great people to work for," Josh says. He has remained at Best Cellar as head chef for eight years.

Josh had read Anthony Bourdain's *Kitchen Confidential.* "It really influenced me, opened my eyes to what a chef can do and be," he says. "I also saw a side of the kitchen in that book that I had not experienced. His stories about conflict, about crazy things happening, were just so entertaining."

Josh's decision to stay with Best Cellar was to some extent a product of a summer working at Planet Hollywood in Myrtle Beach. "I saw a huge difference comparing a volume kitchen, with a lot of prepared foods, to what we had been doing at Best Cellar," he says. "At Planet Hollywood, I spent almost all my time microwaving brownies, versus everything made from scratch in a smaller setting the way we do at Best Cellar."

Friendships at the restaurant constitute one of the most appealing aspects of Josh's work as a chef. And he loves living in the mountains. "If you don't like the weather, just wait a little while and it will change. Within 10 minutes of anywhere around here, I can find a hiking trail and spend the rest of the day in silence in nature. And of course, the local people are great. Everybody waves when you walk by."

When not cooking at Best Cellar, Josh likes "anything Italian," he says.

"My uncle lives in D.C. His mother is a short, small Italian lady, and I remember her meatballs like yesterday, they are so delicious." He goes out to other restaurants on dates but tends to stay home when he's alone. "If I cook at home, for myself, it's usually breakfast. I snack all the time at work, because I taste what I am cooking. If I would not eat it, I won't serve it."

The Restaurant

The Best Cellar is the restaurant inside the historic Inn at Ragged Gardens in downtown Blowing Rock. A large, open fireplace occupies the center of the living room. Stone columns and floors support chestnut-paneled walls. Many of the furnishings are antique. Overnight accommodations are available in 13 guest rooms.

The several small dining areas yield an intimate ambience. The main dining room and a smaller annex look out into the lighted flower garden, which is lovely in three seasons. Seating in another room surrounds an open fireplace. A "cave" area, completely enclosed in the cellar, is especially well suited for private events. The wine cellar features one large table in the center of the restaurant's large wine collection.

Thinking about his approach to cooking and the concept behind the restaurant menu, Josh concludes, "I just want everybody to leave happy and full." The kitchen makes sauces such as Béarnaise and hollandaise from scratch. "It took awhile to get those two right," Josh says. "But the most tedious sauce is demi-glace. We bake off veal bones for about three hours, transfer them to a stockpot, then add wine and vegetables and seasonings. Everything is simmered about seven hours. We strain it, then reduce the liquid several more hours until it reaches the consistency we want."

The Best Cellar utilizes beef and sometimes other meats from nearby North Fork Farm (see page 56) in the summer. Fresh pastas are prepared by The Pasta Wench (see page 99). Produce comes from Lett Us Produce in Boone, which buys from local farmers.

Josh was the subject of a feature article in *Bangle*, a local magazine for women.

The Recipes

Prosciutto-Stuffed Pork Chop with Hot Red Pepper Relish
Serves 2

Stuffing
⅔ cup chopped fresh basil
6 slices prosciutto, diced
⅔ cup provolone cheese

Hot Red Pepper Relish
3 red bell peppers, diced
enough olive oil to brush peppers
2 tablespoons unsalted butter
1 teaspoon minced garlic
2 tablespoons minced fresh rosemary

Pork chop
2 7- to 10-ounce pork chops, bone in
2 teaspoons salt
2 teaspoons pepper
1 teaspoon garlic powder
pinch of oregano

STUFFING

Mix all ingredients in a small bowl. Set aside.

HOT RED PEPPER RELISH

Slice peppers open and remove seeds. Cut into quarters. Brush with olive oil. Roast peppers at 400 degrees for 8 to 10 minutes until skin begins to blister. Allow to cool, then peel skin. Cut peeled peppers into ¼-inch-wide strips. Melt butter in a saucepan over medium heat. Add garlic, rosemary, and roasted red peppers to melted butter. Sauté about 2 minutes until soft.

Cut a small opening on side of pork chop. If cut is too big, stuffing will slide out when it gets hot. Insert as much stuffing as possible. Sprinkle with salt, pepper, garlic powder, and oregano. Preheat oven to 400 degrees. Bake pork chop for 30 to 40 minutes until a meat thermometer inserted into thick portion reads about 155 degrees.

TO PRESENT

Spread relish in center of plate. Place pork chop over relish. Suggested side vegetable: mashed potatoes.

Prosciutto-Stuffed Pork Chop with Hot Red Pepper Relish
Photo by John Batchelor

Sautéed Pineapple and Orange with Bourbon Butter Sauce
Photo by John Batchelor

Sautéed Pineapple and Orange with Bourbon Butter Sauce

    1 tablespoon unsalted butter
    ½ cup pineapple chunks
    ⅓ cup orange slices (small)
    2 tablespoons brown sugar
    ½ teaspoon cinnamon
    2 teaspoons bourbon
    1 large scoop vanilla ice cream

Melt butter in a saucepan over medium heat. Add pineapple, orange slices, brown sugar, and cinnamon. As soon as sugar begins to caramelize, add bourbon. Expect a flame. Let simmer for a few seconds. Serve over ice cream.

Michael Barbato

Michael Barbato
*Photo provided by
Chetola Resort*

Chetola Resort

North Main Street
500 Main Street
P.O. Box 17
Blowing Rock, N.C. 28605
800-243-8652
www.chetola.com

The Chef

Michael Barbato, a Boston native, started out as an engineering major in college and began cooking while he was in the army from 1975 to 1978. He reasoned that anything he actually enjoyed in the army had career potential. When he got out of the service, he went to the Culinary Institute of America in Hyde Park, New York.

Michael spent the early 1980s at The Breakers in Palm Beach, Florida, gaining expertise in banquet production, as well as breads and pastries, soups, sauces, and cold food preparation in the context of German, French, and American menus. His primary role eventually became that of saucier. Each day, he prepared at least 50 gallons of demi-glace, veal stock, and chicken stock, portions of which would be combined and reduced to two cups each of several dozen different sauces. At the end of a nine- to 10-hour day on sauces, he would clock out, then wander down to the bakery and prepare pastries for another three or four hours for no salary, partly in order to learn baking but mostly just because he enjoyed it.

During this period, he earned his certified executive chef's degree through the American Culinary Federation. He was a culinary team member for three functions of the Chaines des Rotisseurs International Gastronomic Society.

Michael recalls one particularly amusing incident from that time. The executive chef was Hungarian. In a kitchen that was producing over a thousand covers per night, the chef would expedite by calling out orders to the line over a microphone. Miscommunications occurred on occasion. One night, a cook on the line prepared three servings of an order. The exec started hollering, "I need six! I need six!" But because of his accent, everyone heard, "I need sex! I need sex!" The line cook called back, "Chef, I can't help you!"

Michael began his life in the North Carolina mountains in Asheville working at the Grove Park Inn in the late 1980s. He spent the mid-1990s in Pittsburgh, Pennsylvania, first with the Westin and Sheraton hotel chains before operating Peppercorns, a 60-seat bistro, with his wife. He returned to a large-scale setting at St. Claire Country Club near Pittsburgh after 2000.

He had often ventured into the High Country to ski while he worked in Asheville. In 2007, he returned to the area to work at Chetola Resort in Blowing Rock. "I really enjoy the quaintness of a mid-sized restaurant such as the one at Chetola, which enables our culinary staff to prepare 99 percent of our items from scratch," he says.

Even now, Michael bakes for fun. One December, he researched fruit cakes and made several, including a Czechoslovakian version that turned out to be the most interesting. "It has to be mixed, then it rests 24 hours, then it is actually baked the next night. After that, it cures with rum and scotch for another week. I serve them for friends and at the resort during Christmas week."

Chef Barbato strives for what he calls "clean cooking." He remarks, "I would not be good in a classic French restaurant because I don't like a lot of heavy sauces with lots of butter and cream. Even when I was in culinary school, during a time when those sauces were popular, I did not like them. I have embraced fresh flavors from the beginning. And especially during the past 10 years, I have tried to focus on quality of health in my recipes. We have implemented a spa menu at Chetola that appeals to some because it is low fat, low calorie.

"I actually like to prepare a different menu every day—just find out what is fresh and build a menu around it. We do that here at Chetola with the Chef's Table. The clients tell us what they want, and we do the rest, especially with wine pairings. We have been offering this service for three years, and it has gone over well. The new kitchen will have a window with a special table for seating at least four guests in the kitchen. Of course, some customers have a favorite dish, and we always accommodate them, so there will always be some repeat items on the menu."

When creating a menu for himself and his family, Michael likes seafood. But in particular, he loves to make pizza. "I found a brand of Italian semolina flour recently, and it makes a crust that is just fabulous. I had heard about it but never used it, and as soon as I started mixing it, it was silky and buttery even without adding olive oil. The first crust came out better than any other I had prepared."

Michael was raised in an Italian family, so much of what he does grows out of that tradition. "We bought a whole pig from one of the local farms recently and made our own prosciutto this winter. The quality of the meat you can get around here is just great!" He is pleased that Blowing Rock has a close-knit chefs' community. "We visit each other, we share ideas," he relates. When he learned that a young, new chef in Blowing Rock was struggling with bread making, he went over and provided baking lessons for several afternoons.

The Restaurant

Chetola Resort spans 87 acres overlooking a pristine lake on the edge of downtown Blowing Rock. The name comes from a Cherokee word meaning "haven of rest." A way station and stable operated on the property before the Civil War. They were expanded into a summer inn prior to 1890. In 1892, new owners turned the property into a private residence. It remained a sanctuary for subsequent owners until the 1920s. J. Luther Snyder, known as "the Coca-Cola King of North Carolina," bought the estate in 1926. The Snyder family hosted important Blowing Rock social events through the 1940s. Chetola remained a family holding until 1972. Ten years later, it became a resort open to the public. In 1997, Rachael Renar and her son, Kent Tarbutton, from Virginia Beach, purchased the resort. They continue to expand its facilities.

Chetola was operating the casual Headwaters Pub and the Manor House fine-dining venue when a fire severely damaged the kitchen in August 2011. It is expected to reopen in the spring of 2012. In addition to continued casual options, a new formal restaurant will open. Since 2004, Chetola has been affiliated with Bob Timberlake, one of North Carolina's most famous artists. Timberlake's, the new fine-dining restaurant, will be decorated in harmony with the painter's celebrations of rural and mountain life in North Carolina. Food will include some game meats—elk, for example, at least in winter—as well as game birds such as pheasant and quail.

The restaurants at Chetola have always sought local suppliers. Today, they buy produce, meats, and cheeses from New River Organic Growers (see page 34). The kitchen purchases chickens, eggs, cheeses, and Angus beef from Mountain Memories Farm in Elk Creek, Virginia. The chefs grind beef to make hamburger patties in-house. With the exception of some sliced bread for sandwiches, all breads, including burger buns, are prepared on the premises. The kitchen blends homemade ketchup from local tomatoes. Tended by Chetola's groundskeepers, a garden of about 400 square feet produces tomatoes, zucchini, squash, peppers, cucumbers, pole beans, eggplant, and herbs. Chetola maintains an additional 12-acre vegetable plot on the owners' property nearby.

Southern Living has rated Chetola "one of the best stays in the Blue Ridge." One of the resort's recipes was selected for publication in the *Orvis Guide to Great Sporting Lodge Cuisine*. Chef Barbato has provided cooking demonstrations on WBIR-NBC television in Knoxville, Tennessee. And the Chetola team won the Fire on the Rock Chef's Challenge in 2011.

The Recipes

Grilled Bison Loin with Maple and Bacon Bourbon Butter
Serves 2

> 1 tablespoon cracked pepper
> 1 tablespoon honey
> 1 tablespoon kosher salt
> 1 tablespoon minced garlic
> 12-ounce bison strip loin steak, cut into two portions
> ½ cup minced yellow onion
> 1 tablespoon butter
> 2 slices high-quality bacon
> ¼ cup salted butter, softened

2 tablespoons maple syrup
2 tablespoons bourbon
fried or sautéed Vidalia onions for topping (optional)

Combine pepper, honey, salt, and garlic to create a rub. Rub steak with mixture. Sauté onions in 1 tablespoon butter in a small pan until light brown. Place in a small bowl. Cook and rough-chop bacon. Place bacon in a medium bowl. When bacon is cool, add softened butter, maple syrup, and bourbon. Add onions to bacon mixture; combine and chill. Grill bison steak to your liking; medium-rare works well. Top with a scoop of butter mixture and fried or sautéed sweet onions, if desired.

Grilled Bison Loin
Photo by Chetola Resort

Grilled Boar Tenderloin with Blackberry Glaze and Pear, Red Pepper, and Bacon Slaw
Serves 2

Boar
>   1 cup apple juice
>   1 tablespoon dried ground thyme
>   1 tablespoon dried sage
>   1 tablespoon paprika
>   black pepper to taste
>   kosher salt to taste
>   8-ounce boar tenderloin

Blackberry Glaze
>   1 cup diced yellow onion
>   ½ cup chardonnay
>   1 cup fresh blackberries
>   1 teaspoon mesquite spice
>   1 teaspoon thyme leaf
>   1 teaspoon minced garlic
>   1 teaspoon ground cumin seed
>   1 tablespoon chili powder

Pear, Red Pepper, and Bacon Slaw
>   1 red pepper, julienned
>   2 tablespoons julienned red onion
>   1 tablespoon minced garlic
>   ¼ cup cider vinegar
>   ½ cup chardonnay
>   1 red pear, cored and sliced thin, skin on
>   1 cup bacon, cooked and chopped
>   2 tablespoons maple syrup
>   1 tablespoon lemon juice
>   2 cups shredded Napa cabbage
>   salt and pepper to taste

BOAR

Combine first 6 ingredients in a glass bowl with a lid with boar tenderloin. Marinate for 2 hours.

Grilled Boar Tenderloin
Photo by Chetola Resort

Blackberry Glaze

Combine all ingredients and simmer 2 to 3 minutes. Remove from heat and chill.

Pear, Red Pepper, and Bacon Slaw

Add red peppers, onions, and garlic to a medium-sized pan. Sweat in pan with vinegar and chardonnay. Toward end of sweating, add pear, bacon, maple syrup, lemon juice, and cabbage. Toss gently. Adjust to taste with salt and pepper.

To present

Grill boar tenderloin to medium-rare (internal temperature 145 degrees). Allow to rest 3 minutes. Slice boar. Place slaw in center of plates. Place boar on top of slaw. Ladle sliced boar with Blackberry Glaze.

Apple Brandy Beef

3746 Mountain View Road
North Wilkesboro, N.C. 28659
336-696-2721
www.applebrandybeef.com

Seth and Jenn Church have operated Apple Brandy Beef since they graduated from college in 2004. Seth grew up on the family farm, then went to North Carolina State University, where he earned a degree in agriculture business management. He met his wife, Jenn, at N.C. State. Her degree is in animal science. She also operates Hidden Creek Stables (www.hiddencreekstables.net), a facility for riding lessons and horse training.

Apple Brandy Beef is truly a family business. For the first two years of the operation, Seth's mother and aunt made all the deliveries, in order to hold down costs. Seth's mother is still the bookkeeper, Jenn handles advertising and web design, and Seth's father, although supposedly retired, is on hand every day. The operation has now grown enough to add an employee for deliveries.

The Churches share pasture land with other family farms that raise cattle of the same breeds. The Apple Brandy Beef line is the "best of the best" of the cattle raised on the property. The Hereford and Angus cattle eat all-natural diets completely free of animal by-products. "For generations, our family has selected specific genetics in an effort to produce a superior cow herd," the Apple Brandy Beef website says. "We know the pedigree and complete history, including exact age, of each animal that goes into our beef program. On our farms we do not use synthetic hormones or antibiotics, except for medical necessity."

Cattle are finished on a specially formulated diet that enhances marbling and flavor. They are harvested at an appropriate age, then the meat is dry-aged for a minimum of 14 days. Cattle are processed at Thomas Brothers Abattoir in North Wilkesboro, a fourth-generation family business that is USDA-inspected and -certified.

The Chop Shop in Asheville is the Apple Brandy Beef retail outlet. Beef packages can also be purchased directly from the website and shipped frozen. Christmas gifts of frozen packaged beef are especially popular. Orders from the website are shipped all over the United States.

Stan Chamberlain

Stan Chamberlain
*Photo by Des Keller
Courtesy of
Crippen's
Country Inn
& Restaurant*

Crippen's Country Inn & Restaurant

239 Sunset Drive
Blowing Rock, N.C. 28605
877-295-3487

The Chef

Stan Chamberlain grew up in his grandparents' BBQ restaurant, the popular Bill Stanley's Barbecue and Bluegrass in Asheville. In Stan's family, "food was always a way to bring people together," he recalls. "Everyone was in the kitchen cooking dinner, not just one person with everyone else scattered about the house." As he got older, he developed a love of fine dining from going out to dinner with his parents and other family members. Those experiences led him to start reading about cooking and restaurants.

He learned to cook primarily from his grandparents by helping with barbecue catering while he was in high school. Before graduating from Appalachian State University, he worked part-time at the Red Onion Café in Boone. "There, I learned how much fun restaurant work can be. It was at the Red Onion that I decided I wanted to be a chef. And I realized that in order to do that, I needed to learn much more that I knew at the time. After the Red Onion, I went to work at Crippen's for James Welch. This is where I became a perfectionist, because at a place like this, it has to be perfect." Stan moved from Crippen's to Storie Street Grille. "There, I learned about management and volume. After working for Storie Street for a couple of years, I was invited to come back to Crippen's as chef.

"Crippen's is a place where you can get food that you can't get anywhere else. I want my menu to be different. That's why I stay away from fried green tomatoes, for example. You can get them at too many other places nearby. People expect more from Crippen's. I try to let ingredients drive the menu ideas. When something great comes in, I want the customers to be as excited about it as I am. I want the customers to see how great something can be, whether it's beef tongue or watermelon."

During the summer, when the restaurant experiences a lot of traffic, Stan doesn't cook at home often. But in the off-season, "I cook for my wife and kids," he says. "My kids are not too picky, so that is fun. They will try just about anything. Mondays are 'Meatless Monday,' so that helps with health and weight."

The Restaurant

Owner Jimmy Crippen sums up his duties in two words: "Booze and schmooze." He is quite a personality, greeting regulars as well as new guests, circulating constantly to provide hospitality and entertainment. Significant renovations in 2010 and 2011 have softened the ambience and generally made both the inn and restaurant more comfortable. On most nights, a pianist plays in the bar.

Upstairs, Crippen's Country Inn provides bed-and-breakfast-style lodging in eight guest rooms. A cottage adjacent to the main building has its own separate entrance. The ground floor houses the restaurant. A sofa lounge is to the left of the entryway. Additional sofas face the fireplace to the right, leading into the bar. Down the hall past the kitchen, a single large dining room provides some of the mountains' best food. The décor fits the country-inn theme.

Chef Chamberlain took the helm at Crippen's in 2010. Since his arrival, the restaurant has been invited to supply recipes for a dinner at the American embassy in Denmark. Ambassador Jim Caine is a regular Crippen's customer. Crippens tied for third place in the 2011 Best Dish North Carolina competition.

The kitchen uses produce from New River Organic Growers (see page 34) as much as possible. "It's tough here because the growing season is much shorter and winters are cold and often harsh. But using local, seasonal food makes menu creation easier because it gives us some direction," explains Chef Chamberlain.

Jimmy Crippen's family had a vacation home in Blowing Rock, so it was a fairly natural step to relocate to the mountains after he spent time at Mark's Place in Miami. Jimmy conceived and initiated the Fire on the Rock Chef's Challenge. The restaurant hosts challenge events on Tuesday and Wednesday nights during February, March, and early April, at which diners join professional judges to complete rating sheets on each of three dishes prepared by each chef, for a total of six courses. The results eventually determine the two finalists. Crippen's has often hosted guest chefs, including several James Beard Award winners.

Jicama-Crusted Mahi-Mahi
Photo by Des Keller
Courtesy of Crippen's Country Inn & Restaurant

The Recipes

Jicama-Crusted Mahi-Mahi with Watermelon Couscous, Shaved Radish, and Watermelon Vinaigrette
Serves 4

Shaved Radish
¼ cup sliced red radish, cut into thin strips
¼ cup sliced daikon radish, cut into thin strips

Watermelon Couscous
1 medium watermelon
1 cup Israeli couscous
½ cup sugar

Watermelon Vinaigrette
    1 shallot, chopped fine
    1 tablespoon sugar
    ¼ cup red wine vinegar
    ½ cup extra-virgin olive oil

Mahi-mahi
    2 tablespoons olive oil
    ½ teaspoon kosher salt
    4 pieces mahi-mahi
    1 cup grated fresh jicama

    4 cups thinly sliced salad greens
    black sea salt (optional)

Shaved Radish

Toss ingredients together.

Watermelon Couscous

Cut watermelon in half. Remove seeds and rind. Set 1 half aside. Cut other half into pieces small enough for the blender. Purée watermelon to liquid consistency. Strain to remove any pieces. Combine couscous, 2 cups watermelon juice, and sugar in a saucepan. Set aside additional watermelon juice to use later. Bring mixture to a boil over medium-high heat. Cook for 2 minutes. Remove from heat and cover with a tight-fitting lid. Bring to room temperature. Chill.

Watermelon Vinaigrette

Combine shallots, 1 cup of reserved watermelon juice, and sugar in a bowl or large measuring cup. Add vinegar. Slowly add olive oil, whisking constantly.

Mahi-mahi

Preheat oven to 400 degrees. Place a skillet or sauté pan on high heat and add olive oil. Sprinkle salt on both sides of mahi-mahi. Press jicama into top of each fillet, covering entire surface. When oil is very hot, carefully place fish jicama side down into skillet. When jicama starts to brown around edges, cook for 30 more seconds. Remove fillets from skillet and place on a greased baking sheet skin side down. Bake 5 to 7 minutes, depending on desired doneness.

Cut four 6-by-6-inch, ½-inch-thick squares of watermelon from reserved watermelon half. Place a watermelon square in center of each of 4 serving plates. Arrange greens to 1 side of watermelon square. Fluff couscous with a fork. Spoon ½ cup couscous on top of watermelon. Evenly sprinkle radish mixture on top of couscous. Drizzle each plate with Watermelon Vinaigrette, pouring some on top of radish mixture and greens and some around watermelon. Place fish slightly askew on top of couscous and radish. Sprinkle black sea salt on top of pooled vinaigrette, if desired.

Cornmeal-Dusted North Carolina Trout with Creamed Cauliflower, Collard Greens, and Creamy Red-Eye Gravy
Serves 6

Chef's Note

"Make the collard greens and cauliflower first, then make the gravy. Your last step will be to fry the trout and plate the dish. These dishes are flavorful enough to be enjoyed separately, too!"

Collard Greens
   4 slices bacon, diced (so fat renders all the way out)
   ½ yellow onion, chopped
   6 cloves garlic
   2 pounds collard greens, cut into 1-inch ribbons
   ½ cup sugar

Cornmeal-Dusted North Carolina Trout
Photo by Des Keller
Courtesy of Crippen's Country Inn & Restaurant

Cauliflower purée

    1 head cauliflower, cut into florets, core removed
    1 cup heavy cream
    ¼ cup butter
    salt to taste

Creamy Red-Eye Gravy

    ½ pound country ham, diced
    2 tablespoons olive oil
    ½ cup strong coffee or espresso
    1 quart heavy cream
    ¼ teaspoon salt (optional)

Trout

    12 4- to 6-ounce trout fillets, skin on
    ½ teaspoon kosher salt
    1½ cups yellow cornmeal
    3 tablespoons olive oil

Collard Greens

Combine bacon, onions, and garlic in a large Dutch oven or heavy stockpot. Sauté over medium heat until golden brown. Add collards to pot, along with enough water to cover half the greens. Reduce heat to low and simmer covered for 1 hour. Add sugar. Cook an additional hour covered. Drain. Return to pot and keep warm.

Cauliflower purée

Cover cauliflower with water in a medium saucepan and bring to a boil. Cook 20 minutes over medium-high heat. A knife will cut through cauliflower with no resistance when it's done. Drain cauliflower. Place in blender with cream and butter. Purée until smooth. Add salt.

Creamy Red-Eye Gravy

Brown country ham in olive oil over medium-high heat in a frying pan, cast-iron skillet, or Dutch oven. Add coffee and scrape bottom of pan to loosen brown bits. Reduce coffee about 1 minute until it is barely visible. Add cream. Reduce heat to medium-low and simmer 20 to 30 minutes. Add salt, if desired; country ham is already salty enough for most people. Place in a glass casserole dish and keep warm.

Trout

Sprinkle fillets with salt and coat with cornmeal. Place oil in a frying pan over medium-high heat. Add fillets to hot pan, skin side up. Sauté 2 to 3 minutes until golden brown. Turn fish and cook 1 minute or until done.

To present

Using a ladle or serving spoon, place ½ cup cauliflower purée in center of each of 6 plates. Using tongs, place 1 cup Collard Greens on top of cauliflower. Place 2 fillets in an X on top of collards. Ladle ¼ cup Creamy Red-Eye Gravy around base of trout.

James Welch

James Welch
*Photo provided by
Green Park Inn*

Green Park Inn

9239 Valley Boulevard
Blowing Rock, N.C. 28605
828-414-9230
http://greenparkinn.com

The Chef

"Daddy, give me a kiss."

Chefs work late hours. By the time they arrive home, the rest of the family has usually gone to bed. Chef James Welch often crossed paths with his daughters, Deanna and Melissa, as he was getting ready to leave for work in the afternoon and they were coming home from school. Their "give me a kiss" ritual grew out of those encounters. The "kisses" were Hershey's Chocolate Kisses. He always carried some in the pocket of his chef's jacket.

Late one night, after the staff had broken down the kitchen, James was sitting in the bar eating a steak. He was also sipping espresso, and the complementary blend of the two flavors struck him. Toward the end of the meal, he reached into his pocket on impulse and took out his last remaining Kiss. Restaurant kitchens are hot, and the Kiss had partially melted. Rather than throwing it away, he squeezed what he could out of the wrapper and ate it with his last sip of espresso. Chocolate and espresso: the flavors are a classic match. James wondered, if chocolate matches espresso, and espresso goes well with beef, what about some combination of all three?

Chocolate Kisses turned out to be far too sweet. But after several experiments, James settled on the combination he now uses, as specified in the recipe on page 32.

James served the dish at a cystic fibrosis fundraising dinner in Charlotte. At the end of the evening, eight chefs were introduced, along with the dishes they had prepared. When the creator of the "Chocolate Steak" was announced, he received the only standing ovation from the crowd, as well as applause from the other chefs.

James is a native of Greensboro, where his parents owned the Steak and Egg Diner. He grew up in restaurants and was washing dishes at age 12. His parents later opened the more upscale Steak and Ale in Friendly Shopping Center. James began cooking there at age 15. By 17, he was managing the kitchen. After his parents sold the property, the new owners opened Wellington's and retained James as general manager.

He subsequently moved to Franklin's Off Friendly. When the Sheraton opened downtown with a fine-dining restaurant, James was hired as saucier. He was later promoted to banquet sous chef.

After his wife graduated from college, James followed her to Miami, where she had received a job offer. He signed on at the Sheraton Bal Harbour, where he oversaw operations at three restaurants. When an opportunity arose at the smaller but more prestigious Mark's Place, he started cooking on the line and soon moved up to sous chef. While at Mark's Place, he traveled with the chef-proprietor, Mark Militello, to cook with famous chefs and celebrities including Julia Child, Jean-Louis Palladin, Mark Miller, Paul Bocuse, and Emeril Lagasse. Chef Welch was part of the team that the James Beard Foundation named "Best in the Southeast" in 1992.

While in Miami, James met Jimmy Crippen, who was then the assistant manager at Mark's Place. He moved with Jimmy to Blowing Rock to open Crippen's Country Inn & Restaurant, where he remained as executive chef for 18 years.

Chef Welch's teams have won the Best Dish North Carolina competition (Fine Dining Division), the North Carolina Pork Council's Best Dish award, and the Fire on the Rock Chef's Challenge (twice!).

James moved across town to the "new" Green Park Inn in 2010.

The Restaurant

The Green Park Inn, which opened in 1891, is named for its original owners, the Green family, and for its location, on acreage in Blowing Rock originally known as "Green Park." Illustrious guests have included Annie Oakley, John D. Rockefeller, Eleanor Roosevelt, Calvin Coolidge, Herbert Hoover, and Margaret Mitchell, who is reported to have written part of *Gone With the Wind* while a guest at the hotel. Named to the National Register of Historic Places in 1982, the Green Park Inn is the last of the "grand manor hotels" in western North Carolina. It is the state's second-oldest operating resort hotel.

In May 2010, New York hotel investors Eugene and Steven Irace purchased the property. Through the summer and early fall of that year, the hotel underwent extensive repair and modernization. The furniture was completely replaced with products primarily from North Carolina—Thomasville, Lenoir, and High Point especially. The inn is now a luxury property, although it retains its historic ambience. Of a planned 80 rooms plus luxury suites, most are now open.

After selecting James as executive chef, the new owners offered him an almost free hand. The kitchen was stripped nearly to the walls, new plumbing and wiring were installed, and modern commercial appliances with the capacity to serve several hundred guests were put in place. The Laurel Room, the property's fine-dining restaurant, reopened on July 1, 2011, with Chef Welch at the helm. Weddings, rehearsal dinners, and corporate meetings are well within the property's purview.

The restaurant has already developed a following for its food. James describes the eclectic cuisine at Green Park as "influenced by . . . French [but] not guided exclusively by any particular cuisine. Influences arise from the Caribbean and Asia, as well as traditional American." The menu changes quarterly.

Local produce includes baby greens from Charlotte's Green House in Valle Crucis; squash and blackberries from J&M Produce in Boone; jams, jellies, cheeses, some eggs, and sometimes lamb from Bella Rooster in Valle Crucis; and tomatoes, butternut squash, and other vegetables from New River Organic Growers (see page 34).

North Carolina Watermelon Salad
Photo by Tom Santay

The Recipes

A Best Dish North Carolina 1st place winner
North Carolina Watermelon Salad with Sage Flatbread, Fresh Mozzarella, and Toasted Almonds
Serves 4

Flatbread
> ½ cup semolina
> ¾ cup flour
> ½ teaspoon salt
> 1 tablespoon chopped fresh sage
> ¼ cup extra-virgin olive oil
> ¾ cup water

Vinaigrette
    ½ cup balsamic vinegar
    2 cups extra-virgin olive oil
    1 teaspoon garlic
    1 teaspoon shallots
    2 tablespoons sugar, plus extra if desired
    salt to taste

    18 to 20 leaves mixed baby greens
    3 cups watermelon, diced about ¼ inch
    1 cup mozzarella, diced to same size as watermelon
    ½ cup toasted almonds
    sliced basil for garnish

FLATBREAD

Combine all ingredients in a non-reactive mixing bowl. Roll out on a sheet tray. Bake at 350 degrees for 12 to 15 minutes until outsides of flatbread start to brown.

VINAIGRETTE

Combine first 5 ingredients in a mixing bowl. Whisk. Season with salt and additional sugar.

TO PRESENT

Lay out greens. Include a small leaf in center. Lay out bread in a triangular pattern between greens. Mix diced watermelon and mozzarella with vinaigrette. Place in center of plate. Sprinkle toasted almonds and sliced basil on top.

Chocolate Beef Tenderloin with French Green Beans and Au Gratin Potatoes
Serves 6

Au Gratin Potatoes
9 large potatoes
1 pint heavy cream
5 eggs
⅔ cup Parmesan cheese
2½ teaspoons salt
⅔ cup pistachio nuts, chopped
⅔ cup goat cheese

Chocolate Beef Tenderloin
Photo by Tom Santay

Baileys sauce
    1 quart heavy cream
    ¼ ounce espresso grounds
    1 cup sugar
    2 ounces Baileys Irish Cream

French Green Beans
    48 French green beans, cleaned, strings removed, ends trimmed
    3 tablespoons salt
    clarified butter for sautéeing

Beef tenderloins
    6 7-ounce beef tenderloins
    2 ounces fresh coffee grounds
    6 ½-ounce pieces bittersweet chocolate

AU GRATIN POTATOES

Can be prepared a day in advance. Slice potatoes (horizontally, not lengthwise) ¼ inch thick and place in water to prevent browning. Spray an 8-inch springform pan with nonstick spray. Arrange a layer of potatoes starting in center and working toward edges. Blend cream and eggs. Pour 1 ounce cream and egg mixture and 1 ounce Parmesan over first layer of potatoes and sprinkle with ½ teaspoon salt. Repeat for 5 layers. Sprinkle chopped pistachios on top layer and crumble goat cheese over nuts. Cover top with plastic wrap, then wrap pan with aluminum foil. Bake 1 hour and 45 minutes at 350 degrees. Let cool and reserve. Reheat and cut into wedges before serving.

BAILEYS SAUCE

Combine cream, espresso grounds, and sugar. Simmer 5 minutes over medium heat. Remove from stove. Stir in Baileys Irish Cream.

FRENCH GREEN BEANS

Blanch beans in salted boiling water. Pour off hot water. Shock in an ice-water bath. Just before serving, melt clarified butter in a pan, add beans, and sauté until hot.

Roll tenderloins in coffee grounds. Grill to desired doneness; approximately 7 minutes per inch per side for medium, 5 minutes for medium rare. Cut a slice into center of each tenderloin and insert ½ ounce chocolate.

TO PRESENT

Place beef tenderloin in center of plate. Place Au Gratin Potatoes at top center (12 o'clock position). Place French Green Beans in X arrangements at other outside positions on plate (5 o'clock, 6 o'clock, 7 o'clock, and 8 o'clock). Pour ½ ounce Baileys sauce over tenderloin.

New River Organic Growers

P.O. Box 1223
West Jefferson, N.C. 28694
828-773-1588
http://newriverorganicgrowers.org

New River Organic Growers is a nonprofit cooperative organization that markets the products of over 30 farms in the High Country. The co-op provides a link between farmers and individual and commercial consumers. The farms produce fresh produce grown under organic guidelines, as well as humanely raised meats from animals that have not been treated with hormones or drugs outside normal veterinary procedures. The co-op helps farmers by assisting with transportation, purchasing supplies in bulk to reduce costs, facilitating communication between producers and consumers, and providing information to the public about sustainable local farming and consumption.

The initiative is sponsored in part by the North Carolina Department of Agriculture Cooperative Extension Service. Richard Boylan, one of the agriculture agents who serve the High Country, was particularly helpful in starting the initiative. Additional funding and support have come through the state's efforts to adjust to the decline in tobacco. In 1998, the attorneys general of 46 states reached a settlement with four of the nation's largest cigarette manufacturers wherein the manufacturers committed to paying more than $200 billion to the states over a period of 25 years. North Carolina has used the funds to establish three initiatives. One of those initiatives, the Tobacco Trust Fund, assists people formerly engaged in tobacco farming or tobacco-related businesses to move into other "qualified agricultural programs." A grant from the Tobacco Trust Fund purchased a refrigerated truck for New River Organic Growers in 2008. That truck enabled the co-op to expand from vegetables to cheese, eggs, and meats, which require refrigeration in transportation.

The co-op delivers orders two or three times a week during the summer and once or twice per week through the winter. Heirloom vegetables have become a particular focus recently. Chefs and home consumers value them for their flavor and fragrance. Although opinions about what constitutes "heirloom" vary, the term generally refers to varieties of fruits and vegetables that existed in the same form before hybridization, grafting, and genetic modifications began to occur—that is, roughly prior to 1950.

Caleb Crowell, executive director of the co-op, is devoted to quality vegetables. He grew up in Boone and went to Appalachian State University, graduating with a degree in geology with a concentration in environmental science. Afterward, he and his wife sold vegan products at the Watauga County Farmers' Market through their business, Hold the Heat Raw Food Makery. They also grew organic vegetables and sold them primarily to restaurants. Crowell has worked in several area restaurants, including The Eseeola Lodge. He remarks that chefs and farmers sometimes speak "different languages," so his job often involves bridging the gap between what chefs want and what farmers need to know in order to provide it. Crowell works with NROG farmers on production schedules, evaluating market trends to help pick specialty crops that will have a higher value to both buyers and growers.

Consumers can purchase New River Organic Growers products from Bare Essentials Natural Market in Boone, from the High Country Community Supported Agriculture organization, and from booths maintained by growers themselves at the Watauga County and Ashe County farmers' markets.

Guy Thomas

Guy Thomas
Photo courtesy of
Fire on the Rock

The Porch Swing

1128 South Main Street
Blowing Rock, N.C. 28605
828-295-9683

The Chef

Guy Thomas was born in De Leon Springs, Florida, near Daytona Beach. As a child, he often came to the mountains on vacations with his family. When the Thomases had to leave, "I would get sick to my stomach," he recalls. "All year long, I would daydream of the time I would get to live here. The beauty, majesty, and down-home feel of these mountains have always been close to my soul. Now that I finally do live here, my life could not be better. Every day is an adventure. It's like being on vacation full-time, even though I work long and arduous hours. But just knowing I'm here has given me a new lease on life."

Guy was cooking by the time he was about nine years old. His father worked as a butcher at a Superette Market, preparing his own sausage, seasoning blends, and rubs. He slaughtered and butchered hogs, cattle, and wild game, fried fish for neighborhood gatherings, and conducted oyster roasts, game dinners, and barbecues. He was well known in the area around De Leon Springs for his culinary abilities. Guy tried to absorb everything his father, mother, and grandmother were willing to teach. His desire to cook professionally was evident by his mid-20s. He was a drywall installation expert until that point. "What a transition! I had never before felt the excitement and enthusiasm that this new career choice brought to me."

From his family, he learned about flavors, how to season, how to process cuts of meats, and how to bone and fillet fish, poultry, and game. Eventually, he took a kitchen management course at Cornell University, a nutritional program through the Culinary Institute of America, and an advanced baking curriculum at Central Piedmont Community College in Charlotte. He has been actively involved with the American Culinary Federation and has entered numerous ACF-sanctioned competitions. Through ACF, he became a certified chef. He has built quite a professional culinary library to keep up with current trends and increase his knowledge base.

Chef Thomas gained a great deal of knowledge from other chefs. "I would work off the clock just for the opportunity to learn and experience what these great chefs had to offer," he says. Over a career spanning approximately 30 years, he has opened seven restaurants, one Sheraton hotel, one private country club, and a catering business, as well as being the executive chef of several restaurants and clubs in North Carolina, South Carolina, and Florida. His career has included many 80-plus-hour work weeks and many three-day periods without a break as he produced banquets and catering events, got ready to open new properties, or prepared for culinary competitions. "Working to make an event the best it can possibly be has always been of particular interest and importance to me," he says. "I try to be an inspiration to all who work under my supervision, motivating, training, and challenging them to give 100 percent effort in all their culinary endeavors. I continue to hear from those who have worked for me in the past, telling me how much they learned, how they enjoyed working for me, and how they have now become chefs in their own careers. That appreciation is very satisfying and fulfilling."

One incident stands out among the situations Guy has encountered as a chef. "The year was 1987," he says. "The owner of a beautiful country club I had opened as the executive chef purchased a state-of-the-art mobile barbecue cooker-smoker at a price of about $8,000. A young man who worked for me assured me he had a lot of experience cooking outdoors. I charged him with lighting the cooker and adding a bag of charcoal. I intended to cook several inside top rounds of beef.

"After about 30 minutes, some club members came charging into the kitchen to tell me the cooker was on fire! I ran out to find that the guy had turned on both gas tubes, placed three 40-pound bags of chunk charcoal over the fire tubes, and on top of that, he had added seven huge split logs of hickory. When I arrived on the scene, the cooker was glowing like a nuclear reactor, the tires were smoking, the taillights were melting, and black smoke was billowing out in torrents. The scene was horrifying. I managed to get the doors open, burning my hands and forearms in the process, and the fire leapt out like a dragon's breath. I commandeered a pitchfork from one of the golf-course maintenance workers and began skewering the 18- to 23-pound top rounds and tossing them behind me. It looked like medieval soldiers tossing flaming balls of pitch over the ramparts down onto their enemies! The beef rounds rolled through the grass, causing quite a sensation for all the club members, who were there enjoying our Olympic pool and Fourth of July festivities.

"I eventually got everything under control, and eight hours later, after trimming all the excessive char off the meat, I was able to place them back in a cooled-down cooker and slow-roast them. They tasted great! Members still talk about that incident at the club."

Chef Thomas considers his style "Southern comfort cuisine. I have worked with the classics of French, Italian, Spanish, Pan-Asian, U.S. regional, and some Japanese, Thai, Korean, and Chinese cuisines. But my most satisfying cooking style is Southern regional, especially coastal, Low Country, Cajun, and Caribbean-style, along with simple country foods. Finding and utilizing the finest, freshest ingredients and treating them with respect and simplicity are the keys to great-tasting food. I am also a firm believer in buying as locally as possible, keeping my supply chain at least within the state or region. Sustainable agriculture practices are also a priority in sourcing my foods, as much as possible. The extra money these foods cost has to be passed along to customers in the form of somewhat higher menu prices, but not a lot higher, and the finished product stands out and brings customer satisfaction to the forefront. You get what you pay for."

Prior to The Porch Swing, Guy was executive chef for almost four years at the Meadowbrook Inn in Blowing Rock. Before that, he opened the Valle Café in Valle Crucis with Bill and Eileen Gaddy of Gadabouts Catering, also based in Valle Crucis.

When cooking for himself, family, and friends, Guy enjoys "the simple, satisfying comfort of pan-fried chicken, pork backbones, fried whole freshwater bream, speckled perch, or catfish, roast fresh chicken, a hearty breakfast of eggs, homemade sausage, creamy slow-cooked grits, biscuits, and gravy, and, of course, a simple char-broiled or even pan-fried hamburger with a thick slice of heirloom tomato, sweet Spanish onion, and mayonnaise with plenty of black pepper. Nothing pretentious, nothing overboard. A big plate of dry white rice topped with simple stewed potatoes has always been a major favorite of mine. My favorite birthday dinner from my grandmother was always a pot of hog chitlins, mustard greens, and pan-fried pork chops with stewed tomatoes and rice. Yum!"

The Restaurant

The Porch Swing, formerly Glidewell's, sits in a prime location on Blowing Rock's Main Street. It's an easy place to drop into while exploring the downtown. It went through some difficult times during the owners' divorce in 2011. After Mary Kelly Glidewell took over, she brought in Chef Thomas to run the kitchen and gave the restaurant a new name to make a clean break with the past. The Porch Swing thus opened in spring 2012.

The concept is based on Southern regional food. The restaurant utilizes fresh local ingredients. The menu changes according to the seasons and the availability of produce and meats.

Chef Thomas has partnered with several small farms in the area, with New River Organic Growers (see page 34), and with conventional suppliers willing to obtain regional meats, produce, and seafoods. He also visits the Watauga County Farmers' Market regularly.

Chef Thomas has participated in the Fire on the Rock Chef's Challenge twice, won the Chili Cook Off during Winterfest two years running, and received various medals from ACF competitions throughout the years. He is especially proud of his ACF President's Trophy for "Best North Carolina Chef," presented in 1984.

The Recipes

Panko-Fried Catfish Fillets with Sweet Potato Fries
Serves 6

Sweet Potato Fries
>   vegetable oil for frying
>   2 large sweet potatoes, peeled and cut into ¼-inch strips
>   1 gallon water
>   1 teaspoon kosher salt or sea salt, plus extra sea salt to taste

Catfish
>   vegetable oil for frying
>   6 catfish fillets (4-6 ounces each), split lengthwise down center
>   2 tablespoons Old Bay seafood seasoning
>   juice of 1 lemon
>   ½ teaspoon pepper
>   2 cups all-purpose flour
>   2 eggs, lightly beaten
>   2 cups milk
>   3 cups breadcrumbs (preferably panko)

>   tartar sauce of your choice

SWEET POTATO FRIES

Preheat oil to 360 degrees. Place cut sweet potatoes in water with 1 teaspoon salt. Bring to a boil and cook about 4 minutes. Drain well and dry on paper towels. Drop potatoes into oil and fry 3 to 5 minutes. Once fries rise to top, let cook 1 minute more. Drain on paper towels and season with sea salt.

CATFISH

Heat oil to 360 degrees in a frying pan. Season fillets with Old Bay, lemon juice, and pepper. Lightly coat fish with flour, knocking off any extra. Beat eggs and milk together to make an egg wash. Place fish in egg wash, then in breadcrumbs, pressing crumbs to adhere to fillets. Place fish in hot oil and fry until fillets are golden brown and float on top for at least 1 minute. Do not crowd pan. Fry 2 at a time if temperature of oil drops. Drain on paper towels and serve with tartar sauce and Sweet Potato Fries.

Panko-Fried Catfish Fillets
Photo by John Batchelor

Bronzed Breast of Chicken
Photo by John Batchelor

Bronzed Breast of Chicken
with Fried Oysters and Étouffée Sauce
Serves 4

Étouffée Sauce

    ½ cup vegetable oil
    ¾ cup all-purpose flour
    1 cup chopped andouille sausage
    1 cup chopped yellow onion
    1 cup chopped green pepper
    ½ cup chopped celery

2 tablespoons minced garlic
1 quart shrimp stock
2 bay leaves
2 tablespoons Cajun seasoning
1 tablespoon Worcestershire sauce
½ tablespoon pepper

Chicken

enough oil to brush chicken
4 6-ounce boneless, skinless chicken breasts
2 tablespoons Cajun seasoning
1 tablespoon clarified butter, melted

Oysters

enough oil to cover oysters when frying
16 large fresh oysters, shucked
1 tablespoon Cajun seasoning
½ teaspoon pepper
1 teaspoon Worcestershire sauce
2 cups all-purpose flour
2 eggs, lightly beaten
2 cups milk
3 cups breadcrumbs (preferably panko)

parsley and/or green onions for garnish

Étouffée Sauce

Heat oil in a cast-iron frying pan until it begins to smoke. Add flour, whisking vigorously. Stir thoroughly until well blended. Place pan in a 400-degree oven for 20 minutes. Remove pan from oven. Stir well, making sure to scrape sides and bottom. Return pan to oven and cook 15 minutes more to achieve a near copper-penny color. Add sausage, onions, peppers, celery, and garlic and let residual heat cook ingredients for about 10 minutes. Add stock and remaining ingredients and bring to a boil. Reduce heat to a simmer and cook about 20 minutes, stirring every 5 minutes.

Chicken

Lightly oil chicken on both sides and coat with Cajun seasoning.

Bronze chicken in butter in a hot cast-iron pan for about 2 minutes per side. Place in a 375-degree oven and finish cooking for 10 minutes.

Oysters

Heat oil to 360 degrees in a frying pan. Season oysters with Cajun seasoning, pepper, and Worcestershire. Place oysters in flour to coat lightly. Beat eggs and milk together to make an egg wash. Place oysters in egg wash, then in breadcrumbs, pressing to assure adhesion of crumbs. Fry oysters in hot oil about 2 minutes until light and golden. Do not crowd pan. Fry in batches of 4 if pan is not large enough to retain heat after oysters are dropped into oil.

To present

Place about ½ cup Étouffée Sauce on each of 4 plates and place chicken on sauce. Top each breast with 4 oysters. Decorate with finely chopped parsley and/or green onions.

Michael Foreman

Michael Foreman
Photo by
John Batchelor

Restaurant "G"
at Gideon Ridge Inn

202 Gideon Ridge Road
Blowing Rock, N.C. 28605
828-295-3644
http://gideonridge.com

Bistro Roca and
Antlers Bar

143 Wonderland Trail
Blowing Rock, N.C. 28605
828-295-4008
http://bistroroca.com

46

The Chef

Natalie Nelson and a female friend were having lunch together at the Augustine Grill in Castle Rock, Colorado, a restaurant popular not only with local residents but especially with professional athletes. Players for the Denver Broncos and PGA Tour golfers were among the regular customers. When Natalie inquired about dessert, the waitress replied that the best choice was not on the menu. "The best dessert is a new guy in the kitchen, and his name is Michael," she told Natalie and her friend. Michael Foreman played a big-brother role for the staff of waitresses. Laughs at the table led to an introduction, which led to an acquaintanceship, which eventually led to marriage.

Natalie and Michael Foreman have been together 12 years. They share three languages, in addition to English. Although he was born in Gadsden, Alabama, Michael grew up in the Baja Peninsula of California, so he is fluent in Spanish. He also speaks what he calls "culinary French." Natalie is fluent in French and Japanese. She is editor in charge of graphic novels for McFarland Publishing.

Michael started cooking as a child. "I had family that put out a buffet every time anyone visited. This was the spark that lit the fire. I started experimenting early with classic meals, poorly prepared." While attending Auburn University as a chemistry major, he worked part-time at the Auburn University Hotel and Conference Center. "The chef, Christine Healey, pushed me harder than I had ever been pushed before. She insisted that I was wasting my time in college, that my talent was in the kitchen. So I left Auburn and attended Trenholm Culinary Institute, the Southeastern Olympic Culinary Team training facility, then went on to Cordon Bleu in London, when there were only two Cordon Bleu campuses in the world, the other one in Paris. I spent every minute of my time reading, watching, and studying other chefs and their styles. I used my organic chemistry background to manipulate natural flavors. I formed a merged style of seeing dishes deeper than just a combination of flavors and ingredients. I see flavors in colors. It's about putting together spectrums of color, constructing several layers into the flavor profile."

His first sous chef job was at the Partridge Inn in Augusta, Georgia. There, he made connections with Kevin Goldsmith, who offered him the position of executive chef at Pullman Hall Catering in Augusta. "His approach was awesome," Michael recalls. "No waste. Everything could be made into something better. And never serve what everyone expects."

In the mid-1990s, Michael moved into the executive sous chef position for the Augusta National Golf Club, where he helped cook the famous celebratory dinner for Tiger Woods's first Masters championship. The winner of the Masters chooses the menu for the Champion's Meal. One of the pros who had been on the tour for some time made a sarcastic remark to the effect that if Tiger Woods won, the Champion's Meal would probably be fried chicken. When Woods did win, his P.R. people contacted the kitchen staff and requested fried chicken, a not-so-subtle retaliation.

From Georgia, Chef Foreman went to New Mexico to open his first restaurant as an owner. "That was a life lesson," he says. "After selling my share, I moved to Colorado to take on a corporate job with Quality Dining International as one of eight corporate chefs. The subsequent move to Augustine Grill was a great experience, providing total freedom. This, I feel, was when I finally blossomed."

Michael and Natalie subsequently decided to move. They threw a dart at a United States map, and it landed on Asheville. Michael became executive chef at the Highland Lake Inn in Flat Rock in 2000. But an opportunity for him to work with one of the world's most famous chefs led the couple to relocate to France. Michael cooked in Lyon under Chef Paul Bocuse, honored by the Culinary Institute of America as "Chef of the Century" for his work with fresh ingredients and his de-emphasizing of heavy sauces based in butter and cream. Chef Foreman then opened another Bocuse restaurant, Julienne, in the Opera District in Paris, in what was originally a costume shop for the opera. The couple remained in France for about two years, the duration of Michael's contract.

The Foremans came to the High Country in 2002, when Michael took the position of executive chef at the Gideon Ridge Inn. "The High Country offers everything we loved about Colorado, but with all the charm of a small town," he says. Michael has used vacations for stages—interim positions working with some of the nation's most important chefs. He was guest chef at Charlie Trotter's for Restaurant Week two years in a row and was part of the grand opening at Central with Michel Richard in Washington, D.C.

When not cooking professionally, Michael likes French and authentic Hispanic food best. "I could eat those every day. It is pure love in every bite. At home, I cook a lot of classic Southern, mainly vegetarian, and Hispanic." Outside the kitchen, he participates in mixed martial arts tournaments.

The Restaurants

Michael is executive chef of two restaurants—Restaurant "G" at Gideon Ridge Inn and Bistro Roca.

Gideon Ridge Inn sits atop the like-named ridge near the Blowing Rock, the formation for which the town is named. Accommodations are provided in 10 guest rooms. Restaurant "G" is one of the High Country's most relaxed and elegant experiences. The view from the patio, where guests often enjoy before-dinner cocktails as well as meals, is one of the most panoramic in the area. The main dining room is decorated in European style. Other amenities on the property include stone terraces, garden walkways, flower gardens, a library with a stone fireplace, and a billiards room.

Devoted to fine dining, Restaurant "G" serves an eclectic blend of fresh mountain ingredients prepared in classical culinary style, its American cuisine often accented with flavors and techniques from France. Chef Foreman seeks to provide simple food of the highest quality, prepared from local, seasonal ingredients. The small menu changes often—sometimes every day. The food follows the seasons and the weather. "The same way that a good wine has overtones and undertones of distinctive flavors," Chef Foreman explains, "my menus strive for a subtlety and a complexity of flavors—flavors that complement each other, not compete. One day, we want the food to be part of a clear view of the mountains. Another day, it's cloudy, and we want food that is darker but will improve your mood. You could eat here five nights in a row and not get bored."

Chef Foreman describes his style of cooking this way: "No cheating, no compromise! The minute you are willing to cut corners in preparing a dish, you will start to do it every time. Only choose the best ingredients. You don't have to serve huge portions. Great ingredients have more flavor, so less is more."

Michael lives with his family on a 10-acre farm in Ashe County, so he is able to visit area farms to see what they grow. "My best trick is to send my five-year-old daughter to the farmer's booth first. She butters them up, then I come in and make the deal for the restaurant. Our farmers are our passion!" He buys regularly from Carolina Bison, New River Organic Growers (see page 34), Stick Boy Bread Company, Owl Creek Breadworks (wood-fired-oven rustic breads from freshly ground grains), and Mountain Memories Farm (chicken). He also buys salad greens and some vegetables grown in nearby Valle Crucis.

One afternoon while prepping for dinner at Gideon Ridge, Michael answered the phone almost by accident, since the hostess wasn't at the phone station at the time. "This guy says he wants to come and stay three days, but his presence must be absolutely private. He asks what kind of food we serve. I tell him French-American fusion, with Latin American influences. He starts talking about being used to eating in the best restaurants in the world. 'How do you compare?' he wants to know. Like any young, brash chef, I tell him we're as good as any of the places he has named. So this guy comes in on a Friday afternoon, and I immediately recognize him. It's Charles Nelson Reilly, the actor, on a brief hiatus while touring in a one-man show. At the end of the weekend, he calls me over to the table and presents me with a copy of *The Metropolitan Opera Cookbook*, which had been given to his mother and signed by Luciano Pavarotti. He had reinscribed the book, 'To Michael of the Mountains.' I still have it, of course."

Four years after Michael took over the kitchen at Gideon Ridge, he and owners Cobb and Cindy Milner decided to open a property devoted to less formal fare. "We wanted the sort of place where our friends would want to go for lunch every day," Michael says. Thus, Bistro Roca was born in 2004. Bistro Roca strives to be a restaurant locals can call home, in addition to being a popular, casual destination for visitors. A rustic, rough-sawed wood exterior encloses Antlers Bar, located to the left of the entry-way. Antlers is widely considered the oldest continuously operating bar in western North Carolina. Its walls are decorated with photos of customers' dogs. It's easy to spend time here just being entertained by the moments the photographs have captured.

The kitchen at Bistro Roca is organized around the only wood-fired oven in the High Country, made from bricks salvaged from the original Antlers Bar, constructed on the property in 1932. Bistro Roca's menu is based on American bistro fare—salads, sandwiches, burgers, and appetizers, as well as French-influenced comfort-food entrées and homemade desserts. The restaurant's specialty is hand-tossed, wood-fired, Neapolitan-style pizzas. The menu is stable, although experimentation is always under way. Changes occur when the availability of ingredients dictates.

Chef Foreman is an approved mentor for the New England Culinary Institute and has served on the advisory board for the Caldwell Community College culinary program.

The Recipes

Shrimp Brochettes
with Winter Vegetable Chow-Chow and Corn Salad
Serves 2-4

Chef's Note
"This flavorful appetizer plays the sweetness of the corn against the tartness of the chow-chow. A chow-chow is a Southern pickled

Shrimp Brochettes with Winter Vegetable
Chow-Chow and Corn Salad
Photo by Scott Pearson Photography

relish that can be made from many different vegetables. This is a great winter dish because of the availability of good frozen sweet corn in the organic section of most supermarkets. As the season changes, vary the vegetables in the chow-chow."

Corn Salad

> 3 tablespoons olive oil, divided
> 2 cups fresh or frozen shoepeg or Silver Queen corn
> 2 cloves garlic, crushed
> ½ cup diced red onion
> ¾ cup diced red bell pepper
> 1 cup grape tomatoes, halved
> 1 tablespoon chopped parsley
> 1 tablespoon fresh oregano leaves
> 2 tablespoons red wine vinegar
> salt and pepper to taste

Winter Vegetable Chow-Chow
   ½ cup water
   1 cup rice vinegar
   ¼ cup sugar
   salt to taste
   1 tablespoon red pepper flakes
   4 sprigs thyme
   ½ cup diced sweet onion
   ¼ cup cauliflower florets
   ¼ cup butternut squash, peeled and diced
   ¼ cup celery, chopped
   ¼ cup parsnips
   ¼ cup garlic cloves, quartered

Grilled shrimp
   12 bamboo skewers soaked in water
   12 large shrimp (16–20 size)
   enough olive oil to coat shrimp

Corn Salad

In a large sauté pan, add 1 tablespoon of the olive oil and sauté corn, garlic, onions, and bell peppers until lightly browned. Remove from heat and add next 4 ingredients. Mix thoroughly and add salt and pepper. Refrigerate.

Winter Vegetable Chow-Chow

Bring water, vinegar, sugar, and salt to a boil. Reduce to a simmer and add red pepper flakes and thyme. Add vegetables and garlic and simmer for 5 minutes. Refrigerate for 24 hours. Serve cold.

Grilled shrimp

Skewer shrimp, brush with olive oil, and grill lightly just until red on each side. Serve hot grilled shrimp with scoops of Corn Salad and chow-chow.

Grilled Angus Strip Loin over Butternut, Wild Mushroom, and Potato Ravioli with Butternut Purée

Serves 4

Ravioli

    3 cups butternut squash, peeled and cut into ½-inch cubes
    1 tablespoon chopped garlic
    2 tablespoons chopped sweet onion
    3 tablespoons butter
    2 cups sliced or chopped mushrooms
    2 tablespoons fresh thyme leaves
    ½ cup shredded Parmesan cheese
    salt and pepper to taste
    1 pack large egg-roll wrappers

Purée

    1 cup beef or chicken stock
    ½ cup cream
    salt and pepper to taste
    1 tablespoon butter

Grilled Angus Strip Loin over
Butternut, Wild Mushroom,
and Potato Ravioli
with Butternut Purée
*Photo by Scott Pearson
Photography*

    3 cloves garlic, peeled and crushed
    1 teaspoon kosher salt
    1 teaspoon black pepper
    2 teaspoons Chinese 5-spice mix
    1 tablespoon olive oil
    2 16-ounce New York strip steaks (Certified Black Angus works best)

    chard for garnish
    favorite vinaigrette

RAVIOLI

Sauté squash, garlic, and onions in butter over medium heat until ¾ cooked through. Reserve ½ of squash mixture for sauce. Add mushrooms to remaining squash and cook until tender. Remove from heat and let cool. Add thyme, Parmesan, and salt and pepper. Lay 16 egg-roll wrappers on a flat surface. Place 1 tablespoon squash mixture on 8 of the wrappers. Moisten all edges of wrappers with warm water. Top with plain wrappers and press firmly to seal. Set aside.

PURÉE

Put reserved squash mixture, stock, and cream in a saucepan. Bring to a boil, then purée in a blender. Return to pan and adjust salt and pepper. Add butter while whisking sauce.

STEAK

Mix first 5 ingredients in a small bowl, then massage into steaks until well coated. Grill steaks over a hot fire until they reach desired degree of doneness. This should take 10 to 15 minutes, depending on the fire. Steaks should be cooked to an internal temperature of 145 degrees for medium-rare.

TO PRESENT

Blanch ravioli in boiling water for about 5 minutes. Heat purée. Place 2 ravioli on each of 4 plates. Spoon purée generously over ravioli. Slice steak and fan over ravioli. Garnish with chard or other mild greens tossed in your favorite vinaigrette.

MICHAEL FOREMAN 55

North Fork Farm

680 North Fork Road
Zionville, N.C. 28698
828-297-5755
http://northforkfarmbeef.com

Jimmy and Sheila Greene purchased their farm in June 1993. The family operation consists of the couple and son Seth, all born and raised in the High Country. The Greenes started out raising beef cattle to sell to family, friends, and neighbors. That phase continued for several years. Then, after figuring out that many people didn't have freezer space for a quarter-, half-, or whole beef, they applied for and received a meat handler's license in October 2009.

Having also received requests for pork and chicken, the Greenes added those meats to their line and began selling packaged products to individuals and restaurants and at farmers' markets. They continue to sell quarter-, half-, and whole beef and half- and whole hog, custom-cut and vacuum-packed. Their beef products include steaks, ground beef, roasts, short ribs, stew, and dog bones. Among their pork products are sausage, roasts, pork chops, ribs, chunked ham, country backbones, and bacon. Chicken products include boneless, skinless breasts, tenders, and whole chickens. They also sell farm-fresh eggs from their laying hens.

In 2011, North Fork became the first meat CSA (Community-Supported Agriculture) organization in the High Country. The farm offers individuals the opportunity to pay a lump sum and receive a variety of beef, pork, and chicken once a month for five months. This not only gives individuals and families a variety of locally raised meats but also helps them if they have limited freezer space.

The farm is home to cattle, 56 laying hens, two roosters named Mr. Speckles and Leo, a cat named Stetson, and a dog named Chico. All farm animals are raised without added hormones or antibiotics and contain no preservatives. Beef cattle are purchased locally and finished on the farm. Pork is raised by a local farmer dedicated to healthy, all-natural hogs, who then markets it to North Fork. Chickens are purchased from an all-natural farm, where they are raised according to the same standards as the pork and cattle.

Jimmy's role involves buying, transporting, and caring for the cattle and chickens. He also works outside the farm, managing Avery Rent-All in Banner Elk. Sheila processes and delivers orders and performs bookkeeping and marketing duties. She sometimes fills in as a substitute teacher at Mabel Elementary School. Eight-year-old Seth assists with feeding the cattle and chickens and is in charge of the eggs, which he collects daily. The hens lay about 40 to 45 eggs per day. Seth also helps wash the eggs and put them in cartons.

Seth and Leo
Photo by Sheila M. Greene

Recently, North Fork Farm began participating in an animal rehabilitation program through the Blue Ridge Wildlife Institute at Lees-McRae College in Banner Elk. The Greenes allowed a great horned owl, Hoot, to be released at their farm and also welcomed a bantam chick that the institute could not keep. That chick, Leo, is now a full-fledged bantam rooster and the North Fork Farm mascot.

Nate Curtis

Nate Curtis
Photo by
Alistair Burke

Rowland's at Westglow Spa

224 Westglow Circle
Blowing Rock, N.C. 28605
800-562-0807 or 828-295-4463
www.westglowresortandspa.com

The Chef

Nate Curtis has lived in the North Carolina mountains most of his life. His first cooking job was at an outdoors camp at age 14. The first day there, he made 300 grilled cheese sandwiches. While a student at Appalachian State University, he worked part-time at Crippen's in Blowing Rock, where all components were made in-house. He found it satisfying to prepare food that way. This approach still guides his style. "Anything else is inferior cuisine," he says.

Working under Chef James Welch at Crippen's, Nate moved from an entry-level position as a prep cook to the cold side, then to sauté. "It was an invaluable learning experience to understand the processes and dynamics of a busy restaurant. I learned the fundamentals—from knife skills, sauce preparation, braising, and searing to timing and overall kitchen organization. The culture there was fast paced. Everyone had to contribute, but we worked together as a team, and that's where I learned the value of having a talented group in the kitchen."

Chef Curtis credits Grant Achatz of Alinea in Chicago for instilling the philosophy that food must please all the senses and create an emotional connection for guests. "A true chef considers all factors when creating a signature cuisine," Chef Curtis says. "For me, I love a dish that can evoke a childhood memory—the aroma of your first fresh biscuit, the sweetness of a fresh summer watermelon, or the comfort of your mom's sweet potato casserole. It's these intangibles that add something much more memorable and unique to the dining experience of our guests."

Above all, Chef Curtis wants his food to be personal. "There should be something about the cuisine that puts customers right at home, yet still brings something new to them. They should want to know what's in it, how this or that was done. There should be some wonder and intrigue, or everything becomes passé. But to make food intricate just for the sake of intricacy takes the focus off the food."

Nate maintains that level of focus when he cooks at home. "I do a lot of roasted and grilled vegetables. Something about quick-blanched *haricots verts* with butter and kosher salt seems perfect to me. Handmade chicken pot pies are another frequent dish at my home. When I eat out, I like to order something out of the norm. I probably would never order chicken at a restaurant. I want something interesting and new that might in turn inspire me to create."

Nate Curtis was Rowland's executive sous chef for two years before being promoted to executive chef.

The Restaurant

Westglow Spa is housed in the restored and updated Greek Revival mansion that was once the summer home of renowned artist and author Elliot Daingerfield, one of America's best-known landscape painters at the turn of the 20th century. The mountaintop setting of this elegant white-columned structure is framed by a large lawn. Panoramic windows provide forever views. Overnight accommodations, spa and salon options, and exercise, massage, wellness, and other renewal activities are among the services provided.

Westglow is one of only 50 members of the Relais & Châteaux family of luxury hotels and restaurants in the United States. The property was voted "Best Boutique Spa in the World" in a Reader's Choice poll by SpaFinder (www.spafinder.com), earning four "Best Category" awards for Best Boutique Hotel, Best for Romance, Best for Hiking, and Best for Cuisine.

According to Chef Curtis, Rowland's, the restaurant at Westglow, is "based on the concept of creating an upscale, metropolitan dining experience while maintaining a strong connection to North Carolina roots. We create a polished, intimate dining experience through our attention to detail, impeccable service, and formal, elegant surroundings." The menu is divided into "Indulgent" and "Spa Cuisine" sections, allowing guests to choose between unrestricted fine dining and options that limit fat and calories. The wine list is extensive.

Local products—organic when feasible—are a focus in food preparation. "Local products in the High Country have virtually exploded over the past seven years," Chef Curtis explains. "Farmers in the area have done an amazing job of branching out into different varieties and maintaining impeccable standards. The sourcing of different local products also greatly determines my style. Rather than shopping for what I need to make a certain recipe or dish, I buy what is fresh and available and tailor what I'm going to do from there. The ingredients are the answer. Cooking them fills in the equation."

The staff at Rowland's works with one produce supplier in particular: New River Organic Growers (see page 34). "They are a cooperative and have really connected farmers with area chefs," explains Chef Curtis. "Everything is beautiful, uniform, and delicious. American farmers have seen declines for decades, and it's time that chefs do everything within their capability to support and grow their local providers. This single issue will, in my mind, become more and more important to our nation and our economy in the coming years."

The Recipes

Beef Cheek Timbales with Date Purée, Pickled Swiss Chard, and Roasted Fingerling Potatoes
Serves 6

Pickled Swiss Chard
    1 cup water
    ½ cup rice wine vinegar
    ¾ cup sugar
    ⅛ cup salt
    1 whole clove
    1 teaspoon yellow mustard seed
    1 teaspoon black peppercorns
    1 teaspoon minced ginger
    ½ jalapeño pepper, seeds and ribs removed, minced
    stems from 1 pound Swiss chard (reserve leaves for timbales)

Date Purée
   3 medjool dates
   ¼ cup extra-virgin olive oil
   1 tablespoon lemon juice
   ½ tablespoon brown sugar
   ½ cup hot water

Beef cheek
   2 pounds beef cheek
   salt and pepper to taste
   ¼ yellow onion, chopped
   ¼ fennel bulb, chopped
   ¼ large carrot, peeled and chopped
   1 cup Cabernet Sauvignon
   1 cup veal or beef stock
   ½ bay leaf

Roasted Fingerling Potatoes
   ½ pound fingerling potatoes
   salt and pepper to taste

Timbales
   leaves from 1 pound Swiss chard
   ½ tablespoon grapeseed or olive oil
   1 pound portioned beef cheek (from above, after braising)
   ¼ pound dried chorizo sausage, sliced thin
   ⅜ cup goat cheese

   1 cup colorful micro greens or chopped parsley
   truffle oil for sprinkling

PICKLED SWISS CHARD

Prepare a day ahead. In a saucepan, combine all ingredients except Swiss chard stems and bring to a boil. Stir to ensure that sugar and salt dissolve. Strain mixture through a fine-meshed sieve and pour over Swiss chard stems. Cover stems with cheesecloth soaked in the liquid to keep stems submerged. Let cool to room temperature, then refrigerate overnight. Dice Swiss chard stems in the morning.

Beef Cheek Timbales
Photo by Alistair Burke

DATE PURÉE

Prepare ahead and reheat, if desired. Combine all ingredients except hot water in a food processor. Pulse until a thick paste forms, stopping constantly to scrape the edges and break up clumps. Slowly add enough hot water to soften purée.

BEEF CHEEK

Preheat oven to 325 degrees. Season beef cheek with salt and pepper, then sear until golden brown on all sides. Remove meat from pan and place in a large baking dish. Sauté onions, fennel, and carrots in a pan until tender and lightly caramelized. Add to the baking dish. Deglaze pan with wine, add stock, and pour liquid into baking dish. Add bay leaf and braise at 325 degrees for 4 hours. Remove from oven, allow to rest for 5 minutes, then slice beef cheek on the bias, removing any tendon or excess fat.

Roasted Fingerling Potatoes

Preheat oven to 400 degrees. Peel potatoes, if desired. Bake for 25 minutes. Add salt and pepper.

Timbales

Preheat oven to 400 degrees. Blanch Swiss chard leaves, then shock them in an ice-water bath. Remove from bath and blot completely dry with paper towels. Oil a paper towel with grapeseed oil or olive oil and rub the insides of 6 medium-sized (approximately 2- to 3-inch) ramekins. Place Swiss chard leaves inside ramekins, overlapping the edges. Make sure plenty of leaf comes over the sides, as these will make the sides and base of the timbales. Layer ramekins with ½ inch of sliced beef cheek, then sliced chorizo, then goat cheese. Fold overhanging Swiss chard leaves to cover tops of timbales, tucking excess into ramekins with the back edge of a knife. Bake timbales for 15 minutes.

Note: Potatoes and timbales can be cooked in the same oven. If you put the timbales in after the potatoes have baked 10 minutes, both should both be done at the same time.

To present

Smear a swath of Date Purée from center toward corner of plates. Lay a line of pickled chard stems next to Date Purée. Use a small knife to ease timbales out of ramekins. Place timbales in the corner of plates next to Date Purée, slightly toward the center. Stack Roasted Fingerling Potatoes in other corner of plates. Garnish with colorful micro greens or chopped parsley sprinkled lightly with truffle oil.

Braised Beef Short Ribs
Photo by Alistair Burke

Braised Beef Short Ribs with Parsnips, Mushrooms, Spinach, and Jus
Serves 6

Chef's Note

"In this dish, I am trying to capitalize on the theme of 1970s high-end New York steakhouses. The idea was to create a modern dish that grows out of the traditional beef staples of potato, demi-glace, and creamed spinach. But substituting the parsnips for potatoes lightens the dish and helps create better balance. The spinach powder melts in the mouth, creating the texture of creamed spinach, but in a new, fresh approach. The dish evokes nostalgia, but it is fresh and modern."

6 pounds bone-in beef short ribs (will yield about half this quantity in
  meat after cooking)
½ yellow onion, chopped
½ large carrot, peeled and chopped
½ fennel bulb, chopped
2 cups port wine
1 cup Cabernet Sauvignon
3 cups veal or beef stock
1 pound parsnips, peeled and chopped
1 vanilla bean, split
4 cups water
½ cup heavy cream
salt and white pepper to taste
1 cup maltodextrin (a tapioca derivative that transforms fat-based liquids
  or other solubles into a powder until eaten, when the texture turns back
  to a liquid)
1 tablespoon spinach powder
⅓ cup plus 2 tablespoons extra-virgin olive oil, divided
¾ pound French horns or other hearty mushrooms
1 tablespoon saba (a syrup made from grape must)

Preheat oven to 325 degrees. Sear short ribs in a large sauté pan until thoroughly browned. Remove and place in a large roasting pan. Drain grease. Sauté onions, carrots, and fennel in sauté pan until soft and lightly caramelized. Remove from sauté pan and reserve with short ribs in roasting pan. Deglaze sauté pan with port and Cabernet Sauvignon. Add stock. Bring liquid to a simmer. Pour liquid over short ribs and vegetables in roasting pan. Cover roasting pan with aluminum foil and braise in oven for 6 hours.

Combine parsnips, vanilla bean, and water in a medium pot and bring to a low boil over medium-high heat. Boil 20 minutes or until ingredients are completely softened. Strain parsnips. Reserve liquid in a bowl. Remove vanilla bean. Place parsnips in a blender. Add heavy cream. Blend on high, gradually adding reserved liquid. Blend until parsnips are completely smooth and desired texture is reached. Result should look similar to mashed potatoes; you may not use all the liquid. Season with salt and white pepper.

Place maltodextrin and spinach powder in a food processor and pulse to mix. Gradually add ⅓ cup olive oil. The fats in the olive oil will cause mixture to come together, creating granulation. Pass mixture through a medium-holed sieve.

Preheat oven to 400 degrees. Toss mushrooms with saba and remaining 2 tablespoons olive oil. Season with salt and white pepper. Roast in oven for 15 minutes.

Divide roasted short ribs into 8-ounce portions. In a hot pan, sear 1 side of each short rib portion. Drain excess grease, then add braising liquid from short ribs and simmer until jus thickens.

Place each 8-ounce short rib portion on a plate. Mound parsnip purée alongside, create a well in center, and spoon jus into well. Place mushrooms on other side of plate. Spoon spinach powder over edge of short ribs.

Andrew Long

Enter as Strangers ...
Leave as Friends!

Storie Street Grille

1167 Main Street
Blowing Rock, N.C. 28605
828-295-7075
www.storiestreetgrille.com

68

The Chef

Andrew Long grew up in Baton Rouge, Louisiana, and went to college at the University of New Orleans. Hired to manage the kitchen at a fitness camp in western Massachusetts, he found that he and the camp director got along well. Really well. They were married a year later. Although they loved the mountains, they wanted to be in the South, "where neighbors are friendly and you don't get a hundred inches of snow in the winter," Andrew says. They relocated to Charleston, South Carolina, but soon got a chance to move to Blowing Rock. "We have been here six years now and love it. It is a great place to raise our two young children, and we enjoy camping, hiking, and my all-time favorite activity, fly-fishing for native trout."

Andrew started in the restaurant business as a dishwasher and bus-boy when he was 14. At 15, he moved into the kitchen as a line cook at George's in Baton Rouge, a popular bar-and-grill. "We served a ton of seafood, po' boys and gumbo," he recalls. "On Fridays during Lent, the line would be wrapped around the building, and I would fry catfish as if my life depended on it. I learned that cooking was honest work. And if you were willing to pay your dues, you could have a good life."

After high school, he moved to New Orleans to study hotel, restaurant, and tourism administration in college but eventually grew frustrated with the program's concentration on the hotel and casino side of the business. "I was learning a lot more in the kitchens of New Orleans, especially at Ralph Brennan's BACCO, in The Ambassador Hotel. That's when I decided to stay in the kitchen and focus on being a chef."

He transferred to culinary school, graduating from Johnson & Wales University in Charleston. But Andrew cautions that "culinary school alone does not make a chef. I've been fortunate to work for some great chefs and with some great cooks, and I have learned, and continue to learn, from them all. The biggest professional influence for me has been Chef William Merelle of Rouge Restaurant in West Stockbridge, Massachusetts. William is from the Provence area of France, and he taught me a refined but unpretentious technique for modern French cuisine. The most important lessons I learned from him, however, were that family comes first, and respect everyone in the restaurant, especially your dishwashers. I continue to educate myself through seminars, conferences, books, websites, and blogs." Just prior to Storie Street Grille, he was the chef at Laura Albert's Tasteful Options, a wine shop and café on Daniel Island near Charleston, where he learned about matching food flavors with wines.

Andrew says that some of his experiences taught him "what *not* to do. There was a steakhouse in New Orleans where I learned how to fabricate and cook meat, and also how to work hundred-hour weeks. I helped open a bar before I was old enough to legally drink, and I learned a lot about dealing with salespeople and purveyors." Being a chef is "mostly a grueling profession that is far from glamorous. How about a *Chef TV* show where you see who can scrub a floor the fastest? That's what I'm waiting to see!"

Outside the Storie Street kitchen, Chef Long likes to eat "anything that someone else cooks for me. At home, we make a lot of big batches of stews and soups. My wife is an expert gardener, and we always have frozen or canned vegetables in the winter. Last week, we bought a quarter-cow from a friend down the street, and I'll be enjoying that all winter!"

The Restaurant

Although Storie Street Grille is a casual restaurant, Chef Long "want[s] people to be pleasantly surprised by the quality of our product. We focus on local and natural meats and produce, and while a lot of restaurants are doing that now, that was not the case five years ago when we started in this direction. The relationships we've established with local producers are well worth the extra effort, because not only do we support our local economy, I am able to get a superior raw product that, in turn, I believe, gives me a superior end product."

Although Chef Long will always find room "for a little Louisiana love" on his menus, his dishes show influences from East Asia and Europe as well. "When I am working on menus, I first look at what is available locally and build from that," he says. "Good chefs that want to serve a quality product have always used local ingredients. It's pretty simple. If your pota-toes were harvested two weeks ago and came off a truck that has traveled 3,000 miles, and my potatoes came out of the dirt yesterday, mine are go-ing to taste better. But it wasn't until a few years ago, after reading Michael Pollan's *The Omnivore's Dilemma* and Barbara Kingsolver's *Animal, Vegeta-ble, Miracle*, that I went to hear Joel Salatin of Polyface Farms speak. And I realized that not only should chefs source locally to get a superior product, but we should do it because it's the right, or sustainable, thing to do."

Andrew cites area resources that link chefs and farmers, such as the Appalachian Sustainable Agriculture Project (see page 198) and New Riv-er Organic Growers (see page 34). "Where I used to have to track each farmer down individually and drive all over town picking up product, now I can just send Caleb at NROG an email, and my groceries show up at my back door two days later, freshly harvested. Both the farmers and the chefs have come a long way to building a local food system in this area."

Storie Street has been a finalist in the Best Dish North Carolina com-petition—sponsored by the North Carolina Department of Agriculture and *Our State* magazine—several times, taking third place in 2007. Its team made it to the semifinals of the Fire on the Rock Chef's Challenge in 2010. Storie Street also helped to start the FARM (Feed All Regardless of Means) Café in Boone, a pay-what-you-can restaurant whose purpose is to provide a healthy, locally sourced meal option for local people in financial need. Opening was in spring 2012; visit www.farmcafe.org for more information.

The Recipes

Grilled Radicchio Salad with Beets
Serves 8

Chef's Note

"The intention of this dish is to create a light and fresh-tasting salad that is still hearty enough for winter. Grilling the radicchio mellows out the bitterness of the leaves and adds a smokiness that is especially nice with the sweetness of the beets and the chevre."

Beets
2 or 3 medium golden beets (any beet variety may be substituted)
2 tablespoons grapeseed or other neutral oil
salt and pepper to taste

Grilled Radicchio Salad
Photo provided by Storie Street Grille

Balsamic reduction
    2 cups balsamic vinegar
    4 cloves garlic
    1 sprig rosemary
    ¼ cup honey

Salad
    1 cup walnuts
    2 heads radicchio, outer layer removed
    2 tablespoons grapeseed oil
    coarse sea salt to taste
    freshly ground pepper to taste

    8 ounces chevre (preferably from Ripshin Goat Dairy or another
      North Carolina goat dairy)
    2 tablespoons extra-virgin olive oil

BEETS

Preheat oven to 400 degrees. Place beets in a small baking dish, drizzle with grapeseed oil, sprinkle with salt and pepper, cover with foil, and place in oven. Beets are done when a small knife or metal skewer can be easily inserted. This will take 30 to 45 minutes, depending on size of beets. Allow to cool. Peel beets and slice ⅛ inch thick.

BALSAMIC REDUCTION

While beets are roasting, combine vinegar, garlic, and rosemary in a small saucepan over medium heat. Gently simmer until liquid is reduced by ½, then add honey and continue to simmer until the consistency of light syrup is achieved. Mixture should coat the back of a spoon. Keep an eye on the reduction while it is cooking, as it will burn quickly if left unattended. Reduction has a variety of uses and may be stored in the refrigerator for up to 3 weeks.

SALAD

Toast walnuts in a skillet over medium heat for 4 to 5 minutes until they become aromatic and slightly brown. Prepare a charcoal or gas grill for indirect grilling. Quarter the radicchio through the stems, leaving them intact to keep them from falling apart on the grill. Rub with grapeseed oil and sprinkle with sea salt and pepper. Grill wedges for 3 minutes on each surface, rotating to achieve cross-hatch grill marks.

TO PRESENT

Fan sliced beets on plates. Top with a wedge of radicchio. Add 1 ounce each crumbled chevre and walnuts. Drizzle with olive oil and a small amount of balsamic reduction.

Pan-Seared Scallops with Candied Bacon and Golden Raisin Bourbon Sauce
Serves 6

Sauce

    1 cup golden raisins
    2 cups water
    2 tablespoons bourbon (rum is a good substitute)
    1 bay leaf
    ½ cup sugar

Candied Bacon

    ½ pound smoky bacon, diced ¼ inch
    2 tablespoons shallots, diced small
    ¼ cup sugar
    ½ cup red wine vinegar

Scallops

    12 large, U-10 sea scallops, fibrous "foot" muscle removed
    salt and freshly ground pepper to taste
    2 tablespoons butter
    1 tablespoon canola oil

    chives for garnish

74 BLOWING ROCK

SAUCE

Combine all ingredients in a medium saucepan over high heat. When mixture starts to simmer, reduce heat to medium-low. Continue to simmer for 30 to 40 minutes until a light syrup consistency is reached.

CANDIED BACON

Add bacon to a cold sauté pan over medium-high heat. Cook bacon until slightly crisp, remove from pan, and place on paper towels. Drain fat from pan. Return pan to high heat and add shallots, sugar, and vinegar. Simmer for 5 to 7 minutes until thick. Remove from heat and add bacon.

Pan-Seared Scallops
Photo provided by Storie Street Grille

Preheat oven to 400 degrees. Place an oven-safe sauté pan or cast-iron pan on medium-high heat. Make sure scallops are dry. Season with salt and pepper. Add butter and canola oil to sauté pan. When butter is a dark golden brown and stops bubbling, carefully add scallops. Do not crowd pan; cook scallops in batches of 5 or 6 to ensure desirable sear. Gently shake pan to prevent scallops from sticking. After a nice golden color is achieved, use a spoon or a pair of tongs to gently flip scallops. Immediately place entire pan in oven. Finish in oven for 8 to 10 minutes until scallops are slightly undercooked. Place scallops on a plate. After a few minutes, juice will accumulate under scallops. Add juice to raisin sauce and stir in.

TO PRESENT

Spoon sauce on each of 6 plates. Place scallops on sauce and spoon Candied Bacon over scallops. Garnish with chives. If serving as an entrée, increase the number of scallops accordingly and serve with sautéed seasonal vegetables.

Boone

Jessica Grogan

Jessica Grogan
wtih Chocolate
Del Fuego
Martini
Photo by
John Batchelor

Crave World Inspired
Tapas and Martini Bar

203 Boone Heights Drive
Boone, N.C. 28607
828-355-9717
www.craveboone.com

The Chef

Jessica Grogan says she was "born, raised, and stayed in Boone. A lot of people move here, but I was born here, and I love it. After high school, I thought about moving away, but then I wondered, 'Why would I leave?' We have four distinct seasons, Appalachian State University is an amazing school, and all my family is here. It was where my heart is, and I couldn't leave. But a vacation once in a while to the beach is great, though."

She started cooking when she was young. "I can remember being five years old and pushing up a stool to the stove and making my own grilled cheese sandwiches. I have always been very independent and really enjoy eating and cooking. I grew up in my mom's restaurant, The Corner Palate in Banner Elk, and worked every shift. When I was 18, I decided to learn more about the kitchen and began training heavily.

"I did not go to culinary school. I think it is a good choice for some people, but having grown up in the business, and always being around it, cooking just became part of me. I have it in my blood. I learned a lot from my mom, and she is my strongest influence. But another part of my inspiration is just going to other restaurants and eating, seeing what they are doing, tasting food in other places, and then developing my own ideas."

Jessica has worked in many restaurants, primarily in the front of the house. "I first started cooking at The Corner Palate. I think of it as a staple in the community, because a lot of very influential chefs and business owners in the area have worked there at some point in their career. The Corner Palate not only taught me how to cook but also how to get timing right and to multitask."

She finds working in restaurants interesting. "Between the customers and the employees, you always have a story to tell. One time, we had a server who was on a student exchange from Russia. She was going to the local college. It was a really busy night, and she came back flustered about ringing in an order. She said that the man at her table ordered a Beefeater and wanted it done well, but she couldn't find it in the computer. It turned out she was looking at the entrées, trying to ring in a steak for him. And she had even asked how he wanted it—rare, medium—and he responded, 'I want it done well.' I guess he left off the 'duh.'"

Jessica does not consider herself to be following a particular style or philosophy when it comes to cooking. "I like a lot of different flavors and styles. I base what I cook on my ingredients and how I feel that day. For example, if I saw some beautiful artichokes at the market, then I would be inspired to create a dish with those. I guess you could say my style is inspired by the seasons and the availability of items." In an article in the *Blowing Rock News*, she mentioned admiring Thomas Keller (of The French Laundry) and watching *Top Chef* and *Iron Chef*.

When she eats on her own, she is "a huge fan of cheese, so I eat a lot of different artisanal cheeses. And I like things that are either warm and gooey or light and refreshing. At home, though, I have kids, so I have to accommodate what they are willing to eat, so I cook a lot of lasagna, meat loaf, and peanut butter and jelly sandwiches."

The Restaurant

Jessica and her husband, Josh, opened Crave in 2009, a few months after they sold Char, their first restaurant venture, which is still open in downtown Boone. "For Char, we had gone with a classic Americana, steakhouse feel, complete with the wooden tables and neutral wall colors," Jessica explains. "For Crave, we wanted something with a little more pop, and it all started with the dining room." Jessica picked the purple and orange colors they used. "I had my doubts, but she pulled it off," Josh recalls. "Jessica is the backbone of the restaurant, and she has been a big reason we've been successful. Not only is she a talented baker, but she is also a good cook in her own right, yet she somehow finds time to manage all of our paperwork, train the front-of-the-house staff, and raise our two boys, Xander and Zane, all while pursuing a master's degree."

Customers often comment that the dining room has a "modern Manhattan" feel to it. The goal was to create a setting where the food would be enjoyable without being overly recognizable, but rather different and exciting. The Grogans decided on tapas for several reasons, according to Jessica: "It's healthier, since studies have shown that one problem with obesity in America is that people will eat with their eyes more than they will listen to their stomachs. If you're served a big plate of food, you tend to eat until the plate is empty. With tapas, you can pace yourself better. Another reason we decided on tapas is that we felt it would be more economical for our customers, especially considering the times we live in. All of our menu items are under $12, and there are over 70 to choose from. So customers can decide how much they want to spend. There are plenty of cozy date-night restaurants with expensive menus, and plenty of budget-friendly places with sports memorabilia all over the wall. Why not have a unique place that's both inviting for anyone and priced for any occasion?"

Chef Grogan purchases from local farms and utilizes other North Carolina providers through farmers' markets, produce stands, and growers' co-ops, as well as "just having the door open to farmers and growers who stop by."

Crave has been recognized by Talk of the Town as one of the top restaurants in Boone for both years it has been open. Just recently, it received a top rating from yelp.com.

The Recipes

Braised Short Ribs with Tomato Jam
Serves 2 to 4

Tomato Jam
    ½ cup diced onion
    4 tablespoons olive oil
    2 cups water
    1 cup sugar
    2 cups peeled tomatoes, chopped
    4 tablespoons tomato paste

1 cup apple cider vinegar
1 tablespoon garlic powder
1 teaspoon red pepper flakes
salt and pepper to taste

Short ribs

salt and pepper to taste
1 pound beef short ribs, cut into 2½-by-3-inch pieces
¼ cup flour
¼ cup olive oil or other cooking oil
1 large yellow onion, chopped
1 large carrot, chopped
1 or 2 cloves fresh garlic
½ cup zinfandel (red)
½ cup beef stock

Sauce

1 Ruby Lager or other lager beer
braising liquid from short ribs

Braised Short Ribs with Tomato Jam
Photo by John Batchelor

Tomato Jam

In a medium saucepan, sauté onions in oil until they begin to soften. Add water and sugar. Bring to a boil. Reduce heat to medium and simmer, stirring constantly, until mixture turns golden brown. Remove immediately from heat and stir in tomatoes, tomato paste, and vinegar. Return to low heat. Add garlic powder and red pepper flakes. Stir well to combine. Cook until mixture is reduced by ½ and tomatoes are falling apart. Remove from heat. Let cool to room temperature and season with salt and pepper.

Short ribs

Preheat oven to 300 degrees. Salt and pepper short ribs, then dredge them through flour. In a large, heavy-bottomed sauté pan, add oil and heat to medium-high. Sear ribs about 5 minutes each on all sides; ribs should have a dark brown sear. Remove ribs from pan and set aside. Reduce heat to medium. Add onions, carrots, and garlic and sauté about 5 minutes until soft. Add wine to deglaze pan. Stir, making sure to incorporate dark brown residue (called fond) from bottom of pan into cooking liquids. Add beef stock and reduce liquid by ½ over medium heat. Space ribs out in a shallow baking pan and add reduced liquid. Make sure liquid dispenses evenly through pan. Cover with foil and cook in oven for 2½ hours. Check for tenderness. Meat should be fork-tender. Set aside and let cool. Cut ribs into ½-inch-thick pieces, making sure you cut against the grain. Strain and reserve liquid.

Sauce

Add 1 part Ruby Lager to 3 parts strained braising liquid in a saucepot. Simmer over medium heat until reduced by ⅓.

To present

Array short ribs on top of appropriate vegetable, such as mashed potatoes or polenta, and ladle with sauce. Cover with Tomato Jam.

S'mores Pots
Serves 10

1 cup egg yolks
1 quart heavy cream
¼ teaspoon salt
¼ teaspoon cinnamon
½ cup cocoa
¾ cup sugar
4 ounces high-quality dark chocolate, chopped into small pieces
graham crackers
miniature marshmallows
chocolate syrup for drizzling

S'mores Pot
Photo by John Batchelor

Preheat oven to 300 degrees. Place ten 3- to 4-ounce ceramic soufflé cups in a large roasting pan about 4 inches deep. Add water to pan to a level about halfway up cups. Place egg yolks in a large bowl and set aside. In a medium pot, combine cream, salt, cinnamon, cocoa, and sugar and bring to a simmer. Pour in ¼ of the egg yolks and slowly whisk to blend mixture into eggs without cooking them. Continue to add eggs slowly until fully incorporated. While mixture is still hot, add chocolate pieces. Whisk until completely melted and blended. Divide mixture among soufflé cups and bake for about 45 minutes. Mixture should still jiggle slightly when done. When you remove pan from oven, carefully remove cups from water bath or mixture will continue to cook. Place cups in refrigerator to cool.

Crumble graham crackers over tops of chilled S'more Pots. Add miniature marshmallows, covering all the graham crackers. Use a torch or long lighter to brown marshmallows. Drizzle with chocolate syrup, if desired.

Sam Beasley

Sam Beasley
*Photo provided by
The Gamekeeper*

The Gamekeeper

3005 Shulls Mill Road
Boone, N.C. 28607
828-963-7400
www.gamekeeper-nc.com

The Chef

Sam Beasley refers to himself as "a military brat." Born in Fairbanks, Alaska, he subsequently spent 10 years with his family at Pope Air Force Base in eastern North Carolina. As a teenager, Sam moved a little south to Wrightsville Beach, where he developed a love for the ocean and surfing and an aversion to schoolwork. In visiting almost every major city in the United States while following the Grateful Dead for almost a decade, he learned about the rich diversity of cultures, foods, and dialects.

He moved to Boone in 1991 to pursue his love of rock climbing. "The High Country is a mecca for climbing and is recognized worldwide for the abundance and quality of the rocks," he says. Now, he considers the area home. "There is so much to do outdoors here—hiking, climbing, biking, swimming, caving, snowboarding, just to name a few."

Sam started cooking almost as soon as he could stand. "I tried to fix breakfast for my parents by making toast on the radiator," he recalls. "Soon, I had the eggs out and the grits in a pot by the time my mom woke up. After that, it was making school lunches for my siblings. My brother still doesn't like Miracle Whip, because I slathered the sandwiches with it." The passion continued beyond his school days. "My late best friend was a chef, and he traveled all over the country working at different places. We ended up working together for a while, and I realized it wasn't a bad way to make a living. Little did I know I would be sacrificing weekends, holidays, and normal days off for the rest of my life."

Pizza Hut was his first job. His other work locations included the Bridge Tender in Wrightsville Beach, 300 East in Charlotte, The Corner Palate in Banner Elk (where he learned to roll sushi), and The Mothership in Boone, a vegan restaurant with an outer-space theme and "a really cool smoothie and juice bar," Sam says. "We had smart drinks for studying and healthy juice shots for your immune system."

Sam learned more advanced techniques by working with other chefs. "Chef Dean Mitchell of Morels in Banner Elk was an awesome mentor, as well as James Welch, formerly of Crippen's. Those were the most painstakingly detailed and meticulous places I had ever worked. If what you did was not perfect, it was thrown away, and you started over." Learning to make classic sauces highlighted his tour at Crippen's; maintaining elegance within simplicity characterized the approach at Morels. Sam was working at Casa Rustica in Boone when he was offered the chef position at The Gamekeeper.

When he's not at The Gamekeeper, Chef Beasley likes sushi and raw bars. He especially enjoys oysters. "When I go home, it's late, I'm tired, and I don't want to cook anything, so it's Ritz crackers and peanut butter. But on my days off, I like to grill—baby back ribs, chicken, fish, and veggies."

The Restaurant

The Gamekeeper is perched on a hill overlooking the Yonahlossee Resort and Hound Ears Club. Most seating in the 1950s stone cottage provides panoramic views of the surrounding mountains. The ambience is chic, yet casual. Owner Ken Gordon is a former chef.

The staff coined the term "modern mountain cuisine" to characterize the restaurant's style. The menu includes buffalo, elk, pheasant, wild boar, antelope, mountain trout, and wild-caught, day-boat seafood. Chef Beasley focuses on farm-to-table fresh local ingredients that go with wild game. "The average morsel of food Americans consume has travelled 1,800 miles. Tell me something from five miles down the road isn't fresher!" he says. Much of The Gamekeeper's produce and meats comes from New River Organic Growers (see page 34). Ostrich comes from Forsyth County, buffalo from Carolina Bison, and pork from Watauga Farms. All the fish—except salmon, of course—swam in North Carolina waters.

Chef Beasley likens his cooking to the "First, do no harm" portion of the Hippocratic oath. "I will never serve anything I would not eat myself, regarding taste, freshness, and cleanliness," he explains. "If there is any doubt in my mind, the food is not going out. When thinking about what to pair with certain game, I like to imagine what the animal ate—berries, mushrooms, corn, wild onions, for example—and I try to match that as best I can, within reason. I would describe my style as classic French and Americana with creative fusion. Randomness, to me, is also a feature. Keeping an open mind with a little bit of common sense will carry you far in the chef world."

Although known for game and meat dishes, Chef Beasley prides himself on his vegetarian preparations as well. The menu always includes non-meat options.

The Gamekeeper has been recognized by Open Table as one of the top 50 restaurants in the United States. AAA has awarded it Four Diamonds for five years in a row. In 2010, The Gamekeeper team won the Fire on the Rock Chef's Challenge. Endorsements have come from the *Charlotte Observer* and *Southern Living, High Country*, and *Our State* magazines. Author Mary Flynn, a regular customer, set a scene in her recent novel, *Three Gifts*, in The Gamekeeper.

The Recipes

Pork Saltimbocca
Serves 6

> *Chef's Note*
> "*Saltimbocca* means 'to jump in the mouth'."

White truffle mashed potatoes

 3 pounds Red Bliss potatoes, rinsed and scrubbed
 ½ cup heavy cream
 4 tablespoons butter
 1 teaspoon salt
 pinch of pepper
 ½ teaspoon white truffle oil
 1 tablespoon chopped parsley

Pork chops

 6 6- to 7-ounce pork chops
 2 tablespoons chopped sage

Pork Saltimbocca
Photo provided by The Gamekeeper

salt and pepper to taste
6 1-ounce slices country ham
1 cup flour for breading
2 tablespoons olive oil
1 pint red and yellow plum tomatoes
2 tablespoons green onions, sliced on the bias
2 tablespoons chopped parsley
1 tablespoon minced shallots
1 teaspoon minced fresh thyme
4 tablespoons capers
juice of 2 lemons
1½ cups white wine, divided
4 tablespoons butter

6 sprigs thyme for garnish

WHITE TRUFFLE MASHED POTATOES

Quarter potatoes and boil in salted water about 6 minutes until tender. While potatoes are boiling, add cream and butter to a small saucepan and heat until butter is completely melted. Drain potatoes when done, then add cream mixture. Mash potatoes. Season with salt and pepper and add truffle oil and parsley.

Preheat oven to 350 degrees. Lay pork chops on a cutting board and cover with plastic wrap. Using a meat mallet, tenderize and flatten chops with 3 to 4 hits. Remove plastic wrap and put a pinch of sage on each chop. Season with salt and pepper. Place a ham slice on each chop and press firmly. Use 1 or more ovenproof pans; do not crowd chops. Dredge chops in flour. Heat olive oil in pan(s) on high. When oil begins to smoke, reduce heat to medium-high to temper oil so it doesn't burn. Place chops in pan, ham side down. After about 3 minutes, flip. Add tomatoes, green onions, parsley, shallots, thyme, capers, and lemon juice and sauté 1 minute. Deglaze pan with 1 cup of the white wine and combine with flour left from dredging pork. Place pan in oven for about 8 minutes until chops are cooked through. Remove from oven and return to stovetop on medium-high. Caution: pan will be very hot. Add remaining ½ cup wine and butter. Shake pan to incorporate wine and butter and simmer another minute.

TO PRESENT

Put a scoop of mashed potatoes in center of each plate. Lean pork chop on potatoes at an angle. Pour sauce over pork and potatoes. Garnish each plate with a sprig of thyme.

North Carolina Day-Boat Snapper with Avocado-Jalapeño Ice Cream and Mango-Pecan Brown Butter
Serves 6

Avocado-Jalapeño Ice Cream
> 2 ripe avocados, mashed
> 1 cup half-and-half, or ½ cup milk and ½ cup cream
> ⅓ cup sugar
> ½ cup sour cream
> 3 tablespoons lime juice
> ½ teaspoon salt
> 1 jalapeño pepper, seeded and chopped

North Carolina Day-Boat Snapper with
Avocado-Jalapeño Ice Cream and Mango-Pecan Brown Butter
Photo provided by The Gamekeeper

Sauce

    8 tablespoons butter
    3 ripe mangos, peeled and diced
    1 cup chopped pecans
    pinch of salt

Snapper

    6 5- to 6-ounce portions snapper
    salt and pepper to taste
    1 cup panko breadcrumbs
    2 ounces peanut oil
    ½ cup white wine

    12 to 18 slices star fruit
    12 ounces micro greens
    pinch of parsley
    pinch of cilantro

AVOCADO-JALAPEÑO ICE CREAM

Mix all ingredients thoroughly with a whisk and freeze in an ice-cream machine to consistency of soft-serve ice cream. Remove and place in freezer.

SAUCE

Place butter in a sauté pan on high heat. Heat until butter turns a hazelnut color (beurre noisette). Remove from heat. Add mangos and pecans. Shake pan to incorporate all ingredients. Add salt.

SNAPPER

Preheat oven to 350 degrees. Season snapper with salt and pepper and lightly dredge in breadcrumbs. Temper oil in a large, oven-proof sauté pan. Carefully add fish to pan skin side up and sauté about 2 minutes until browned. Flip fish and deglaze pan with wine. Place pan in oven for about 5 minutes until fish is cooked completely through.

TO PRESENT

Place fish in center of plates. Pour sauce over fish. Garnish each plate with 2 or 3 slices starfruit and top with a pinch of micro greens, parsley, and cilantro. Pause. Respond graciously to compliments.

Gina Paolucci

Gina Paolucci
*Photo provided by
Gina Paolucci*

Paolucci's Italian Bar and Grill

783 West King Street
Boone, N.C. 28607
828-268-7525
www.paoluccisitalianrestaurant.com

The Chef

Gina Paolucci was born in Westbury, New York, but has lived most of her life in the Cary/Raleigh area of North Carolina. She moved to Boone in fall 2009 to help her family open and run Paolucci's. She has learned to enjoy the calming, laid-back atmosphere and the beautiful natural surroundings of the High Country.

She cannot remember a time in her life when she was not cooking. Her parents began teaching her and her siblings how to cook and take care of themselves when they were young. "We pretty much always had home-cooked family dinners," Gina recalls. "My parents always stressed the value of cooking everything from scratch. With that instilled in my mind, and my dad always working in restaurants and eventually owning his own restaurant in Cary, I picked up a lot of knowledge over the years. After moving to Boone to work at Paolucci's, I grew tired of just working in the front of the house and started training in the kitchen. There, something just clicked. I had often thought of culinary school as an option when I was in high school. Now, I could really see if it was something I wanted to do. After the past year and a half, I cannot imagine myself doing anything else.

"My cooking training has just been a culmination of years being around the kitchen and my family. Being raised in an Italian family, there's really no way to avoid food. It has always been how we spend time together and bond. From that part of my life and also working our family's restaurants, life just kind of became about food. Once I ended up in the kitchen, it spiraled. Now, I pretty much eat, sleep, and breathe cooking. I have no formal culinary training yet, but now that I know what direction I want to take, my next move will be attending culinary school.

"I guess my entire life has been a lesson in cooking, it seems. Most of my memories are somewhat connected to food. From each family gathering, to being raised around our first restaurant, to working every position possible in two different restaurants, I have become who I am. I owe all my knowledge and experience to my family. My grandparents, parents, sister, brother, and extended family have all influenced me and my cooking. They have given me the upbringing that has allowed me to see what it is about food and cooking that fascinates me. I can't get enough of food and cooking. I am thankful to all of them for showing me the value of a home-cooked meal, the hard work that goes into it, and the impact and memories it can provide."

Gina considers her style of cooking to be fairly simple. "At this point in my life, being only 22 years old, I'm still learning a lot about techniques and ingredients, so I have a lot of room to grow as a chef. But for me, cooking with quality ingredients and respecting them for what they are is key. Well-balanced flavors and textures are the basis of my food. You can't force cooking or make it do anything it shouldn't. When I start thinking of a meal, I start with one ingredient or concept and then think about what I want people who eat my food to experience and take from it. All in all, I would say my style of cooking is well thought, balanced, and explorative."

When cooking for herself and friends or family, Gina likes a wide variety. "I love to make things I crave but can't normally find on menus," she says. "I love lots of fresh vegetables, and I play around with flavor combinations that interest me. I often find myself intrigued by Thai and Asian styles of cooking when I am outside of work, because of their delicate use of ingredients but depth of flavors."

The Restaurant

The theme of Paolucci's Italian Bar and Grill is comfort. "Whether you're referring to the food or the atmosphere, it feels almost like home. And as a family-owned and -operated restaurant, I believe that's an important quality to provide," Gina says. "We offer many traditional Italian cuisine options on our menu, but we also leave space to bring some other inspiration into our dishes. Having a wide variety of options and flavors allows us to present a delicious meal to all of our customers. In the kitchen, we focus on putting out fresh, quality food for an affordable price, which is another comfort we bring. You won't leave hungry, and you won't break the bank eating a meal here. If you're hungry, you should always be able to find something that catches your eye."

Gina has been with the restaurant from the beginning. "After my parents spent months finding the location, it has been a large effort from a hardworking, close-knit group, doing construction, decorating, creating the menu, advertising, and anything else involved in creating Paolucci's. I began working in the front of the house as a server, host, manager, bartender, or anything else. But with the persuasion and help of my brother, I ended up in the kitchen, where I found my niche. After a year and a half of working for my brother, he had to move back to Raleigh, and that placed me in the position of head chef."

The Recipes

Vegetable Lasagna
Serves 15

Chef's note

"Our Vegetable Lasagna is one of my favorite dishes. It is just one of those delicious Italian comfort-food options that bring up a lot of memories of family and working in our restaurants. I may not be a vegetarian, but I prefer it over meat lasagna because it is filling like lasagna should be but not quite as heavy on the stomach. This recipe is one that we have been preparing over the years, and people are well satisfied with it. It has versatility, in that you can use whatever variety of seasonal and local vegetables you like the most and play around with a lot of different combinations."

16 lasagna noodles of choice
3 cups diced roasted eggplant
2 cups spinach
1½ cups diced zucchini
1 cup diced yellow onion
1 cup sliced mushrooms

Vegetable Lasagna
Photo provided by Paolucci's

½ cup olive oil
3 tablespoons chopped garlic
1 teaspoon salt
1 teaspoon pepper
1 teaspoon crushed red pepper
2½ pounds ricotta cheese
1 cup breadcrumbs, preferably Italian-style
1 egg
12 ounces marinara or sauce of choice, plus extra for serving
1 cup Romano cheese
2 cups mozzarella cheese, plus extra for serving

Preheat oven to 350 degrees. Place noodles in a pan with hot water for 10 to 15 minutes to partially soften. Noodles should be pliable but should remain mostly hard, since they will cook more in oven later. Sauté all vegetables in olive oil with garlic, salt, pepper, and red pepper. Do not overcook vegetables, since they will also cook more when lasagna is baked. Let vegetables cool. Mix ricotta, breadcrumbs, and egg together. Coat a 12-by-10-by-2-inch pan with vegetable oil or olive oil. Layer the following in order in pan: marinara sauce to cover bottom; 4 lasagna noodles;

⅓ of ricotta mixture; ⅓ of vegetable mixture; ½ cup Romano; 4 lasagna noodles; ⅓ of ricotta mixture; 1 cup mozzarella; 4 lasagna noodles; remaining ricotta mixture; remaining vegetable mixture; ½ cup Romano; 1 cup mozzarella; 4 lasagna noodles; and marinara sauce to cover top layer. Cover lasagna with parchment paper, followed by aluminum foil. Place lasagna pan in a larger, deeper pan containing ½ inch water. Bake in oven for about 45 minutes until an internal temperature of 155 degrees is reached. Remove from oven and cut into portion sizes. Just before serving, top each portion with more marinara and mozzarella. Bake portions for another 5 minutes to melt cheese.

Porcini Mushroom Ravioli with Chopped Chicken and Beet-Bacon Cream Sauce
Serves 2

14 store-bought porcini mushroom ravioli
2 cups beets
olive oil for sautéeing
3 strips bacon, diced
3 boneless chicken breasts, diced
½ cup quartered mushrooms
½ cup chopped yellow onion
¼ cup white wine of choice
½ cup chicken stock
½ cup heavy cream
2 tablespoons butter
¼ cup fresh basil chiffonade
¼ cup Parmesan and Romano cheese blend
salt and pepper to taste

Cook ravioli according to package directions. Set aside and keep warm. Roast beets at 350 degrees until fork-tender. Peel and dice. Heat a large sauté pan and coat bottom with a small amount of olive oil. Add bacon and cook 75 percent to render fat. Remove bacon from pan and set aside. Add chicken, mushrooms, onions, and beets. Sauté about 3 minutes, then add bacon back into pan. Once chicken and bacon are thoroughly cooked,

Porcini Mushroom Ravioli with Chopped Chicken and
Beet-Bacon Cream Sauce
Photo provided by Paolucci's

deglaze pan with wine, scraping bottom with a wooden spoon to loosen bits of bacon. Add chicken stock. Simmer until reduced by ½. Stir in heavy cream, butter, and basil. Continue to simmer until sauce thickens. Add Parmesan and Romano and season with salt and pepper.

To present, place ravioli in center of plates and cover with sauce.

The Pasta Wench

P.O. Box 2303
Boone, N.C. 28607-2303
828-262-1040
www.PastaWench.com

Andrea Morrell christened her business The Pasta Wench because "I thought it was a cool, memorable name," she says. She also operates Andrea's Organics, a USDA-certified organic farm just outside Boone that grows most of the herbs used in the pastas.

The Pasta Wench partners with the Appalachian Sustainable Agriculture Project (see page 198) and New River Organic Growers (see page 34). Pastas are prepared in small batches using all-natural ingredients. Almost all ingredients that Andrea does not grow herself are sourced locally. Andrea describes Pasta Wench ravioli as "unlike others on the market today, buttery thin gourmet pasta on the outside and several times the filling of traditional ravioli."

Andrea, of Sicilian descent, has been involved with food all her life. She describes her mother as "an amazing cook, who spent hours driving around to specialty stores for different ingredients long before buying local was popular. She was not much of a supermarket shopper for our meals. This was inspiring! My father also cooked a great family breakfast every Saturday morning. So I've been a foodie since a very young age."

Andrea moved to the High Country around 2008. Her husband, Pony, is a former chef and an author of nonfiction books. They love to backpack and be near great arts and food, and Boone has the perfect combination. "Plus, I wanted to be an organic farmer, and this is where I could make that dream come true," Andrea says. "I love the mountain lifestyle, the people, the culture, the feeling of community, and meeting neighbors even when they are a few miles down the valley. These mountains ooze the feeling of home."

When she moved to North Carolina, Andrea intended to sell produce from her farm, primarily at farmers' markets, according to an article by Michael Hastings in the *Winston-Salem Journal*. But as the date to open her stand grew near, she realized that everything she had grown was small and not ready to harvest, so she made some pasta—"the kind our family made growing up." She sold out quickly on the first day and made more the next week. Shortly thereafter, The Pasta Wench was born. Employees—who now number about eight—are classified as Wenchlets and Man-wenches, terminology that is typical of the playful ambience in the production kitchen at The Pasta Wench.

Andrea's favorite foods at home are soups—"all different kinds, especially from whatever I can pick out of the garden or greenhouse, depending on the time of year," she says. "Great soup with a good loaf of bread can't be beat for comfort food, unless of course you have some of my pasta on hand."

Pasta Wench products can be ordered directly from the website or purchased at the Watauga County and Asheville farmers' markets, as well as several other farmers' markets around the state. The Pasta Wench provides fundraising programs for schools and other organizations looking for products to sell. Whole Foods Market and North Carolina–based grocers Harris Teeter and Earth Fare frequently sell Pasta Wench products.

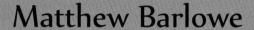

Matthew Barlowe

Matthew Barlowe
Photo by
R. Martin Stewart

The Table
at Crestwood

3236 Shulls Mill Road
Boone, N.C. 28607
828-963-6646
www.crestwoodnc.com

The Chef

Matthew Barlowe, a native of Granite Falls, North Carolina, moved to Boone in fall 2005 to finish a baccalaureate degree at Appalachian State University, where he majored in English. He especially likes not having to use air conditioning in the summer. While he was in college, he started washing dishes "because I needed to pay the rent," he says. "And from that, I eventually just fell into cooking and moving up the line because I wanted more money. At some point, though, I realized that I enjoyed what I was doing, and that was when I decided to pursue becoming a chef as a full-time career."

His training came on the job in the form of "enough chefs yelling at me when I screwed up so that I eventually learned how to do it the right way. I also supplemented that training by constantly reading cookbooks and trade magazines to get new ideas, and experimenting at home. As far as my style is concerned, I'm not really sure because I'm still experimenting so much. I wouldn't say I have one set style, except to say that I cook what I like to eat, and I hope customers enjoy it as much as I do. Mainly, I try to follow what I know to be the fundamentals of quality cooking. If you don't do that, whatever else you try to do in the kitchen will always be subpar."

Matthew's first titled position was sous chef at Crippen's Country Inn & Restaurant in Blowing Rock, where he was a member of the team that won the 2007 Fire on the Rock Chef's Challenge. He did two stints as a personal chef for area families. Before moving to The Table at Crestwood, he was sous chef at Hound Ears Club, working under Executive Chef Luke Fussell. Matthew was responsible for setting up the line for each evening's service, creating nightly specials, assisting the executive chef with menu preparation, ensuring proper setup and preparation for banquets, and overseeing quality control. On the business side, he managed spreadsheets for cost and inventory control.

His favorite food is scallops "in any way, shape, or form," he says. But he acknowledges that he spends too much time in the restaurant kitchen to do much cooking at home.

The Restaurant

The Inn at Crestwood perches on the edge of a mountain just off the scenic drive along Shulls Mill Road. Guest accommodations are provided in 15 rooms and two suites in the main building, four cottages (two of them pet-friendly) large enough for families or other large parties, and several three-story villas that can be reserved as individual rooms or in their entirety. All accommodations have far-ranging views of the mountains; many have private terraces, fireplaces, and whirlpool tubs. An indoor pool, a sauna, and a fitness center are available for guests. Facilities for tennis, bocce ball, shuffleboard, and croquet are located outdoors on the property. A gallery displays works by local artists.

Weddings and rehearsal dinners, corporate and other large group meetings, and retreats are hosted fireside on the terrace, in the library, and on the lawn.

The Dawg Star Bar is the inn's casual facility. Seating in The Table at Crestwood, the fine-dining restaurant, is on two levels. A balcony overlooks the main dining room, floored in Brazilian cherry hardwood. A large fireplace occupies center stage. Diners look out a panoramic picture window 30 feet tall. The long-range views of the surrounding mountains are especially inviting at sunset.

The menu is organized around the belief that food should be really good, yet not too fussy. The fare can be characterized as casual but upscale Southern with European influences. The restaurant's website vows, "The team at The Table are firm believers in the 'farm to table' philosophy about food. [We utilize] as many local and fresh ingredients as possible to develop ongoing and sustainable relationships with farmers and fishermen." Listed suppliers include Ripshin Goat Dairy, New River Organic Growers (see page 34), Hickory Nut Gap Meats (see page 264), Charlotte's Greenhouse, and Inland Seafoods, which provides catches from the North Carolina coast.

Matthew Barlowe's Table at Crestwood team competed in the 2012 Fire on the Rock Chef's Challenge. The Table took second place in 2010 and third place in 2009 in the Best Dish North Carolina competition.

The Recipes

Port-Poached Pear Salad with Gorgonzola, Pecans, and Lemon Vinaigrette
Serves 4

Chef's note

"This can be prepared in advance, then assembled just before serving."

Vinaigrette

¼ cup lemon juice
1 teaspoon garlic, small dice
1 teaspoon shallots, small dice
1 teaspoon minced parsley
¾ cup canola oil
salt and pepper to taste

Pear salad

2 cups port wine
2 cups water
2 tablespoons brown sugar
2 sticks cinnamon
2 pears, cored, peeled, and quartered

1 pound mesclun greens
4 tablespoons chopped pecans
4 tablespoons Gorgonzola cheese crumbles

VINAIGRETTE

In a non-reactive bowl, mix lemon juice, garlic, shallots, and parsley together. While whisking mixture, slowly drizzle in canola oil until emulsified. Add salt and pepper. If prepared in advance, mixture may separate. If it does, just whisk until re-emulsified.

Port-Poached Pear Salad
Photo by R. Martin Stewart

Pear salad

Combine all ingredients in a saucepan and place on high heat until mixture comes to a boil, then reduce to a simmer. Cook until pears become fork-tender. Remove from heat and chill pears in cooking liquid.

To present

Toss greens in vinaigrette and place them on plates. Top each salad with 1 tablespoon each of pecans and Gorgonzola crumbles. Strain pears from cooking liquid and place to the side on plates.

Chipotle Bourbon-Glazed Salmon with Herb-Steamed Basmati Rice and Mustard Crème Fraîche

Serves 4

Chipotle Bourbon Glaze

½ cup canned chipotle peppers
1 cup honey
¼ cup plus 2 tablespoons bourbon
1 tablespoon brown sugar

Mustard Crème Fraîche

1½ cups heavy cream
¼ cup sour cream
⅓ cup whole-grain Dijon mustard

Basmati rice

2 cups basmati rice
3 cups water
1 tablespoon minced parsley
salt and pepper to taste

Salmon

2 tablespoons canola oil
4 6-ounce salmon fillets, skinned
1 tablespoon kosher salt

CHIPOTLE BOURBON GLAZE

This can be made in advance. Purée chipotle peppers in a food processor. Mix peppers with honey, bourbon, and brown sugar until thoroughly combined.

MUSTARD CRÈME FRAÎCHE

Combine heavy cream, sour cream, and mustard in a saucepan and reduce until mixture coats the back of a spoon.

Chipotle Bourbon-Glazed Salmon
Photo by R. Martin Stewart

BASMATI RICE

Place rice, water, and parsley in a saucepan on high heat until water is boiling. Reduce to a simmer and cover. Cook for 10 minutes, then remove lid. Fluff with a fork and season with salt and pepper.

SALMON

Preheat oven to 350 degrees. Add oil to a sauté pan and place on high heat. Season salmon fillets with salt. Once oil begins to shimmer and slightly smoke, place fillets in pan 1 or 2 at a time, depending on size of pan. Sear on both sides. Remove fillets to a sheet tray and coat with Chipotle Bourbon Glaze. Finish cooking salmon in the oven for 4 to 5 minutes until fillets reach an internal temperature of 130 to 135 degrees.

TO PRESENT

Place ¼ cup Mustard Crème Fraîche on each plate and swirl until entire plate is covered. Place rice in center of plate. Top with finished salmon.

MATTHEW BARLOWE 107

Sam Ratchford
Photo provided by
Sam Ratchford

Vidalia

831 West King Street
Boone, N.C. 28607
828-263-9176
www.vadaliaofboonenc.com

The Chef

Samuel Ratchford is a native of the High Country, born and reared in Blowing Rock. "I like living in the North Carolina mountains because my family has planted roots here," he says. "I fit into the laid-back mentality. And honestly, I just feel like large cities were never for me." He started washing dishes at a local restaurant when he was 16 and learned over time to work the various stations. "I felt like I had a knack for it, I enjoyed the camaraderie, and cooking provided me with a self-fulfilling creative outlet."

Preparing for the profession, he graduated from New England Culinary Institute in Montpelier, Vermont. He then interned as a sauté cook at Trapp Family Lodge in Stowe, Vermont (operated by the family from *The Sound of Music*), where he learned to function in a fast-paced atmosphere, and at Cafe Terigo in Park City, Utah, where he was allowed to create off-menu specials. He moved back to Blowing Rock for his first head chef position, at Storie Street Grille, where he learned the business aspect of the enterprise. For a couple of years after that, he worked as a restaurant consultant, designing concepts and layouts.

In his own restaurant, Chef Ratchford maintains a tradition of playing practical jokes on interns and new cooks. "Chefs and cooks are their own breed, and there is always a sense of playful amusement in the air of a kitchen from day to day, from witty banter to hazing."

At home, he likes to eat comfort food. "We grill out a lot, make barbecue. And Italian food." Mac 'n' cheese and hot dogs are the house favorites, though. He likes to go to other restaurants in the area so he can "try to see what everybody else is doing."

The Restaurant

Vidalia is located in downtown Boone across from the county courthouse. Chef Ratchford owns the restaurant with his business partner and wife, Alyce, who is manager and oversees the wine list. The couple met while working together in the restaurant business. They term the food at Vidalia "creative American cuisine." "We try to do simple soul/comfort food with a creative twist, developing the most flavor from the ingredients, using what's locally at hand as much as possible, keeping things new and fresh," Samuel says. "We have a proactive wine list that doesn't feature wines that you can get at a grocery store or is dictated by point systems, and it changes quite regularly as we discover new and interesting wines. We feel like there are few restaurants such as ours in the area. We change the menus according to the seasons and trends and availability of local goods. The kitchen is open to a small, 45-seat dining room, giving people a view of the inner workings of the kitchen. And we also have a Chef's Table and bar overlooking our plate and prep areas."

Vidalia is a member of the Appalachian Sustainable Agriculture Project (see page 198). The Ratchfords partner with New River Organic Growers (see page 34). Local farmers often come to the restaurant to sell their products. Chef Ratchford also connects with local farmers by visiting the Watauga County Farmers' Market.

The Vidalia team has competed in the Fire on the Rock Chef's Challenge. It has also participated in the Girl Scout Cookie Cook Off and other local charity events.

The Recipes

Poached Pear Salad
Serves 4

Pears

    4 Anjou pears, peeled and halved lengthwise, cores removed with melon baller
    1 bottle white wine (expensive wine is not necessary)
    1 cup sugar
    2 stars anise
    2 sticks cinnamon
    1 tablespoon whole coriander seed

Poached Pear Salad
Photo provided by Sam Ratchford

Salad

mixed salad greens, enough to cover bottom of salad plate
½ cup pecans, toasted and salted
enough blue cheese (your favorite brand) to scatter over salad
dried cranberries or cherries
your favorite cranberry or raspberry vinaigrette

PEARS

Place pears in a small stockpot. Cover with wine just until pears float. Add sugar, anise, cinnamon, and coriander. Weigh pears down with small plates so they stay submerged. Bring to a boil, then reduce to a simmer for 20 minutes. Chill entire contents, including liquid and spices, in refrigerator overnight.

Remove pears from liquid. Strain liquid, removing spices and debris. Simmer on low heat to reduce liquid until it reaches the consistency of syrup. Let cool.

SALAD

Assemble salad greens on bottom of plate. Sprinkle pecans, blue cheese, and dried fruit over top. Slice poached pears lengthwise and fan over top. Drizzle wine reduction syrup over salad. Serve with your choice of vinaigrette.

Smokin' Chicken Mac 'n' Cheese
Serves 4

Smokin' Chicken Mac 'n' Cheese
Photo provided by Sam Ratchford

1 cup kosher salt
1 cup sugar
4 cups water
4 6-ounce chicken breasts
ice to cover
3 or 4 sprigs fresh rosemary
wood chips for smoking, per directions on chips and smoker
2 cups heavy cream
1 cup milk
½ cup sun-dried tomatoes, rehydrated
½ cup shredded sharp cheddar cheese
½ pound cavatappi or macaroni pasta, cooked al dente and chilled
salt and pepper to taste

To make brine, bring salt, sugar, and water to a boil to dissolve salt and sugar. Place chicken in a 4-quart container and cover with about 2 inches of ice. Break up rosemary and place on top. Pour hot brine over chicken and ice and let sit for 10 to 15 minutes. Remove chicken from brine and smoke until done, following instructions on smoker. Allow to cool.

Pull chicken by separating meat from bone and pulling meat into strips. Set meat aside. Bring cream and milk to a simmer. Reduce until thick and until large bubbles form. Reduce heat to low. Stir in tomatoes, cheddar, and chicken. Stir slowly until cheese melts. Add pasta and mix well. Season with salt and pepper.

Valle Crucis

Randall Isaacs

Randall Isaacs
Photo by Bernard Russo

The 1861 Farmhouse

3608 Broadstone Road (N.C. 194)
Valle Crucis, N.C. 28679
828-963-6301
www.1861farmhouse.com

The Chef

Randall Isaacs is a mountain man, born in Sugar Grove, near Valle Crucis. He has lived in the High Country all his life and would never think about moving anywhere else. "I tried it once," he recalls. "Got as far as Hickory. But I had to come back to my mountains. I love being outdoors, working in the garden, collecting fresh vegetables to prepare for dinner, and sawing timber."

His interest in cooking began when he was young. He describes standing on a stepstool beside his grandmother and watching her in the kitchen. "I thought she could do anything," he says. "I loved watching her make biscuits. Sometimes, she would let me help and show me how to do things.

"I grew up in a house that was only a half-mile from my grandparents' house. I would walk to their house every morning, and my grandmother would cook a hot breakfast for me. Sometimes, my whole family would go, but often it would be just me. Fresh eggs from her hens, country sausage she had made herself, hot biscuits with homemade butter, and her delicious homemade apple butter. Mmm! I would never miss a meal that my grandmother cooked! She would also fix a delicious lunch for us every day—just simple country cooking like chicken and dumplings with a big pot of pinto beans and collard greens. She always made fresh biscuits. I loved being there right when she took them out of the stove. They smelled so good, and—oh, my goodness—they were so soft and fluffy! Then I would slather on her homemade butter. My grandfather owned a sawmill. She would cook lunch for him and his workers every day. She didn't have to twist their arms to make them come up and eat!

"My grandmother, Celie Guy, was a strong woman—a true mountain woman, very independent. She cooked from a wood stove until she was in her nineties. She would not have a modern electric range in her house. She said her food 'would not cook right.' She also did not have plumbing in her house until the late 1990s. She had fresh spring water running right into her kitchen through a pipe in the kitchen window. She kept her milk and her butter in a cold spring-water trough. No refrigerator. Long after my grandfather had passed away, she continued to raise two hogs every year. She would make her own country sausage, can vegetables from her garden, and make jams and jellies from fruits picked here in the mountains. She lived to be over a hundred years old.

"Another great memory of growing up is lunch on Sundays at my aunt Blanche Presnell's house. She would cook the best meals I have ever had, even to this day. We would go to her house after church, and she would turn out the most wonderful fried chicken, country-style steak, and fresh vegetables straight from the garden, then apple pie for dessert."

Making the transition from such wonderful home cooking to restaurant kitchens began when Randall was in his teens. He went to work at the Green Park Inn, first washing dishes and shucking oysters, then moving to prep cook and line cook positions. But as he worked his way "up the line" in restaurants, he realized how much he needed to learn. He looked into culinary schools and was "really happy" when he saw how good the program was at nearby Caldwell Community College. He completed the program in the early 1980s, earning his certified culinary chef's degree. He moved on from the Green Park Inn to several other local restaurants, including the Banner Elk Café, before eventually settling at The 1861 Farmhouse.

Developing a chef's career did not go smoothly. At one point, he was unable to support his family on restaurant work, so he became a lumberjack. "That's pretty different from cooking, isn't it?" he says. He worked in lumber for 18 years. "Now, that was some truly hard work. Some nights, I would come home, and as much as I love food, I would just go to bed, I was so tired. But my heart was always in cooking. About eight years ago, I came back to it. Now, I really love being a chef. I love the creativity."

Experience has helped him realize that leading a professional kitchen requires attention to detail and careful communication. "I was training a new prep cook, and I told him how to mix our Southern potato salad," he recalls. "He was listening very carefully. I got busy doing something else and left him alone to make potato salad. I saw him dice the potatoes and then start mixing away. When he finished, he gave it to me to taste. I realized that he had not cooked the potatoes first! That made me understand that when you are explaining a recipe, you really have to take it slowly and explain every step. You can't assume anything!"

Randall says his method starts with fresh ingredients. "It is always my goal to bring out the best in a food, to show what's already in it, rather than to use a lot of heavy sauces to change the inherent flavor of something. Although I am a trained chef, and I feel that I can compete with the best of them, I would have to say that my style is fairly simple, because I was raised on a farm and I have a deep appreciation for fresh ingredients, especially vegetables. I love taking something fresh and cooking it perfectly, so that the simple, natural flavors come through. I love to take things slowly as much as possible, and not rush anything."

When he cooks for himself, Randall's favorite meat is pork. "I also love potatoes, and I can prepare them a hundred different ways. My table at home is always loaded with fresh vegetables—slow-cooked lima beans with pork, fresh sliced tomatoes with a little salt and maybe fresh basil, plus collard greens and corn bread. That is a perfect meal to me."

The Restaurant

Steve and Alison Garrett spent two years reconstructing a Civil War–era farmhouse in order to create a restaurant and winery. Listed on the National Register of Historic Places, the house is located in the heart of Valle Crucis across from the historic Mast General Store. Patrons feel a warm, welcoming country atmosphere as soon as they arrive. Many guests sit in the rocking chairs on the porch, sip wine, relax, take in the view that spans the valley, and experience a sense of peace. A deck out back overlooks a mountain stream. Tables are set on the porch and deck for outdoor dining during the summer and early fall.

Inside, three dining rooms, each with its own unique character, provide the setting for cozy fireside dining. The "wine room," located in the original brick part of the house, offers an Old World feel. Its walls are over a foot thick, constructed of bricks that Henry Taylor, the original owner, made by hand. Henry also built and operated the Mast General Store before selling it to the Mast family. His wife, Victoria, was postmistress of Valle Crucis for more than 30 years; residents came to the house to collect their mail. Even in the 1800s, the farmhouse was widely known for welcoming visitors. Today, the solid hemlock floors remain intact, and diners enjoy views of the valley through the original wavy glass in the 150-year-old windows. The owners have taken care to re-create the look and feel of Sunday dinner at Grandma's house, complete with mismatched china set on lace-covered antique tables.

Chef Isaacs met the Garretts while they were renovating the house. He auditioned by cooking a dinner for them. The restaurant opened Memorial Day weekend in 2011 and began drawing crowds right away.

Valle Crucis resident Charles Church heads an organization of area farmers that sells produce to area restaurants; the kitchen at The 1861 Farmhouse tries to get first pick of local vegetables. In addition, the Garretts have begun planting a garden on the premises. They plan to grow tomatoes, cucumbers, onions, potatoes, and herbs.

Patrons have given high scores to The 1861 Farmhouse on www.highcountrydining.com/. Chef Isaacs and his team competed in the 2012 Fire on the Rock Chef's Challenge.

The Recipes

Chicken Cabernet
Serves 4

Author's Note

Chicken Cabernet is the result of a collaboration between Chef Isaacs and Alison Garrett, owner of The 1861 Farmhouse. One afternoon as Randall began to prepare Chicken Kiev, he realized the chicken breasts would not be thawed early enough for the advance preparation required. He needed to prepare something for the nightly special that could be made to order. In stepped Alison. She had a favorite dish that she fixed for her

Chicken Cabernet
Photo by Bernard Russo

family using chicken, red wine (a switch from white wine, more commonly used with chicken), and mushrooms. Chef Isaacs added a veil of melted Swiss cheese and added cream to the Cabernet sauce. They christened their collaboration Chicken Cabernet. It was such a hit with customers that night and over the next few weeks that it moved from the special menu to the nightly dinner menu. Chef Isaacs recommends serving Chicken Cabernet with mashed potatoes topped with a bit of the Cabernet sauce and either green beans or grilled asparagus spears.

½ teaspoon sea salt
½ teaspoon pepper
2 large boneless chicken breasts
2 tablespoons olive oil, divided
1 tablespoon butter
1 clove garlic, minced
¼ cup sweet onion, chopped fine
1 tablespoon flour
2 cups chicken stock
1 cup Cabernet Sauvignon, divided

2 tablespoons heavy cream
2 cups sliced mushrooms
4 slices Swiss cheese at room temperature
fresh parsley for garnish

Salt and pepper chicken on both sides. Brown chicken in a skillet in 1 tablespoon of the olive oil. Remove from pan and set aside. Add butter to pan and melt over medium heat. Add garlic and onions. Stir to keep from sticking. Add flour to make a roux, stirring constantly. Slowly add chicken stock while stirring. Stir in ½ cup of the Cabernet. Cook over low heat for about 5 minutes. Whisk in heavy cream as sauce thickens. Remove from heat and set aside. In a separate saucepan, heat remaining 1 tablespoon olive oil over medium heat. Add mushrooms. Toss to combine. Add remaining Cabernet and sauté mushrooms until reduced.

To present, top each breast with ¼ of the mushrooms. Cover each breast with a slice of Swiss cheese. Spoon ¼ of the sauce over each. Garnish with fresh parsley.

Lime Zest Trout
Serves 4

Chef's note

"The 1861 Farmhouse uses only fresh North Carolina mountain trout that has been filleted and deboned. One of our favorite and most simple ways to prepare it is our fresh lime zest version. The lime zest enhances but does not overwhelm the delicate natural flavor of the trout. 'Less is more' is the philosophy behind this recipe. Fresh North Carolina mountain trout is so good that you don't want to do too much to it."

4 fresh trout fillets, approximately 4 ounces each
olive oil nonstick cooking spray
sea salt to taste
finely ground pepper
1 or 2 limes, depending on size

Lime Zest Trout
Photo by Bernard Russo

Spray trout lightly on both sides with cooking spray. Lightly sprinkle sides with sea salt and pepper. Zest limes and sprinkle zest over trout. Squeeze a little lime juice on each piece. The juice of 1 lime should be enough for all 4 pieces. Grill trout face down for 3 to 4 minutes. Flip fillets and grill skin side down another 3 to 4 minutes. Do not overcook.

The 1861 Farmhouse serves trout with a creamy herbed risotto and grilled fresh asparagus spears.

Danielle Deschamps Stabler

Danielle
Deschamps
Stabler
Photo by
John Batchelor

Mast Farm Inn

2543 Broadstone Road
Banner Elk, N.C. 28604
828-963-5857
www.themastfarminn.com

The Chef

Danielle Deschamps Stabler comes from a family that is French on her father's side and Italian on her mother's. Danielle grew up in Haiti, France, Great Britain, Switzerland, and New York. In addition to being chef, she serves as innkeeper, along with her husband, Ken. Other family members maintain various aspects of the Mast Farm Inn's operations.

Danielle relates that since arriving in the North Carolina mountains, she has never wanted to leave. She loves the slow pace of life, the friendly neighbors, and the "amazing" sense of community. With regard to her work as chef, she is particularly attracted by "all the farms and produce we can find around here. All winter long, farmers keep us stocked, and in the summer, we get the opportunity to garden ourselves and use all those beautiful vegetables at the restaurant. I love the mountains!"

She started cooking when she "had to fend for myself" in college. "I never knew I had what it took to be in the food industry," she says. "But when we moved to North Carolina and started with the B&B, I naturally migrated to the kitchen and loved it." She never went to culinary school. "I always say that I went to Mom and Grandma's school. I never met my grandmother, but from what I hear, she was an amazing chef, from making fresh mozzarella to fresh pasta, and Mom passed her knowledge and skills on to me. Mom cooks with me every day at the inn, and we have a ball doing it. We have a great dynamic."

When cooking just for friends and family, Danielle leans toward simple foods, especially fish and lots of vegetables. "When you start with wonderful ingredients, you don't need to do much to them, and that is the real secret to success in the kitchen," she says. Danielle is working on her own cookbook of Mast Farm recipes.

The Restaurant

The Mast Farm Inn was established in the 1700s by Joseph Mast to provide lodging for mountain travelers. A two-room log cabin constructed in the early 1800s remains in use on the property; it is the oldest habitable structure in Watauga County and one of the oldest in North Carolina. The Mast family retained ownership for approximately two centuries, until 1984. The Deschamps family bought the property, along with the nearby Taylor House Inn, in 2006; the family had owned what used to be Camp Glen Laurel, a camp for girls, in Little Switzerland, for 10 years and was looking for a way to operate a business in the mountains on a year-round basis. The Mast Farm property is listed on the National Register of Historic Places.

Although meals at the Mast Farm Inn are served family-style, the food is "more elevated" than traditional family meals. "We cook one meal a night, and everyone gets the same thing," Danielle says. "We serve four courses over two hours. Everything is fresh, everything is made in house from scratch (including our bread), and everything is as organic and as local as it can be."

The restaurant's website cites several influences and recommends books by Alice Waters, Barbara Kingsolver, Michael Pollan, and other chefs and food writers identified with what has come to be called the "Slow Food" movement. Much of the produce used in the restaurant comes from New River Organic Growers (see page 34), which, according to Chef Deschamps, "bridges the gap between farm and restaurant. They compile a list twice a week of what is available within 75 miles of the inn. Once I place an order, it is harvested the next day and brought to me. We also have great relationships with other smaller farms nearer to us, and they let us go in there and pick stuff out as we please. Only up here would such things be allowed—one more reason I love the High Country!"

The Mast Farm Inn's entry came in second in the Best Dish North Carolina competition in 2011; the restaurant was one of 10 finalists the previous year. The inn is a member of the Select Registry of Distinguished Inns of North America. It has been recommended in articles in the *Washington Post*, the *New York Times, Southern Living*, and the *Discerning Traveler*. Chef Deschamps and her mother, Marie-Henriette, operate a cooking school that offers a series of cooking vacation travel packages.

Cream of Carrot Astaire and Jolly Roger Ginger Soup
Photo by John Batchelor

The Recipes

Cream of Carrot Astaire and Jolly Roger Ginger Soup, Dancing to the Tune of Cumin, Cinnamon, Nutmeg, Curry, Orange, Onion, Garlic, White Wine, Extra-Virgin Olive Oil, Butter, and Chicken or Vegetable Broth

Serves 6

2 pounds carrots
1 large onion
4 cloves fresh garlic
1 teaspoon fresh thyme
½ teaspoon cinnamon, ground
½ teaspoon ginger, ground or powdered
1 tablespoon olive oil
salt and pepper to taste
2 tablespoons butter
⅓ cup white wine
zest and juice of 1 orange
½ teaspoon curry powder
4 cups chicken or vegetable stock
⅓ cup heavy cream
pinch of nutmeg

Peel carrots and onions. Dice to approximately ¼-inch pieces. Place carrots and onions in a mixing bowl. Add garlic, thyme, cinnamon, ginger, olive oil, and salt and pepper. Mix to combine. Preheat oven to 350 degrees. Place above ingredients in a roasting pan and bake for 35 minutes. Melt butter in a soup casserole dish. Deglaze roasting pan with wine and pour all above ingredients into soup casserole. Add orange zest and curry powder. Add stock and simmer for 25 minutes. Add orange juice. Purée with a hand blender. Add heavy cream and nutmeg. Serve immediately.

Pepper Cream Steak with Fingerling Potatoes
Serves 4

Crème Fraîche
>   1 cup sour cream
>   ¼ cup heavy cream

Fingerling Potatoes
>   24 fingerling potatoes
>   3 tablespoons butter
>   6 cloves garlic, minced
>   2 sprigs rosemary, chopped
>   6 or 8 sprigs fresh thyme, chopped
>   1 tablespoon chopped parsley

Steaks
>   4 6-ounce filets mignons (preferably all natural, grass fed,
>   and pasture raised)
>   sea salt
>   coarsely ground pepper
>   2 tablespoons butter
>   ¼ cup rum
>   dollop of Dijon mustard

CRÈME FRAÎCHE

In a metal or glass mixing bowl, whisk together sour cream and heavy cream until they become whole. Feel free to add more sour cream

Pepper Cream Steak
Photo by John Batchelor

if mixture doesn't seem thick enough. Refrigerate until ready to use. This French version of heavy cream is thicker and creamier than sour cream. It has a wonderful aroma and taste and is great for use in any pasta, chicken, or fish dish.

FINGERLING POTATOES

Bring salted water to a boil in a saucepan. Boil potatoes until soft. Drain potatoes and pat dry with paper towels. Melt butter in saucepan. Sauté potatoes in butter until tender. Toss in garlic, rosemary, thyme, and parsley.

STEAKS

Preheat oven to 350 degrees. Season steaks with salt and pepper; go heavy on the pepper! Let steaks stand until they reach room temperature. Heat a pan to medium-high on stove. Add butter. Sauté steaks for about 4 minutes on each side, letting them brown. Pour in rum. Using a long match, light rum to flambé steaks. Remove steaks from pan and reduce heat to low. Put steaks on a baking sheet and place in oven for 4 minutes.

Add extra butter to the pan and use a whisk to help butter melt. Add crème fraîche and Dijon. Stir. Simmer until mixture thickens. This will take no more than 4 to 5 minutes. Sauce should be ready by the time steaks come out of oven.

Caution: cream and butter sauces tend to turn if they are overcooked, so keep heat on low while making sauce.

To present

Remove steaks from oven, top with sauce, and serve alongside Fingerling Potatoes.

A Best Dish North Carolina 2nd place winner
Mixed Berry Cobbler
Serves 8 to 12

Fruit

    1 pint blueberries
    1 pint raspberries
    1 pint strawberries
    1 pint blackberries
    2 tablespoons vanilla extract
    1 large stick cinnamon
    2 stars anise
    zest and juice of ½ lime
    1 cup brown sugar
    ⅓ cup brandy
    ⅓ cup cream sherry or liqueur such as Grand Marnier

Crust

    1½ cups flour
    1 cup sugar
    ½ cup sugar in the raw
    1 teaspoon cinnamon
    1 stick butter, melted
    1 teaspoon vanilla extract

    ice cream

Mixed Berry Cobbler
Photo by John Batchelor

FRUIT

This should be prepared the night before and keep frozen in a plastic resealable bag overnight. If you prefer, you can freeze it in individual ramekins so the portion sizes are already done.

Combine all ingredients in a large mixing bowl. Be careful not to break up cinnamon stick. Stir mixture so cinnamon stick settles toward bottom center. Let stand overnight in freezer.

CRUST

Preheat oven to 350 degrees. Mix together flour, sugar, sugar in the raw, and cinnamon. Add melted butter and vanilla.

TO PRESENT

Remove fruit mixture from freezer 30 to 45 minutes before start of baking. Allow mixture to soften a bit. Remove cinnamon stick. Stir to redistribute flavors. Place fruit mixture on bottom of a baking dish or portion-sized ramekins. Spread heavy coating of crust mixture over fruit. Bake approximately 30 minutes until bubbling and thick. For a browner crust, broil for the last 3 or 4 minutes; watch to make sure crust doesn't burn. Serve with ice cream.

Banner Elk

Joshua Grogan

Josh Grogan
Photo by John Batchelor

Hearthstone
Tavern and Grille

3990 N.C. 105 South #9
Banner Elk, N.C. 28604
828-898-3461
www.hearthstonetavern.net

129

The Chef

Josh Grogan is a native of the North Carolina foothills, having grown up in Hickory. He moved to the High Country in spring 2001 after meeting his future wife, Jessica, whose family lived in the area. He loves the seasons, the people, and the opportunities to enjoy the outdoors.

Josh had been involved in corporate restaurants before 2001, but not in the kitchen. Jessica's mother owned The Corner Palate and the Banner Elk Bistro, both in Banner Elk. Josh started working at The Corner Palate as a waiter but eventually found his way into the kitchen. When both of the restaurant's sushi chefs graduated from Appalachian State University and decided to move, the family needed someone to take over the sushi station. Josh bought a few books and learned how to cook rice and make a proper roll. He then studied books on inventive new techniques and a book on the history of sushi. From there, he "found a love for food, and how to create flavors starting from basic ingredients," he recalls.

At the time, The Corner Palate had some "dedicated and experienced chefs who were kind and patient enough to serve as mentors," Josh says. Within two years, he was running the line himself. A constant reader, he bought books on various culinary stylings and became especially fond of traditional Southern, Low Country, and Asian cuisines. Eventually, he left his post at The Corner Palate and worked at several other local establishments, learning from their chefs.

Josh believes the most important factors in food preparation are simplicity and flavor. "It may seem like a cliché, but now more than ever, chefs and cooks get too caught up in appearance and exotic techniques, and some of them seem to forget the fundamentals. 'Do these foods pair together nicely?' Food is art. But it is edible art. Just because you *can* make a stunning red cabbage gelée doesn't mean that you *should* make a red cabbage gelée. That said, I admit that I have started dabbling in molecular gastronomy. But my style is Southern at heart—lots of butter, bacon, and cream, with salt. But I also am very influenced by Asian cuisine. Whenever I can, I try to blend the two. I'm currently working on another restaurant concept with a friend who's also a chef, to be called 'cUt.' We want it to be a Texas-style steakhouse that meets a New York sushi eatery."

When at home, Josh's favorite dish is braised short ribs. "We use Old Hickory Brewery's Ruby Lager as the braising liquid and in the sauce," he says. "And I love pork belly. Last month, we did a wine dinner, and I smoked salmon using slabs of pork belly rubbed with applewood salt. It was delicious. I cook almost all the dinner shifts, so I don't cook at home often. My wife is a baker, so she spends a lot of time in the kitchen with our two boys, experimenting with cookies and cupcakes."

The Restaurant

Josh Grogan took over Hearthstone in winter 2011–12. He and Jessica knew the former owners as well as some of the employees, so when they learned the property was for sale, they decided to open a second restaurant; they also own Crave in Boone (see page 77). Hearthstone is situated at the foot of Grandfather Mountain at the Tynecastle intersection. It was decorated during a previous owner's tenure, after a customer suggested the concept of a combination furniture showroom and restaurant. The customer turned out to be Art Thompson, president of Lane Venture Furniture. The restaurant subsequently closed for a long weekend, and the Lane Venture crew took over. Few other restaurants feature furniture as distinctive. A large stone fireplace centers one wall. A metal gazebo ushers patrons through the entry area.

Hearthstone features a Southern-style menu. The ambience conveys the warm and inviting feel of the mountains. "We complement the menu with the dining-room décor by making it comfortable and approachable while also making it a bit exciting," Chef Grogan says. "A lot of the restaurants in the area focus on a more modern décor or a casual bar atmosphere. At Hearthstone, we are very competitive, with prices falling in the same range as other area restaurants, but we also provide atmosphere that makes customers feel welcome and at home."

Chef Grogan loves to work with local farms and North Carolina products. "We feel it is very important to keep our money local and to support others in our community. We work with the local produce stand in Banner Elk so we can get farm-fresh products. We also work with a few new companies and farms in our area that email us their weekly products, and purchase items from them to use in our kitchen."

Hearthstone has already received recognition. The restaurant won *Wine Spectator* awards for its wine list in 2010 and 2011 and has applied for the honor in 2012. It also received an Open Table Diner's Choice award for 2012.

The Recipes

Fried Green Tomatoes with Cajun Crawfish Cream Sauce
Serves 6

Tomatoes
1 large egg
½ cup buttermilk
½ cup all-purpose flour, divided
½ cup cornmeal
1 teaspoon salt
½ teaspoon freshly ground pepper
3 medium green tomatoes, cut into ⅓-inch slices
1 to 2 cups vegetable oil

Cajun Crawfish Cream Sauce
1 tablespoon olive oil
½ cup tasso ham, diced small
1 tablespoon minced shallot
½ cup crawfish tail meat
1 teaspoon minced garlic
¾ cup heavy cream
salt and pepper to taste

Fried Green Tomatoes with Cajun Crawfish Cream Sauce
Photo by John Batchelor

TOMATOES

Lightly whisk egg and buttermilk together and set aside. Combine ¼ cup of the flour, cornmeal, salt, and pepper in a shallow pan or bowl and set aside. Dredge tomato slices in remaining ¼ cup flour. Dip floured tomatoes into egg mixture, then dredge in cornmeal mixture. Pour oil halfway up a large cast-iron skillet. Heat oil to approximately 375 degrees or until just bubbling. Drop small batches of tomatoes into hot oil and cook for about 2 minutes on each side until golden brown. Use paper towels on a plate to absorb oil as tomatoes cool.

CAJUN CRAWFISH CREAM SAUCE

Heat olive oil in a large sauté pan and add ham. Render for 2 minutes. Add shallots, crawfish, and garlic and sauté for about 1 minute. Add cream and bring to a boil. Reduce to a simmer and cook for 4 to 6 minutes until sauce reduces enough to coat the back of a spoon. Add salt and pepper.

TO PRESENT

Serve sauce over or under hot tomatoes.

Maple-Bourbon Pork Belly
Serves 4

Pork
> 2 pounds pork belly
> 2 tablespoons olive oil
> 3 tablespoons 5-spice blend
> 2 cloves garlic

Maple-bourbon glaze
> ¼ cup quality maple syrup
> 2 cup brown sugar
> ¼ cup bourbon
> 1 cup orange juice
> 4 tablespoons balsamic vinegar
> salt and pepper to taste

PORK

Remove any skin and ribs from pork belly. Place olive oil, 5-spice blend, and garlic in a blender and blend to a paste. Brush pork belly thoroughly with paste, then tightly enclose in plastic wrap. Place pork belly on a flat pan that will fit in the refrigerator. To help ensure even coating, place another pan on top and weigh it down with a few heavy canned items. Refrigerate overnight.

Remove plastic wrap and allow pork belly to come approximately to room temperature. Set grill for direct grilling. Grill pork belly for 5 to 7 minutes on a high heat until all the meat is seared, then remove pork and

Maple-Bourbon Pork Belly
Photo provided by Hearthstone

place it in a rack. Add a roasting tin to the grill and set the pork belly over the tin. Reset the grill to indirect cooking and grill pork for 1 hour.

MAPLE-BOURBON GLAZE

Place all ingredients in a saucepan and gently cook until properly melted together. Lower heat and simmer 10 to 15 minutes until sauce thickens. While pork belly is cooking, cover pork with glaze at regular intervals until roughly ⅔ of glaze is used. The pork will get darker the more you glaze it. Reserve remainder of glaze to drizzle onto pork before serving.

TO PRESENT

Cut pork belly into 4-ounce portions. Hearthstone usually serves this dish in steamed flour tortillas or lettuce wraps with a charred corn and black bean relish.

Patrick Bagbey

Louisiana Purchase

397 Shawneehaw Avenue
Banner Elk, N.C. 28604
828-963-5087
http://louisianapurchasefoodandspirits.com

The Chef

Patrick Bagbey, the son of a home economics teacher and the grandson of an independent grocer, grew up in Clarksville, Virginia. As a child, he spent summers and time after school working on family farms. He began his restaurant career in fast-food when he was a teenager. When he was about 20, he made a trip to the High Country with a friend who was transferring to Appalachian State University. He has never left.

Patrick took a part-time job at Sagebrush in Boone, where he worked prep and learned to butcher whole animals. The restaurant's transition to premade products prompted his move to the Banner Elk Café. A friend then set him up with a dishwashing shift at Louisiana Purchase, where Patrick could pick up a little extra money by covering duties when the friend didn't want to work. The friend's absence led to Patrick's more extended presence—which led to romance, increased responsibility, and eventually ownership of the restaurant.

"I learned here from the crew," Patrick says. "There was a lot to be learned. I have been at Louisiana Purchase since 1998. After washing dishes for a while, I moved to a line-cook role. I didn't really have a title. But I became a full-time employee in 2000."

Laurie Simmons is from Winston-Salem. She came to the mountains for a summer after high school in 1995 and has remained ever since. "You make certain sacrifices for your quality of life here," she says of Banner Elk. "It's cold, and there's only one stoplight. The conveniences of larger cities just aren't here. But it has everything we want. I forgot to lock up one night, but no one bothered anything." By the time Patrick started regular work at Louisiana Purchase, Laurie was floor manager. They were married in 2004. Their son, eight-year-old Ryland, is a frequent presence at the computer in the greeting station. He is growing up in the restaurant.

Patrick thought seriously about culinary school but found he was learning from the other chefs at the restaurant. And he constantly read publications related to food and cooking. His tutors at Louisiana Purchase included some of the High Country's most prominent chefs. "Colin Patience

(on opposite page)
Patrick Bagbey
Photo by Leah Joyner

was sous chef when I came," Patrick recalls. "He took me under his wing and taught me a lot about the basics. He is now executive sous chef at Linville Ridge Country Club. Patrick Maisonhaute was executive chef; he is now the exec at Eseeola Lodge. Fabian Botta, who founded the restaurant, would come back from time to time as guest chef, and I learned from him, too. Chef Luke Fussell, executive chef at Hound Ears Club, provided guidance along the way. I spent most of my time under the watchful eye of chef-owner Mark Rosse, who has always been well respected in the area. It really boils down to just a long period of hard work. I was on my own, taking care of myself, and I just set out to find ways to make myself valuable to the restaurant. I was determined to learn to cook everything on the menu during my first year, and I did. Within a year, I had been promoted to sous chef." By the time a decision about further schooling had to be made, Patrick was already well established in the kitchen at Louisiana Purchase.

"If I'm not cooking for company, I like ethnic, spicy foods—Thai especially," Patrick says. "We serve a staff meal here every day. We cook Thai cuisine and Southern favorites—meat loaf, chicken-fried steak, for example. For Christmas dinner, the staff had pork chops, red-eye gravy, collard greens, and black-eyed peas. You'll see Southern things like that as specials sometimes in the summer."

The Restaurant

Louisiana Purchase is in its third generation of chef ownership. Fabian Botta, formerly of the fabled Tack Room, started the restaurant in 1984. Laurie considers him "a genius at conceptualizing and a personal friend." Fabian sold the restaurant to his executive chef, Mark Rosse. After Chef Botta left, Chef Rosse gave Patrick more responsibility in the kitchen. By the time Mark Rosse decided to retire, Patrick had been elevated to executive chef. That was around 2005. "Mark let the word out that he was going to retire, and my wife and I started looking into how we might be able to take it over," Patrick recalls. "We didn't have a lot of money, but he helped us work it out. It made sense to him, and my wife and I were already managing the restaurant part of the time when he wasn't here. I could never imagine myself moving to a restaurant that was better than Louisiana Purchase already was."

Laurie continues in her role as manager. The couple became owners when Patrick was 28 years old. Laurie reflects on their time in the restaurant: "Earning experience in food service is no easy feat. No amount of education in any culinary program can teach you to wash a pot, dress a duck, plan a menu, or manage a staff. We are so proud of Patrick's accomplishments, especially his ability and willingness to work so hard and continue to be a wonderful husband, a loving dad. We feel fortunate to have had the opportunity to have a family business. What a blessing to set your child on a prep table and talk about the recipe for sourdough bread. And then make it, while your son watches and helps!"

Louisiana Purchase occupies two stories of a small shopping-center storefront. The interior is elegant. A mural of a New Orleans street band extends upstairs into the bar. Original art depicts rural mountain scenes as well as a bit of New Orleans jazz. Black chairs flank white-clothed tables.

Pâtés occupy a special status at Louisiana Purchase; they are prepared from scratch and cured in-house. Everything else is made in-house, too—soups, sauces, bread, ice cream, even the cookie cups the ice cream is served in. "We buy whole fish daily and trim them by hand. Our beef is hand-trimmed as well," Chef Bagbey says.

He buys produce at the Watauga County Farmers' Market, although the growing season is limited due to weather. "We try to be as much farm-to-table as possible," he says. "Our fish—except salmon, obviously—is almost all from the North Carolina coast. I just refuse to buy from Hawaii and the Pacific. We work with Trosley Farms in Elk Park for duck, Cornish game hens, lamb, and pork, plus some vegetables—squash and zucchini especially. Charlotte's Green House in Valle Crucis provides hydroponic lettuce, leaf lettuces, kale, and Swiss chard. The Louisiana Purchase Salad is made with lettuces she grows into a rose shape just for us."

Louisiana Purchase has earned multiple "Best of Awards of Excellence" from *Wine Spectator*, of which there are only slightly over 800 world wide.

BBQ Shrimp
Photo by Leah Joyner

The Recipes

BBQ Shrimp
Serves 2 generously

Grits cake
> package of grits, preferably yellow stone-ground, approximately 12 ounces
> 2 tablespoons ground andouille sausage
> 2 tablespoons grated cheddar cheese
> 2 eggs, beaten, to use as egg wash
> enough flour and breadcrumbs to coat a 3-inch grits cake

Sweet potato threads
> 1 sweet potato

Shrimp
> about 2 tablespoons cooking oil
> heaping tablespoon minced red onion

heaping tablespoon minced shallot
1 tablespoon minced garlic
12 shrimp, preferably 16–20 size, deveined and peeled, tails left on
½ cup dry sherry
2 tablespoons Worcestershire sauce
2 tablespoons Tabasco sauce
2 tablespoons fresh-squeezed lemon juice
1 stick cold butter
1 tablespoon diced scallions

GRITS CAKE

Make grits according to package directions for two portions. Sauté sausage until lightly browned. Add cheddar. Allow to cool. When grits are cold, form 2 cakes. Coat cakes with egg wash and dust with flour and breadcrumbs. Fry on both sides until crusty, approximately 2-3 minutes per side. Set aside.

SWEET POTATO THREADS

Julienne sweet potato (cut into thread-sized strips using a mandoline). Deep-fry at 325 degrees until crisp. Remove, drain, dry, and set aside.

SHRIMP

Heat a sauté pan containing enough cooking oil to coat bottom. Add red onions, shallots, and garlic. Sauté about 2 minutes until translucent but not beginning to brown. Add shrimp. Sauté about 1 minute. Add sherry, Worcestershire, Tabasco, and lemon juice. Simmer until shrimp turn red. Remove shrimp. Simmer remaining liquid until it thickens. Add butter straight out of the refrigerator. Reduce heat. Whisk butter until mixture reaches sauce texture. Add scallions.

TO PRESENT

Place grits cakes in center of plates. Place shrimp over grits. Ladle with sauce. Cover top with sweet potato threads.

Paysan-Style Veal Pâté
Serves 12

Paysan-Style Veal Pâté
Photo by Leah Joyner

Paysan pâté spice

- 1 teaspoon black peppercorns
- 1 teaspoon ground allspice
- 1 teaspoon mace
- 1 teaspoon paprika
- 1 teaspoon cardamom
- 1 teaspoon thyme
- 1 teaspoon rosemary
- 1 teaspoon basil
- 1 teaspoon sage
- 1 teaspoon ground cloves
- 1 bay leaf

Pâté

- 26 ounces veal top round, trimmed and sliced
- 14 ounces pork tenderloin, trimmed and sliced
- 4 ounces salted fatback, washed and trimmed
- ½ yellow onion, julienned
- 1 teaspoon pink salt (curing salt)
- 1½ teaspoons kosher salt
- 6 ounces chicken livers
- 1 cup buttermilk
- 1 pound applewood-smoked bacon

crostini

- spiced mustard
- cornichons
- chopped onion

PAYSAN PÂTÉ SPICE

Using a mortar and pestle, grind all ingredients into a fine powder.

Place veal, pork, fatback, and onions in a mixing bowl. Add salts and 1½ teaspoons Paysan pâté spice. Mix well. Wrap in plastic and refrigerate overnight. In a separate bowl, soak chicken livers in buttermilk overnight.

After meats have been refrigerated overnight, line a terrine with strips of bacon, leaving excess hanging over sides. Grind meat mixture and chicken livers and mix well. Place mixture in terrine and fold excess bacon over top. Cover with terrine lid. Bake in a water bath at 350 degrees until an instant-read thermometer shows 130 degrees in center of terrine. Place in refrigerator and chill.

TO PRESENT

Slice pâté and serve with crostini, spiced mustard, cornichons, and chopped onions.

Hanger Steak with Gorgonzola Glaçage
Serves 2

    12 Brussels sprouts
    4 tablespoons pancetta
    2 butternut squash
    2 6-ounce portions hanging tender beef (hanging tender is the name of
      the cut)
    4 tablespoons cooking oil
    salt and pepper to taste
    ½ cup vegetable stock
    ½ cup heavy cream
    2 tablespoons Gorgonzola cheese
    pinch of salt

Blanch Brussels sprouts by placing them in boiling water until slightly soft but not fully cooked. Drain water, shock in ice water until cooled, then drain and dry. Render pancetta by frying until fat around edges starts to crisp and pancetta is lightly browned. Trim away fat, if desired. Chop into ¼-inch pieces. Peel squash so as to make ribbons from peel. Set aside both

Hanger Steak with Gorgonzola Glaçage
Photo by Leah Joyner

ribbons and squash. Grill steak to no more than medium doneness or it
will be tough. Internal temperature should be 145 to 150 degrees. Allow to
rest. While steak is cooking, heat a pan containing oil. Dice ½ cup squash.
Add squash to pan and season with salt and pepper. Toss in hot oil about 3
minutes until squash begins to soften. Add blanched Brussels sprouts and
lightly brown. Add 1 tablespoon pancetta pieces. Stir and flip to mix and
prevent sticking. Add vegetable stock. Simmer until squash is the texture
you want. In a separate pan, bring heavy cream to a slow boil. Add Gorgonzola and a pinch of salt. Simmer until mixture comes together. This is
the Gorgonzola Glaçage. Place ribbons of squash peel in deep-frying oil
heated to 325 degrees. Fry until curled but not browned.

To present

Place steak in center of a heated dish. Surround with Brussels sprouts
and squash mixture. Ladle top with Gorgonzola Glaçage. Cover with ribbons of fried squash peeling.

Tom Jankovich

Tom Jankovich
and Monte Weber
Photo by
Heather Turner

The Painted Fish Café

2941 Tynecastle Highway
Banner Elk, N.C. 28604
828-898-6800
www.paintedfishcafe.com

145

The Chef

Tom Jankovich was born in South Bend, Indiana, and grew up in Racine, Wisconsin. He moved to the North Carolina mountains in 2000, when he became executive chef at Grandfather Golf & Country Club in Linville, a position he held for 10 years. He says he will always live somewhere in the mountains: "No traffic, friendly, real people, great weather, great place to raise a family, and skiing!"

He started cooking at age 16 at a pizza and fried chicken place. He went to college at the University of Wisconsin in Madison, majoring in art. While there, he took a part-time restaurant job, though he had "basically no credentials." He explains, "Some other guy had gotten the job, but he called in after working two days and said he would rather party. They called all of the other applicants, but no one wanted to start on New Year's, so they finally got to me. Since I needed the money, I took the job, and I have been hooked ever since. I broiled 75 steaks that night, and only one was returned!"

By the time Tom began to consider culinary school, he had already spent a lot of time in professional kitchens. He left art school to check out L.A. "It was the early Spago era," he recalls, referring to Wolfgang Puck's hit creation. He talked his way into two and sometimes three jobs just to make money and learn.

Tom's culinary career took a detour when he decided to try to make the PGA Tour. He moved to Florida to play golf. He actually earned some money but was never able to qualify for the PGA Tour. During that time, he worked as a sous chef and chef in several clubs, which led him back to a culinary career.

He cites one strong influence in particular—"Chef in the Hat" Thierry Rautureau of Rover's and Luc restaurants in Seattle. "I hooked up with him for a year or so and learned more than five years of formal schooling could have done for me," he says. Chef Jankovich has learned in some famous kitchens: Cyrano's in Hollywood; Christiana Inn in Lake Tahoe; Boca West Country Club in Boca Raton, Florida; Mariner Sands Country

Club in Port St. Lucie, Florida; and The Landings in Savannah. As executive chef at The Landings—the largest country club in the United States, with 5,000 members—he was in charge of four clubhouses and 85 employees. "It was the first time in my career that I couldn't physically determine the outcome of each meal," he says. "It's a hard lesson to learn—how to motivate people to cook, act, and think like you, because everyone thinks the chef cooks everything even if he isn't there! Five thousand opinions, and each one is genuine to the person to whom it belongs!"

Tom has been a chef for over 30 years. On his days off, he likes to cook steaks. He is also a big fan of foie gras, truffles, sushi, "really fresh seafood," and oysters.

The Restaurant

The name *Painted Fish* comes from a strange piece of art that Tom coveted during his tenure at Grandfather Country Club; at the time, he thought it was too expensive. Although not a seafood restaurant—the menu is broad ranging—the café offers plenty of seafood.

The restaurant's motto is, "No pretense. Great prices. Homegrown ingredients. Inspired food for friends and family." It summarizes Chef Jankovich's belief "that great, imaginative food does not have to be expensive, pretentious, or unapproachable! The Painted Fish showcases recognizable food with a twist at prices that are affordable enough to allow people to go a few times a month and not feel like they have to budget for every visit." He tries to keep the food simple. "Use great, fresh ingredients, don't overwork anything, and always remember that flavor comes first," he says. "You can make it look pretty after you develop the flavors!"

He works closely with New River Organic Growers (see page 34) and with several local farmers and hydroponic growers. "We buy mushrooms from several foragers and cultivators. Much of our high-turnover stuff comes from the Asheville Market through Clemmons Produce. We get our micro greens from a woman in Boone. And several other farmers call and tell us what they have. We change menus and create featured items based on whatever is available fresh."

The atmosphere is relaxed and casual. Weather permitting, the outdoor seating provides views of Sugar Mountain. The café offers artisanal beers and quality wines especially selected for value.

The Recipes

Bacon Chicken
Serves 4

Chicken

4 chicken breasts, skin on, wing bones attached (skin-on boneless breasts or boneless, skinless breasts can be substituted)
splash of olive oil

Sauce

12 strips bacon, diced small
¼ cup light brown sugar
3 tablespoons Dijon mustard
3 tablespoons white vinegar

CHICKEN

Preheat oven to 400 degrees. Chop off knobs at end of wing bones if you prefer that appearance. Add olive oil to a large, ovenproof sauté pan over medium heat. Place chicken skin side down in pan and cook until a nice brown color is achieved. Turn chicken over and place entire pan in oven for 15 minutes. Remove from oven.

SAUCE

While chicken is cooking, place bacon in a 1-quart saucepan and render over medium-high heat. Just before bacon becomes crisp, remove from stove, leaving grease and bacon bits in pan. Add remaining ingredients,

Bacon Chicken
Photo by Heather Turner

stirring constantly until incorporated. Mixture can be reheated or held warm. If holding warm, stir well before serving. This sauce can be used with many other proteins and salads. Try it warm over a baby spinach salad. Sauce will last in refrigerator for a week.

TO PRESENT

Serve with a starch of your choice, such as potatoes or risotto. Place chicken on top of starch and place a green vegetable to the side. Ladle chicken with sauce.

Thai Curry Scallops Carbonara
Serves 4

Author's Note

This recipe was created by Monte Weber, sous chef at The Painted Fish.

Vegetable "pasta"
    2 large zucchini
    2 large straightneck yellow squash

Sauce
    3 eggs
    ⅓ cup heavy cream
    1 tablespoon red curry paste
    ½ tablespoon rice wine vinegar
    1 tablespoon honey

Scallops
    12 large fresh scallops
    1 cup medium-diced bacon
    ½ medium red onion, chopped
    5 cloves garlic, chopped
    1 cup Parmesan cheese

    3 tablespoons red curry paste (optional)
    2 tablespoons corn syrup (optional)

Vegetable "pasta"

Using a mandoline with a medium blade, slice zucchini and yellow squash into long strands resembling spaghetti, turning vegetables after each slice to utilize only the colorful outer skin. Boil unsalted water in a 3- to 4-quart pot and blanch vegetable strands for 1 minute. Drain and chill quickly under cold water. Set in a cool area until time to plate. This can be done up to a day ahead.

Sauce

In a blender, mix all ingredients until thoroughly combined. Refrigerate until needed.

Scallops

Remove tough "feet" from scallops. Rinse off any grit, drain, and dry thoroughly with paper towels. In a sauté pan over medium high, sear scallops until golden brown on each side. Remove each 1 as it becomes medium-

Thai Curry Scallops Carbonara
Photo by Heather Turner

rare in the center. Place on paper towels and set aside. In a 2-quart sauce-pan over medium-high heat, render bacon until almost crisp. Add onions, garlic, and vegetable "pasta" and sauté until onions are tender. Remove from heat and toss in Parmesan. Add curry mixture and toss to coat.

TO PRESENT

Place scallops back in pan for 15 seconds to reheat. Grab "pasta" mixture with tongs and twist equal amounts into center of plates. Continue to twist tongs until a kind of cylinder forms. Place scallops around vegetable "pasta." For an optional garnish, blend red curry paste with corn syrup. Add a slight amount of water so sauce just coats the back of a spoon. Lace on plates with a squirt bottle.

Nicole and Anthony Palazzo

Nicole Palazzo
*Photo provided by
Sorrento's Bistro*

Sorrento's Bistro

140 Azalea Circle
Banner Elk, N.C. 28604
828-898-5214
www.sorrentosbistrohome.com

The Chefs

Nicole Palazzo is petite, weighing in at barely 120 pounds. But it is not unusual for her to go into a restaurant and order every appetizer on the menu, plus two entrées, just for herself. She may not clean every plate, but she savors every bite. Of more importance, she will probably be able to identify all the ingredients from taste. "I probably inherited a sensitive palate, but my sense of taste has been trained all my life," she says. Nicole loves to eat, loves restaurants, plans vacations around restaurants she wants to visit, and loves being a chef in her family's restaurant.

Born in Hollywood, Florida, sister and brother Nicole and Anthony Palazzo moved to Banner Elk as children. Their grandfather was driving through town on his way to New Jersey and fell in love with the scenery. Eventually, their grandparents and aunts and uncles moved to the area as they retired.

Nicole and Anthony grew up cooking with their grandmother. Nicole remembers sitting in her grandmother's lap and rolling meatballs when she was no more than four years old. Anthony's cooking memories center on "Grandma's homemade gnocchi, ravioli, and pastas. Everybody would be involved—kids, uncles, aunts, everybody. It was very labor intensive." By the time Nicole was seven, she was throwing pizza crusts in Villa Sorrento, the restaurant the family opened in one of downtown Banner Elk's oldest buildings. "People would come in just to watch these little kids cooking their dinner," she recalls.

After Valle Crucis Elementary and Watauga High School, Nicole went to Cape Fear Community College in Wilmington to take art classes. She was creative. She waited tables but mostly enjoyed being a student and going to parties. "I loved the three Bs of college life: booze, beach, and boys." While in college, she got ideas from television cooking shows, then cooked huge five- or six-course meals for her friends. "They had never experienced anything like that, so they started wanting more," she says. Friends would call and ask if they could come over for her to cook for them. She eventually left Wilmington, returned to Banner Elk, and went back into the restaurant as bartender and waitress. But she moved into the kitchen quickly.

Anthony says he cannot imagine life without a restaurant. He became "one of the cool kids in high school because when I got off the school bus, it was at the restaurant. Everybody else got off at home. All the other kids wanted to get off at my stop and come in and eat. I could invite friends into the restaurant and cook for them. So I never even thought about doing anything else for a career."

Since she and her family own the place, Nicole did not have to endure the hazing female chefs often experience. But life in the restaurant's kitchen is still lively and challenging. "It's always fun around here when the power goes off," she says. "We go to the Dollar Store and buy more flashlights. Last year, we had a big storm that dumped snow all over the area. Nobody could get to work." Nicole ran the whole line by herself. Along with one or two other servers, she also waited tables and mixed drinks. In short, she handled the entire restaurant. Sorrento's drew a big crowd because almost all the other area restaurants were closed and because "everybody wants pizza and beer when they come off the slopes." Widespread power outages occur in the area at least once or twice every winter. "Power went out during one round of Fire on the Rock," Nicole recalls, "and we think we won because we had the experience of cooking in the dark. Sorrento's has propane gas tanks, so we can still cook in bad weather, snowstorms, and power outages. We have emergency lighting so we can stay open even if the rest of the town is dark."

At home, Nicole especially likes to cook breakfast. "Potatoes and eggs is a big family tradition. I made a breakfast pizza of potatoes and eggs for my aunt. She had never had that before. I will also make soup out of anything that is in the house."

The Restaurant

Villa Sorrento, named after a town in Italy, was the first restaurant the family owned in the area. It fit all the stereotypes: checkered tablecloths, candles in wine-basket bottles, a menu of mostly pizza and spaghetti. The restaurant burned in 1998. When planning to rebuild, the family decided "to go a little more upscale," Nicole says.

Since the pizza station was in a separate building, the pizza ovens were salvaged. The family moved to a new shopping area closer to the center of town and created Sorrento's Bistro, which offers a menu ranging from pizza to traditional Italian veal, chicken, seafood, and eggplant fine-dining entrées.

Nicole and Anthony try to let the ingredients speak for themselves. The menu still has "family Italian" dishes that people expect to see. But the ingredients in the more ambitious dishes are quite sophisticated. The restaurant uses Provimi veal, Prosciutto di Parma, Roma pepperoni, and San Marzano tomatoes. The Italian rope sausage is imported and fresh-roasted every morning. "You cannot slack on product," Nicole says.

The restaurant purchases most of its vegetables at the farmers' market in Banner Elk. A mushroom supplier who has lived in the area all his life brings in tubs of shiitake, oyster, and cauliflower mushrooms on a regular basis. Boone's Let-Us Produce is another major supplier that buys from local farmers. The kitchen uses no frozen ingredients.

The team from Sorrento's, led by Nicole and Anthony, vied for the championship of the 2011 Fire on the Rock Chef's Challenge. It defeated all competitors in the preliminary rounds and ultimately placed second by a small margin. The Sorrento's team had placed third in 2010 in its first competition.

The Recipes

Ham and White Bean Soup
Serves 4

> 1 large sweet onion, diced
> 2 tablespoons butter
> salt and pepper to taste

Ham and White Bean Soup
Photo provided by Sorrento's Bistro

2 cups good-quality baked ham such as Honey Baked, cut into ½-inch cubes
8 cups chicken stock
2 cans cannellini beans, preferably imported Italian
¼ cup diced fresh parsley
crisp bread

Sauté onions in butter until browned. Add salt and pepper. Add ham. Add chicken stock and bring to a boil. Add beans. Reduce heat and simmer at least 15 to 20 minutes until mixture thickens. Press some of beans against side of pot to mash and release starch. Continue to simmer. Add parsley at the last minute. Serve with crisp bread such as ciabatta.

Shrimp Nikki
Serves 4

Chef's Note
"I typically use reconstituted sun-dried tomatoes in this recipe, but I have used dry as well. If using reconstituted, soak for 5 to 7 minutes in water that has just been removed from boiling. This will produce a deeper tomato flavor, whereas dry will give a crunchy texture. Either option is fine."

Shrimp Nikki
Photo provided by Sorrento's Bistro

4 to 8 jumbo shrimp
4 to 8 thin slices prosciutto di Parma
olive oil
pinch of red pepper flakes
2 cloves garlic, minced
4 sun-dried tomatoes, chopped rough
2 cups heavy cream
salt and pepper to taste
10 fresh basil leaves (6 torn, 4 whole)
handful of Romano cheese
4 slices ciabatta bread, cut into triangles

Wrap shrimp in prosciutto. Sauté in olive oil until crisp. In another pan, sauté red pepper flakes and garlic in olive oil until garlic is very light brown, then add sun-dried tomatoes. Add heavy cream, plus salt and pepper. Reduce over medium heat. Add torn basil leaves and continue to simmer. Drop in Romano and allow to thicken. Meanwhile, grill ciabatta until crisp, with nice grill marks.

To present, drop whole basil leaves in a deep fryer for about 20 seconds until crisp. Remove and add a little salt. Place ciabatta slices on a plate. Position prosciutto-wrapped shrimp on each slice. Cover with sauce. Place basil chips on top.

Stuffed Chicken Breast
Photo provided by Sorrento's Bistro

Stuffed Chicken Breasts
Serves 4

5 eggs
slight amount of milk
4 boneless, skinless chicken breasts, pounded thin
salt and pepper to taste
4 tablespoons chopped fresh rosemary
4 thin slices Italian-style salami with peppercorns
4 thin slices Sopressata sausage
2 whole roasted red peppers
4 slices fresh mozzarella cheese
enough flour to coat chicken
Italian-seasoned breadcrumbs

Prepare an egg wash by beating eggs and adding a little milk to thin. Lay breasts flat and sprinkle them lightly with salt and pepper, then with rosemary. Layer with sausage, salami, and red peppers. Add mozzarella slices. Fold breasts over, fold ends, roll in flour, then roll in egg wash. Roll in breadcrumbs. Flash-fry for about 1 minute until lightly browned. Finish by baking in a 350-degree oven about 15 minutes.

To present, cut whole, stuffed breasts on the diagonal. Fan slices on plates.

Linville

Patrick Maisonhaute

Patrick
Maisonhaute
*Photo provided
by Eseeola Lodge*

The Eseeola Lodge

175 Linville Avenue
Linville, N.C. 28646
800-742-6717 or 828-733-4311
http://eseeola.com

The Chef

Patrick Maisonhaute was born in Saint Etienne in the vicinity of Lyon, France. As a young boy, he was "kind of naughty," he recalls. "I did not like school, and school did not like me. In France, you have to find a different way if you do not fit into the academic program—mechanical education, clothing, woodworking and carpentry, for example, or culinary arts." A friend of his parents ran one of four pastry shops in the village. "I loved cars and motorcycles, but I knew I was terrible at fixing them, and I had no interest in woodworking or clothing, so I enrolled in pastry classes. I worked unpaid for a week in Michael Durand's pastry shop. I liked it because it took me out of my comfort zone. I was surprised at the structure, the clear roles and behaviors that were required in the preparations. It was the best thing for me because I learned discipline and focus." He attended a four-year culinary-school program and passed the exit exam.

He pays special respect to the food experiences he had as a child. "My mother was a nurse. My father was in the air force," Patrick says. "Their jobs required that I live with my grandparents. My grandmother was a retired teacher. She was devoted to food. My grandfather had a garden, and he raised chickens. You don't recognize the value in that when you are young, but now that I am almost 40, I see it. It's like being a horse with blinders on. You only see straight ahead when you are young. The older you get, the wider your vision becomes. I remember my grandmother making a salad dressing—mustard, shallots, vinegar, oil—just for lunch. My grandfather had picked the greens an hour before. In less than two hours out of the ground, the food was on our plates. As a kid, I did not appreciate that. But now, I realize how important it was."

After culinary training, Patrick spent another year of study in a butcher shop learning how to cut meat and make pâtés, sausages, terrines, and galantines. "I trained with some great people," he recalls. When his 20th birthday came, he wanted to sign up for the army but didn't meet the criteria. "I had been looking forward to military service because I wanted to travel. I was restless. I wanted freedom." So he did some traveling in Europe on his own and then went to London, where he was hired by restaurateur Bruno Loubet, who was opening Brasserie L'Odéon. "That's when the next phase of my life really started," Patrick says. He learned how to work in a fine-dining professional kitchen and to speak English. "I spoke very little English until the U.K.," he recalls.

He spent four years in the United Kingdom. During that time, he worked at several places, including the illustrious Mandarin Oriental in London. "I was very lucky to be working with great chefs. I learned to be open minded from them."

Patrick came to the United States after being hired by the Four Seasons to work at its Palm Beach property. "For a Frenchman used to living in London with the rain, [Florida] was like, oh, my God!" he says. "The weather, the sunshine, the ocean! I did not want to go back to Europe after my first taste of warm weather. And there were so many food possibilities because the weather created such a long growing season."

After 18 months, the Four Seasons transferred him to its property on the island of Nevis in the Caribbean. "The only tourism there at that time was this five-star hotel and a few good restaurants. It was small and sophisticated. Soon, we got hit by a hurricane and had to shut down for repairs, so the Four Seasons moved me back to London to open their Canary Wharf property, and then eventually I was transferred back to Nevis."

When he returned to Nevis in 2000, Patrick met Toni Robinson. She was on vacation visiting her sister, a conference manager for the Four Seasons. "I was smitten very quickly," he recalls. "She has traveled a lot, too, so it was a great match."

After the events of September 11, travel slacked off and the economy in the islands deteriorated. "We normally had a lot of customers from New York and Washington, D.C., but no one was flying," Patrick says. "Although I had a good job, it seemed like a good time to think about moving. Toni and I had been carrying on a long-distance relationship, so I decided to move to North Carolina, where Toni lived. I checked out restaurants in the area, sent an email to Mark Rosse at Louisiana Purchase, and we talked on the phone. We met and got along well, and I became the chef there. I stayed for four years. It was a good place to be for me at that time, a small restaurant. I loved summer in the mountains, but I don't like winter weather, although I eventually got used to it."

When he and Toni went to dinner in local restaurants, they often chose The Eseeola Lodge. "Eseeola Lodge is special for us. One night after dinner, I dropped down on one knee and proposed to Toni in the restaurant. That table is still my favorite. Although The Eseeola Lodge has since been renovated, that table is still in the same place."

John Blackburn, Eseeola's general manager, subsequently contacted Patrick about taking over the kitchen. "It turned out to be exactly what I wanted because of my background in luxury hotels," Patrick says. "In the U.S., there is a saying, 'Never trust a skinny chef.' In France, it's 'Never trust a fat chef.' It means he is lazy and he doesn't work hard enough. I have been fortunate. I work very hard, and people see what I do, so when Mr. Blackburn approached me, it made me feel really good. I admire him very much.

"At the end of the day, I am a simple person. I care about the company. I care about my brigade. Our kitchen is like a military system, and it goes back to what [legendary French chef Auguste] Escoffier designed. I follow what my predecessors learned. Chefs have to lead by driving themselves, and that makes others strive to improve as well. You have to bring focus, structure, and established procedures to what you are doing. In this organization, I am the chef, yes, but it all depends on the performance of the entire brigade, from the dishwasher all the way through and including the wait staff. The hardest part for a leader is to guide people with different ideas and different backgrounds to pull together in the same way."

Patrick's task is a considerable one, as The Eseeola Lodge has a kitchen brigade of about 43 people.

The Restaurant

Construction of The Eseeola Lodge began in 1891 under the initiative of Harvard professor William James, who wrote, "I . . . am in the most peculiar and one of the most poetic places I have ever been in." Over the course of about 30 years, the inn developed a following for providing dancing, relaxation, golf, and other resort activities. In 1924, famed designer Donald Ross began directing construction of a golf course, which became Linville Golf Club. A fire in 1936 destroyed the inn, so lodging was moved to the Chestnut Annex, which is the current site of The Eseeola Lodge. Another fire in 1952 destroyed the clubhouse, which was rebuilt in the same location. John Blackburn became general manager in 1983. By the mid-1990s, the lodge and its surrounding land, now part of Linville Resorts, spanned over 3,000 acres. Golf, tennis, swimming, and fine-dining facilities have been steadily expanded. The inn offers 24 rooms and suites, all with private baths and porches. The focus is on personal attention. Linville Golf Club is open to guests of the lodge, in addition to club members; greens fees are not included in room rates. A day camp is available for children. Spa services are provided as well.

Although the cost of breakfast and dinner is included in guest-room reservations, the lodge's restaurants are also open to the public. Custom private dining experiences for groups can be arranged. Jackets are required for gentlemen at dinner. Thursday nights are devoted to a seafood buffet, a longstanding tradition at the lodge. Chef Maisonhaute is proud of the buffet because "it is very popular with local people, not just visitors. It is not inexpensive, but the quality of the food makes it a great value. I love it because people come every season just for that."

Diners on other evenings order from the à la carte menu. Chef Maisonhaute reports, "My style, of course, includes some French, but it has a more international flair. I try to provide what customers want. The buffet was a tradition. It goes back a long way, and I love and respect it. I have such respect for the history of the resort. Few restaurants have this level of character. It's not just a building. There is such a history here." Tom Dale, the current golf professional, is second generation. His father, Burl, was the golf professional for 27 years before him. Likewise, the second and third generations of greenskeepers now work for the company.

Because the volume of guests is huge, especially on Thursday nights, the kitchen must use some ingredients that are always available, regardless of where they are produced. But Chef Maisonhaute tries to use as many local ingredients as possible. "Especially, we buy local ingredients in small quantities for particular dishes," he says. "For example, I make Coq Au Vin only with chickens from Trosley Farm in Elk Park. The chickens are great. It's about respect for the products. They have been raised and fed properly. We only serve as many as we can get without variation in quality." The kitchen buys vegetables from New River Organic Growers (see page 34). "Caleb Crowell at New River Organics has worked for me in the past. He is a vegan, and he is passionate about his vegetables. Amos Nidiffer at Trosley Farm is the same way, just on the meat side."

WNC magazine has published a feature article about The Eseeola Lodge experience. The golf course has been named one of the best in the United States by *Golfweek*.

The Recipes

Coq Au Vin
Serves 4 to 6

> 1 whole chicken
> 1 carrot, diced medium
> 1 large white onion, diced medium
> 1 bunch celery, diced medium
> 1 small bunch fresh thyme
> 2 bay leaves
> 2 cloves garlic
> black peppercorns
> 4 cups Burgundy wine, divided
> 4 or 5 strips raw bacon, sliced fine
> kosher salt and pepper to taste
> flour, enough to dredge chicken pieces
> 1 quart chicken stock
> ½ cup beef stock
> Cornstarch, quantity to achieve desired thickness

Clean chicken and cut into 8 pieces. You will need only the breasts

Coq Au Vin
*Photo provided
by Eseeola Lodge*

and leg/thigh quarters. Save leg pieces for the day of service. Place breasts in bottom of a plastic container, then place ½ of carrots, ½ of onions, ½ of celery, thyme, bay leaves, garlic, and peppercorns on top. Cover with 2 cups of the wine. Cover and marinate in refrigerator for 24 to 48 hours.

On the day of service, render bacon in a pan until just crispy. Reserve bacon pieces and leave grease in pan. Season chicken leg pieces with salt and pepper and dredge in flour. Return pan to high heat and sear leg pieces until brown all over. Remove and set aside. Remove breasts from wine marinade and discard marinade. Dry breasts with paper towels, then season. Sear breasts in same pan as legs. Remove breasts when browned and set aside. Brown remaining vegetables in same pan until golden. Remove pan from heat and deglaze with remaining 2 cups wine. Return pan to medium-high heat and reduce by ½. Return chicken to pan and cover with chicken stock. Cover and simmer on stovetop or in oven for about 45 minutes until chicken is tender and almost falling off the bone. Remove chicken and set aside. Strain remaining liquid and return to pan. Add beef stock and cooked bacon and reduce for 5 minutes. Whisk in flour or cornstarch to make a roux; a flour roux must simmer 5 minutes before final thickness is achieved. Sauce should simmer at least 15 minutes on low heat to blend flavors well.

Let stand 10 minutes before serving. Serve with mashed potatoes, pearl onions, or your preferred sides.

Grilled North Carolina Rainbow Trout
with Succotash and Tomato Emulsion

Serves 4

Tomato Emulsion

6 ripe tomatoes, cut in large pieces
1 medium Spanish onion, cut in large pieces
salt and white pepper to taste
¾ cup extra-virgin olive oil

Succotash

3 ears yellow corn, cooked for 6 minutes in salted water, then removed
   from cobs
3 ears white corn, cooked for 6 minutes in salted water, then removed
   from cobs
1 red bell pepper, diced fine
2 cups frozen shelled edamame beans
1 red onion, diced fine
1 bunch flat-leaf parsley, chopped fine
½ cup extra-virgin olive oil
¼ cup red wine vinegar
salt and white pepper to taste

Trout

4- to 6-ounce, fresh North Carolina mountain trout, filleted and boned
salt and white pepper to taste
melted butter
¼ cup white wine

fresh herbs
edible flowers

TOMATO EMULSION

Place tomatoes, onions, and salt and white pepper in a saucepot and simmer for 30 to 40 minutes. Remove and blend in a blender until smooth. Strain through a sieve and return to blender. Slowly add olive oil until well blended. Set aside.

Grilled North Carolina Rainbow Trout with
Succotash and Tomato Emulsion
Photo provided by Eseeola Lodge

Succotash

Place all ingredients in a saucepan and slowly simmer for 5 to 7 minutes. Remove from heat and check seasonings. Set aside.

Trout

Heat a grill to high. Season fillets and spray with nonstick cooking spray. Place fillets on grill flesh side up just long enough to sear grill marks, then remove from grill. Place in a shallow pan with a little melted butter and white wine. Finish trout in a 350-degree oven for 4 to 5 minutes.

To present

Place 3 to 4 tablespoons Tomato Emulsion on bottom of plate and spread around entire plate. Place about 1 cup warm Succotash in center of emulsion. Place fillets in crisscross pattern on top of Succotash. Garnish with fresh herbs or edible flowers.

Spruce Pine

Nate Allen

Knife and Fork

61 Locust Street
Spruce Pine, N.C. 28777
828-765-1511
www.knifeandforknc.com

The Chef

In late 2008, Nate Allen and his wife, Wendy Gardner, decided to leave Los Angeles, mostly due to the impact of the recession. Nate's parents had retired to North Carolina by then, and Wendy's father lived in the state, so an extended family was already in residence. Wendy is from Burnsville, 14 miles from Spruce Pine. The couple had visited the area for a long time and felt an affinity for the North Carolina mountains.

Since his father worked for the Department of Defense, Nate moved around a lot when he was growing up. Born in the District of Columbia, he has lived in Colorado and several places in the Mid-Atlantic, in addition to Los Angeles. But Nate has always felt North Carolina is his home state.

Intellectual curiosity more than an interest in food drew him into cooking. "I enjoyed learning about how people in different areas related to food," he explains. "Did friends make choices based on religion, conscience (such as vegans), or family, or what? Understanding how people relate to food is key to being a good host and an entertainer. People, rather than recipes, became my primary course of study."

He went to college in jazz composition at East Carolina University, where he met Wendy; Nate still plays the drums for recreation. At college, he hosted a party every Saturday night, cooking for friends and fellow musicians. He found he enjoyed the experience not in the context of a career but rather as what he terms "a celebration of life. It was about entertaining and seeing what happens when you get a diverse crowd together over food and drinks."

Nate transferred from ECU to Johnson & Wales in Providence, Rhode Island. "At the time, I was aware that Johnson & Wales is fully accredited and offers a baccalaureate degree, and I intended to graduate," he says. "But I could not complete the required math classes because of my work schedule in restaurants. So I never completed either degree."

He is conscious of the various demands on chefs that go beyond cooking. "When people think about becoming a chef, they tend to think about learning knife skills and other well-known fundamentals. But they are often not aware that a restaurant owner also has to be a manager of people and time, as well as a plumber, an electrician, and a psychologist." He considers the inevitable stresses that occur in restaurants to be opportunities for growth. "On three occasions this year, on a Saturday, with the restaurant fully booked, I found fuses blown on our only refrigerator, and $3,000 to $4,000 worth of food ruined. We not only had to throw it away, we had to figure out how to completely restock and prepare for our busiest night, in about three hours. In retrospect, that was good experience for participating in the Chef's Challenge."

When he is not meeting the demands of the professional kitchen, Nate likes to visit family. He is also fond of traveling to explore what other restaurants are doing. His trips have included Vieques, Puerto Rico; Apalachicola, Florida, to eat oysters; and return visits to Los Angeles because he "grew up as a chef in some of those kitchens." He is fascinated by the groundbreaking initiatives he has seen there, such as Korean food trucks and the West Hollywood restaurant Comme Ça, which focuses on classic preparations using marrow bones, for example, as well as classic cocktails with chipped ice. He continues to admire his former boss Suzanne Goin and her restaurants A.O.C., named after the governing board for French wines, and Lucques, which has received attention from many state and national publications. "She was on the cover of *Food & Wine* as one of the top 10 chefs in the United States when I was in culinary school. Then I later became her sous chef. She was also a former chef at Chez Panisse. Her influences are still very strong in my compositions."

During his interview for this book, Chef Allen was cooking turkey stock in preparation for Thanksgiving with family. "I particularly enjoy cooking Thanksgiving dinner, then fixing leftovers later—turkey soup and turkey enchiladas especially," he says. "I constantly have a stock on the range. I heat the house with wood, and the stock provides aroma and moisture and just a warm, welcome feeling to the home. I also cook a lot of casseroles at home."

The Restaurant

Chef Allen started talking to a number of area farmers about partnerships and cooperative arrangements in summer 2009. Almost on the same day he and Wendy arrived from Los Angeles, a friend called and told him about a space that was available across the train tracks. He found that the former restaurant had some equipment, but it was not in good condition. It seemed fixable, however, and the county had just passed legislation allowing restaurants to serve alcohol, which helped prospects for the proverbial bottom line.

He initially tried to keep Knife and Fork open year-round but found in his first year that business was just too slow in winter. So for the last two years, the restaurant has been closed in January and February. He was pleased to find that in the restaurant's third year, business improved in spite of the economic downturn.

Chef Allen goes to area farms frequently—some weekly, others daily, depending on their products. "We have a small kitchen, almost no cold storage, so there is no space for long-term acquisitions," he says. "This creates a situation where our vegetables have just come out of the ground, and our meats are really fresh. I scrub and prep and think about how to prepare what I have picked up that day. Our clientele includes a lot of repeat customers. We see the same people every Thursday for lunch, others every Friday for dinner. Some want their favorites, so they order the same thing. Others are interested in something different every time. So I work within the whims of the weather and the seasons to bring about food that is the essence of what this region produces. It's like a farmhouse in that what I serve is what grows here and now, in this weather. . . . It's about my interpretation of the geography and the season and the land."

Knife and Fork has garnered quite a few accolades. *Cooking Light* listed Allen as the best small-town chef in America. "I don't know how they heard about me," he says. "Robin Bashinsky, the magazine's writer, came in on the first night we were open after being closed for two months last winter." *Garden & Gun* named Chef Allen's Rabbit and Red Quinoa one of the top dishes in the South. And the Knife and Fork team won the Western North Carolina Chef's Challenge in 2011, narrowly defeating the team from Biltmore. They also tied for third place in the Best Dish North Carolina the same year.

The Recipes

Rabbit Livers with Roasted Beet Jus, Chilies, Shallots, and Burnt Lemon Vinaigrette
Serves 4

Rabbit Livers
1 pound rabbit livers, cleaned, lobes separated
¼ teaspoon cayenne pepper
¼ teaspoon salt
½ teaspoon pepper
1 teaspoon fresh thyme leaves
2 cups buttermilk
4 cups canola oil
2 cups White Lily self-rising flour

Roasted Beet Jus
6 to 8 beets
enough olive oil, salt, pepper, and thyme to sprinkle beets

Burnt Lemon Vinaigrette
2 lemons, halved
2 tablespoons olive oil
1 teaspoon fresh thyme leaves
¼ teaspoon salt
¼ teaspoon pepper
¼ teaspoon sugar

12 leaves parsley
3 shallots, sliced in ¼-inch rings
2 Thai chilies, sliced very thin in rings

Rabbit Livers
Photo by Nate Allen

RABBIT LIVERS

Place livers, cayenne, salt, pepper, thyme, and buttermilk in a bowl and let stand in the refrigerator for 1 hour. Heat canola oil to 350 degrees in a large pot. Toss livers 1 at a time in flour, then place in hot oil. Fry livers 6 to 8 at a time for 2 to 3 minutes until golden and crunchy. Transfer livers to paper towels.

ROASTED BEET JUS

Rinse and peel beets. Sprinkle beets with olive oil, salt, pepper, and thyme and wrap in aluminum foil. Roast at 350 degrees about 25 minutes until just tender. Reserve the jus that remains.

BURNT LEMON VINAIGRETTE

Place lemon halves cut side down on a hot grill. Leave them for 3 to 5 minutes until cut sides are charred. Remove from grill and let cool. Once you can handle the lemons, squeeze their juice into a bowl, add next 5 ingredients, and whisk together.

Make a puddle of Burnt Lemon Vinaigrette and Roasted Beet Jus on each plate. Divide livers into 4 equal portions. Place over puddles, slightly off center. Sprinkle with parsley leaves, shallots, and chilies.

Trout with Turnips and Turnip Greens, Fig Chutney, and Tomato Fennel Broth
Serves 4

Tomato Fennel Broth
2 large ripe tomatoes, quartered
1 bulb fennel, diced
1 small yellow onion, diced
2 cloves garlic, smashed
2 cups white wine
1 sprig fresh thyme

Fig Chutney
10 fresh figs, chopped rough, stems removed
1 small onion, diced
2 cloves garlic, minced
1 jalapeño pepper, seeded and diced
1 tablespoon cumin seed
½ cup sugar
½ cup red wine vinegar
2 tablespoons olive oil
½ teaspoon salt
½ teaspoon pepper

Turnips and Turnip Greens
2 tablespoons olive oil
20 small white turnips with greens, turnips halved, greens washed and stemmed
salt and pepper to taste

Trout with Turnips and Turnip Greens
Photo by Nate Allen

Trout
    4 6-ounce rainbow trout fillets
    salt and pepper to taste
    4 tablespoons olive oil

TOMATO FENNEL BROTH

Combine all ingredients in a medium saucepan and bring to a boil. Immediately reduce to a simmer and cook for 30 minutes. Strain through a fine sieve or cheesecloth. Keep hot until ready to serve.

FIG CHUTNEY

Combine all ingredients in a saucepan over high heat until thoroughly mixed and until sugar is dissolved. Turn out into a bowl and reserve.

TURNIPS AND TURNIP GREENS

Heat a large skillet on high. Barely coat bottom of skillet with olive oil.

Arrange turnips cut side down so they fill skillet but all cut sides have contact with hot pan. Do this in as many batches as necessary. Once turnips have color on their cut sides, fold in turnip greens to slightly wilt them. Remove turnips and greens onto a platter. Continue until all turnips and greens are cooked and hot. Salt and pepper to taste.

TROUT

Lightly season both sides of fillets with salt and pepper. Place fillets skin side up on a plate. Add olive oil to a large cast-iron skillet and heat to medium-high. Sear 2 fillets at a time skin side down, then flip to meat side after 2 minutes. Cook 2 more minutes on meat side and remove to a warm plate.

TO PRESENT

Spoon ¼ of the vegetables onto each plate. Place trout fillets skin side down on vegetables. Spoon chutney over trout and ladle tomato broth over chutney to form small broth puddles on the plates.

Hot Springs

Chris Brown

Chris Brown
*Photo provided by
Mountain Magnolia Inn*

Mountain Magnolia Inn

204 Lawson Street
Hot Springs, N.C. 28743
800-914-9306 or 828-622-3543
www.mountainmagnoliainn.com

The Chef

Chris Brown remembers spending his first birthday in what is now the Garden House, a guest house adjacent to the herb and berry garden at the Mountain Magnolia Inn. His grandmother owned the house at the time, so his roots here run deep. His first job, at age 14, was mowing grass and mulching gardens on the property over summer break from school.

He did not plan to be a chef. "I just sort of fell into it," he recalls. "I wanted to join the army and signed up in my senior year of high school. Under a two-year pre-enlistment program, I was going into communications systems. But before I ever entered boot camp, I found out that I was going to be a father. Under the army's 'no deadbeat dads' policy, I was given the choice of getting married or not joining. Having a baby was scary enough for a 19-year-old, and I was not ready to commit to marriage. But neither was I willing to leave my little girl without a father. Having grown up never knowing my own father, I was and remain committed to always being there for any children I have, so I consider the development to be serendipitous.

"I moved out of Hot Springs but stayed in Madison County in Mars Hill with my daughter and her mother, supporting my family any way I could—mowing grass, construction work, roofing, concrete. You name it, I did it. But my life fell apart when my girlfriend left me and moved my child 300 miles away. Then my truck broke down, causing me to lose my job. Somebody broke into my house and stole most of my possessions. I was evicted because I had no money for rent. So I went to my grandmother, who raised me, and asked if I could move back in with her until I got on my feet. She took me in. I hitchhiked from Mars Hill to Hot Springs and immediately saw a Help Wanted sign in the window of the Bridge Street Café. I filled out an application and within a few days got a call to come in as a dishwasher. There, I met the chef, who took me under her wing and gave me most of my culinary knowledge. Working for her was like boot camp would have been in the army. She made sure I did things exactly right, or I had to do them again. I chopped so many vegetables for her, I got a callus on my hand from the knife—which I still have to this day! It's a point of pride now.

"She was hired as the executive chef at the Mountain Magnolia Inn, and I went with her as a dishwasher and prep person. Within a couple of years, I received full custody of my daughter, moved into my own house again, bought a truck, and found that things were looking up for me. The owners of the Mountain Magnolia invited me to become head chef at the Iron Horse Station, which they were helping the owner renovate and re-open after a failed lease with another person. After a year at the Iron Horse Station, I was given the opportunity to return to the Mountain Magnolia under yet another chef, who had been a culinary-school instructor for 15 years. I wanted to learn as much as possible from him. Within six months, however, the owners determined he was not working out, and they offered me the executive chef position. I could not have been happier. I still am. I have my dream job with the freedom to cook my own menu items creatively, and I am raising my beautiful nine-year-old daughter in my own hometown!

"Over the past year and a half, I have had the opportunity to hone my own style of cooking, using only fresh local products, organic when available. 'Keep it simple' is my philosophy. I use olive oil plus salt and pepper much of the time, and I do not feel a need to overcomplicate things. Good ingredients speak for themselves, which is why I handpick all that I use myself on shopping trips into Asheville. Included in these trips is a side stop in Fletcher to Hickory Nut Gap Meats (see page 264) to purchase local beef, pork, and breakfast meats. My seafood comes fresh from Blue Water Seafood Company. Using the best ingredients, you get the best results, and buying local items stimulates the local economy and leaves a smaller carbon footprint, which is better for us all in the end."

The Restaurant

The Mountain Magnolia Inn was built in 1868 as the estate of Colonel James H. Rumbough and his wife, Carrie, who owned and operated the

350-room Mountain Park Hotel where the Hot Springs Spa is now located. Carrie earned local fame by riding to Knoxville and negotiating the release of her husband from a Union army prison. The historic inn features Italianate Victorian architecture. The design includes a cupola, angled bay windows, ornate trim, a double-door arch and columns, and a dramatic ceiling rose. The inn's careful restoration was featured in *This Old House* magazine.

The inn can accommodate 35 guests in the main house's five guest rooms and two-bedroom suite; in the Garden House, which has three bedrooms and a full kitchen; and in Fowler's Bend, which has two suites and a small one-bedroom unit. Visitors have panoramic views of Pisgah National Forest, which surrounds the inn. Pete and Karen Nagle have operated the inn for 12 years as a historic property. Exceptional service, great food, and eco-friendly practices are emphasized. Day hiking, whitewater rafting, yoga, and soaking in the nearby hot mineral springs are among the relaxing recreational activities offered. The property is well suited for weddings, rehearsals, and other large functions. A professional event coordinator is available to assist with arrangements. *The Knot*, a wedding magazine/website, has named Mountain Magnolia Inn one of North Carolina's top 10 wedding locations.

Dining at the inn is casual. Breakfast is reserved for inn guests. Dinner is normally offered Friday through Monday to the public as well as to guests, although reservations are requested for non-guests; check the website for current days and hours.

Chef Brown often uses herbs and flowers grown in the inn's gardens as garnishes. For a truly special experience, guests can reserve the Chef's Table, at which they enjoy a five-course meal they design in collaboration with Chef Brown. This meal can also be served in front of the fireplace in winter or in one of several outdoor dining locations in warmer weather.

Squash and Apple Soup
Photo by Chris Brown

The Recipes

Squash and Apple Soup
Serves 8 to 10

1 small hubbard squash, peeled, seeded, and sliced
olive oil, enough to coat squash
salt and pepper to taste
2 cups diced red onion
1 cup chopped celery
1 cup chopped carrot
2 tablespoons butter
3 apples, peeled, cored, and diced
1 teaspoon salt
1 teaspoon pepper
pinch of cayenne pepper
2 tablespoons maple syrup
3 cups vegetable stock or chicken stock
1 cup heavy cream
1 cup water
crème fraîche, parsley, and smoked paprika for garnish

Roast squash ahead of time. Coat squash with olive oil and add salt and pepper. Roast in oven at 350 degrees for about 30 minutes until tender. In a medium pot over medium heat, cook onions, celery, and carrots in butter for about 5 minutes until onions are translucent. Add roasted squash, apples, 1 teaspoon salt, 1 teaspoon pepper, cayenne, and maple syrup. Mix well. Add stock, cream, and water. Reduce heat and simmer about 20 minutes. Purée with a food processor or an immersion blender. Garnish with crème fraîche, parsley, and smoked paprika, if desired.

Stuffed Pork Tenderloin
Serves 3 or 4

18- to 24-ounce pork tenderloin, preferably from Hickory Nut Gap Meats
1 cup dried cherries
1 cup pecans
enough olive oil to coat pork
1 teaspoon salt
1 teaspoon pepper
½ cup creamy blue cheese
1 cup demi-glace

Stuffed Pork
Tenderloin
*Photo by
Chris Brown*

Remove silver skin from tenderloin. Cut into 5- or 6-ounce portions. Using a fillet knife, make a cut into center of each piece; be careful not to go all the way through. Put cherries and pecans into a food processor. Give it 3 or 4 good pulses. Stuff pork with cherry and pecan mixture. Coat each piece of pork with olive oil, salt, and pepper. Sear all sides in a skillet on medium-high heat. Finish in a 350-degree oven for 15 minutes. Remove from oven and let rest 2 to 3 minutes. Slice into medallions, top with blue cheese, and pour demi-glace over top.

This dish goes well with garlic mashed potatoes and roasted Brussels sprouts.

Chocolate Lava Cake with Local Honey Ice Cream
Serves 4 to 6

Local Honey Ice Cream
    1 pint heavy cream
    splash of vanilla extract
    9 egg yolks
    1 cup sugar
    2 cups honey

Chocolate Lava Cake
Photo by Chris Brown

Chocolate Lava Cake
        1 pound chocolate
        4 teaspoons butter
        3 eggs
        ⅓ cup all-purpose flour
        ⅓ cup sugar
        1 teaspoon salt

LOCAL HONEY ICE CREAM

In a saucepan, bring cream to a simmer. Add vanilla. Remove from heat. In a large bowl, mix yolks and sugar. Slowly add cream to egg mixture. Pour into an ice-cream machine. Add honey at end of cycle, after about 40 minutes. Let ice cream set in freezer overnight.

CHOCOLATE LAVA CAKE

Preheat oven to 400 degrees. Melt chocolate and butter over a double boiler. Add eggs, flour, sugar, and salt. Mix well. Pour into ovenproof ramekins and bake for 15 minutes.

Asheville

Damien Cavicchi

Damien Cavicchi
Photo provided by Biltmore Estate

Biltmore
The Bistro/Deerpark/ Cedric's Tavern/ The Dining Room at The Inn

1 Approach Road
Asheville, N.C. 28803
828-225-6260
www.biltmore.com
Note: An admission ticket to the property is required in order to dine in the Biltmore restaurants.

The Chef

Damien Cavicchi is from an Italian family. He grew up in New Orleans. With a background like that, cooking is in his genes! He carries a package of spoons in his pocket and tastes constantly while cooking.

He moved to the North Carolina mountains in 1998 because he was interested in experiencing a different part of the South. He was particularly attracted to the creative spirit, the climate, and the mountains of the Appalachian region. Asheville seemed like a good place to raise children.

Damien recalls from his childhood that he "was always curious about the spices in our pantry. As a teenager, I began to experiment and take over some of the grilling duties at home. My mother was a proficient cook who made scratch meals for our family of six. Cooking lends itself to creativity, and that always kept me coming back to the kitchen. As soon as I started driving, I got a night job at a downtown restaurant as a busboy and dishwasher. I loved the energy and the pressure. I also liked to eat, and I soon worked my way to the fry station on the line. I was instantly hooked on the adrenaline rush of a busy dinner service.

"In New Orleans, everyone seemed to be able to cook, so it was more the expectation, not the exception, that food would be prepared well, and not be bland or boring. On my dad's side of the family, I was surrounded by crawfish boils, tomato sauce, gumbo, and po' boy sandwiches. Everything was highly seasoned or spicy. Then my mother got into health food and started putting tomato-cucumber salads in my lunch—in first grade!—and trying to convince me that a sandwich could be made of chickpea purée and sprouts. As I got older, I started to appreciate where my mom was coming from. We had salad and vegetables at every meal. But my favorite foods were, and still are, red beans and rice cooked with smoked pork; fried oyster po' boys in French bread with mayonnaise, hot sauce, and shredded iceberg lettuce; and *spaghetti aglio e olio*, or spaghetti carbonara without cream. Perfection! To this day, I approach cooking with those Louisiana levels of seasoning, or the comfort of the Italian pasta spirit. Curiosity has always been at the center of my cooking, and that is how I learned to cook from others. After high school, I attempted culinary school, but that lasted only four months. I was after immersion in cooking and wanted to learn only by doing, so I began to travel the country learning from others."

During his rebellious early 20s, Damien decided he didn't want to look the part of a chef, so he cooked in a T-shirt, shorts, and usually Birkenstock sandals with no socks. He found out there is a reason most professional chefs wear traditional kitchen attire. "I was rendering the excess fat out of duck breasts during a dinner service, and some of the molten liquid duck fat spilled into the top of my sockless foot and ran down into my shoe," he recalls. "The restaurant was packed, and I decided to tough it out and finish the rush. After we closed, I went outside to assess the damage to my foot, which was considerable. I still have a scar there to this day. I don't know why I was so committed to that dinner service, but it earned me lots of street-cred points with the other cooks. During another busy dinner rush, the kitchen was about 110 degrees, in the middle of summer. I was wearing pants that day, and right on the line, I decided I couldn't take the heat. I took out my chef knife and cut the bottoms off my pants without taking them off, turning them into shorts, and went right back to cooking."

By the time Damien reached Asheville, he had mellowed a bit. He spent some time as chef at La Caterina Trattoria, located downtown. "There, I was given the freedom to change the menu every day, based on the season," he says. "I learned just how short the local seasons are for certain foods—things like fresh fava beans, ramps, wild mushrooms, and squash blossoms. Also, I learned restraint—that simple cooking can be better cooking. I realized that dishes need only include four or five ingredients, and that limiting ingredients did not mean that I wasn't a good cook or that I lacked ambition. It meant that I was maturing. I pushed the skill envelope by making everything from scratch—bread, pasta, salami, sausage, cheese, desserts. I also learned that much of cooking is variations on a theme, based on cooking methodology, what food is available, and the changing of the seasons."

Chef Cavicchi subsequently owned two restaurants. In 2005, he started Clingman Avenue Coffee and Catering Company and Clingman Café. "I wanted to do something that was deli-inspired but food-forward," he explains. Two years later, he got "the bug to do a fine-dining Italian restaurant, and I fell in love with a space in downtown Asheville. I sold the café [which is still operating] and renovated a new space which would become Sugo. Both restaurants were well received, the latter being exactly what I had always wanted to do—bold Italian food in a romantic, tasteful setting, bringing dining to the guest as an event, with excellent service and commitment to consistency. As chef-owner, I learned two important things from those experiences: restaurants take a lot more money than you could ever imagine, and the instant gratification of a satisfied guest goes a long way in motivating you to keep up with the very unglamorous behind-the-scenes work of running your own business."

He came to Biltmore in 2008 and worked his way up in several of the property's operations. Damien was named estate executive chef in 2011. He describes his style as "primarily seasonal, with decisions based on flavor and impact. I think about what produce is available, and then what meats or other proteins go best with them. I cook like an Italian with love for the American South, who romanticizes the food of Louisiana. Funny thing about Italy and the American South: Both have amazing food and food cultures. Both cultures nurture the family, and that lends itself to everyone gathering in the kitchen. Both cultures are based on seasonal ingredients. Food is one of the few things that we can, hopefully, enjoy on a regular basis that can really have a positive impact on our day. Technique is so important. Seasoning is one of the most overlooked aspects of cooking."

On his own time, he loves to go to restaurants and try what other chefs are cooking. Sometimes, he splurges on foie gras. At home, "I usually cook healthy," he says. "I have five children, and I do almost all of the cooking at the house. Staples include ground turkey, boneless chicken thighs, tough cuts of pork, any husky cut of meat cooked slowly with a sauce made from the juices, along with brown rice, beans, greens, and fish. My kids' favorites are salmon, trout, homemade steak fries with a homemade seasoning, red beans and rice, anything Mexican or Italian, and, of course, mac 'n' cheese, to which I usually add puréed broccoli for extra vitamins."

The Restaurants

As estate executive chef, Damien presides over all food operations for Biltmore Estate except for The Dining Room at The Inn. This includes three full-service restaurants, four casual-dining facilities, Lioncrest (a dedicated banquet and meeting building), and myriad other catering and banquet operations. Biltmore is capable of handling parties of any size for any occasion.

Biltmore's farmers and an agriculture team supply the estate's restaurants with produce, eggs, beef, and lamb. Partnerships with local farmers supplement what the estate supplies. "Western North Carolina has an entrepreneurial spirit," Chef Cavicchi says. "I can't tell you how many times I've been approached by a farmer with a seed catalog in hand, offering to grow anything I wanted. In 2004, I was actually using so many local products, I started an open-air market with about 25 vendors. At Biltmore, we have a history of longstanding relationships with farmers and purveyors. And our purchasing department and chefs continue to participate in new initiatives that make a real difference not only ethically but economically for the people in our region and state."

The Bistro

Seating in The Bistro surrounds an open kitchen where each day's harvest is sautéed and stirred, grilled and flavored. Located next door to Biltmore's winery, The Bistro has a relaxed atmosphere for enjoying fine dining and great wine.

The cuisine is based on modern American food often prepared with European flair. "We pull globally in flavor profiles," one of The Bistro's chefs says. "I think a lot of restaurants put emphasis on reinventing the wheel and pushing culinary boundaries, which is great because food is constantly evolving and new trends are being set every day, making dining experiences that much more exciting. At The Bistro, we believe in simple food with great execution and bold flavors marked with a personalized touch. We want to showcase our food the best way we know how, and we have been successful in that approach.

"Asheville and the surrounding areas have myriad food artisans who we source from and showcase on our menus. Biltmore also has a unique advantage in that we are an operating farm and working estate. Biltmore has a kitchen garden that grows amazing produce just for the outlets on the property. We grow everything from baby lettuce to countless varieties of tomatoes to winter squash and fresh herbs." The estate's pastures provide ample support for cattle and sheep operations, while fields and gardens produce squash, fragrant berries, pumpkins, root vegetables, green beans, lettuces, tomatoes, herbs, and flower garnishes.

The Bistro's culinary team has been widely recognized for excellence in fine cuisine. In 2011, it competed for the championship of the Western North Carolina Chef's Challenge.

Deerpark

Deerpark is housed in a charming rustic barn designed by famous architect Richard Morris Hunt. Conversion into a restaurant included the installation of panoramic windows looking out onto an open-air courtyard surrounded by majestic trees decorated with thousands of twinkling lights. A lush garden courtyard occupies center stage.

Southern regional cuisine is served from a buffet. Roasted meats are a specialty; particular attention is paid to holiday favorites such as hand-carved turkey. Decadent desserts abound. Deerpark is especially family-friendly; discounts are offered for children. Sunday brunch is highly popular.

In addition to casual dining, Deerpark specializes in weddings, receptions, and catered meetings. One of its wedding cakes was featured in *Grace Ormonde* magazine. Restaurant personnel have appeared in *Blue Mountain Living* magazine, on P. Allen Smith's show on PBS, and on the DIY network.

Cedric's Tavern

Cedric's Tavern is named after George Vanderbilt's St. Bernard, who was dearly loved by the family. The tavern is situated adjacent to the village green in Antler Hill Village. It offers a less formal Biltmore dining and entertaining option. The ambience and menu are modeled after pubs in Britain, Scotland, and Ireland.

The Dining Room at The Inn

The Dining Room at The Inn is elegant. Picture windows look out onto extended views of the Biltmore property. Chargers are embossed with the Vanderbilt crest. Chandeliers cast soft light; gas-fired logs flicker from a large fireplace along one wall.

The kitchen staff at The Inn, numbering around 50, provides not only the fine-dining experience of The Dining Room but also banquets, catered events, weddings, receptions, and other large functions. The Inn has its own executive chef; the position was in a state of transition as of spring 2012.

The fine-dining cuisine at The Dining Room has grown out of George Vanderbilt's vision when he bought this land. The Biltmore property is a huge, self-sufficient working farm. From hormone-free beef and lamb to fruits, berries, vegetables, and honey, all are raised on the property. To fill in any gaps, the restaurant works with the Appalachian Sustainable Agriculture Project (see page 198) to source products from local farmers scattered throughout western North Carolina. The list of area suppliers is large, given the volume of production that characterizes Biltmore. It includes Three Graces Dairy in Marshall, Carolina Bison in Asheville, and Spinning Spider Creamery in Madison County, as well as Imladris Farm (see page 248) and Hickory Nut Gap Meats (see page 264), both in Fairview. One of the senior chefs remarks, "We strive to partner with as many local farmers as we can. Biltmore also has an in-house charcuterie program. We make sausage, and we are now making some cheese. We buy local eggs, but we also use our own."

The seasonal menu at The Dining Room is built around whatever is fresh. Two items in particular are likely to be found on the menu at all times: the garden salad, made from greens and herbs grown in estate fields and the property's greenhouse, and the Black Angus fillet, which comes from estate cattle. A field-to-table tasting menu is always available, although what is on it changes.

The culinary team from The Inn won the Western North Carolina Chef's Challenge in 2010. Open Table named The Dining Room at The Inn one of the most romantic restaurants in the United States. The Dining Room has been selected for dinners by Chaines des Rotisseurs. Five years of *Wine Spectator* Awards of Excellence adorn the wall. The Inn at Biltmore is regularly cited among the best hotels in the United States by *Condé Nast Traveler* and *Travel + Leisure*.

The Recipes

Fried Green Tomato Eggs Benedict with Crab Hollandaise
Serves 4 as a brunch main course

Chef's Note

"Fried green tomato is one of the flavors that really are nostalgic, and an authentic representation of the South. I never want to eat regular eggs Benedict, but this recipe just feels and tastes more inspired. It transports me to a New Orleans courtyard on a summer Sunday."

Tomatoes

- 4 large green tomatoes
- 2 eggs
- 1 cup buttermilk
- 1 cup rice flour

½ cup cornmeal
½ cup breadcrumbs
2 teaspoons coarse kosher salt
¼ teaspoon pepper
¼ teaspoon cayenne pepper
1 quart vegetable oil for frying

Hollandaise

4 egg yolks
1 tablespoon freshly squeezed lemon juice
½ cup unsalted butter, melted
pinch of salt
pinch of cayenne pepper
1 tablespoon lemon zest
½ pound lump crabmeat, picked

Eggs

2 tablespoons white distilled vinegar
2 tablespoons kosher salt
8 large eggs

sliced green onions for garnish

TOMATOES

Slice tomatoes ¼ inch thick. Reserve ends for another use. In a large bowl, beat eggs well with a wire whisk and add buttermilk. Add tomatoes to egg mixture, toss well, and reserve. In a separate bowl, combine next 6 ingredients and mix well. Sprinkle some of the dry mixture over a sheet pan. Remove tomatoes from wet mixture, allow excess liquid to drip off, and coat well with dry mixture. Set on prepared sheet pan until all tomatoes are coated. In a large, heavy-bottomed saucepan, heat oil to 360 degrees, using a frying thermometer as needed. Layer a second sheet pan with paper towels. Working in batches, fry tomatoes about 2 minutes per batch until golden brown. Place cooked tomatoes on sheet pan with paper towels.

HOLLANDAISE

In a stainless-steel bowl, whisk yolks and lemon juice vigorously until

Fried Green Tomato Eggs Benedict with Crab Hollandaise
Photo provided by Biltmore Estate

very pale and doubled in volume. Set bowl over a saucepan of barely simmering water and continue whisking. Be careful not to let water touch bottom of bowl or to let eggs get too hot. Once eggs are warm, add melted butter in a slow stream, whisking constantly. Remove from heat. Add salt, cayenne, zest, and crabmeat. Cover and reserve in warm area of kitchen. Sauce can be thinned with a small amount of cold water if it becomes too thick.

Eggs

Fill a 10- to 12-inch sauté pan halfway with water. Bring to a low boil, then add vinegar and salt. Using a slotted spoon, gently swirl poaching water into a slow whirlpool. Carefully add eggs 1 at a time and cook for 3 to 3½ minutes.

To present

Set out 4 large dinner plates. Arrange 3 to 4 tomato slices on each plate. Drain poached eggs in a slotted spoon and set out 2 per plate. Cover generously with hollandaise and green onions. Serve immediately. These are delicious with pan-fried andouille sausage and Biltmore Sauvignon Blanc.

Cast-Iron Seared Shrimp with Panna Cotta, Creamed Corn, and Saffron Hush Puppies
Serves 4 as an appetizer

Chef's Note
"Cast iron is one of my go-to pans. I love the Italian *al mattone*—or 'under a brick'— technique, and sometimes I use two hot iron skillets together to mimic the procedure. The flavor from smoking hot cast iron is rustic and bold. I love the way it pairs with silky panna cotta, which acts as the acid note to the shrimp."

Panna Cotta
1¾ cups buttermilk
1 tablespoon kosher salt
½ teaspoon white pepper
1 sprig fresh thyme
1 tablespoon fresh lemon juice
1 tablespoon lemon zest
4 sheets gelatin

Creamed Corn
2 tablespoons butter
2 cups fresh yellow corn
2 tablespoons all-purpose flour
1 cup whole milk
1 tablespoon kosher salt
1 tablespoon sherry (optional)

Saffron Hush Puppies
4 threads saffron
½ cup all-purpose flour

Cast-Iron Seared Shrimp
Photo provided by Biltmore Estate

½ cup corn flour
¼ teaspoon baking soda
½ teaspoon kosher salt
½ teaspoon cracked pepper
1 large egg
½ cup buttermilk
1 tablespoon hot water
2 tablespoons melted butter
¼ cup minced white onion
2 cups canola oil

Shrimp
12 to 16 shrimp (16–20 size), peeled and deveined, tails on
1 tablespoon kosher salt
2 tablespoons canola oil

PANNA COTTA

Prepare in advance. In a small saucepan, combine buttermilk, salt, white pepper, and thyme over low heat. Bring to a simmer and remove from heat. Stir in lemon juice and zest. Soften gelatin sheets in cold water for about 3 minutes. Drain and add to buttermilk. Mix well and strain. Evenly distribute mixture into an ice-cube tray, cover, and refrigerate.

Creamed Corn

Set a medium saucepan over medium heat. Melt butter in saucepan and add corn. Cook about 3 minutes until corn is tender, lowering heat if necessary. Stir in flour and cook 30 seconds. Add milk and continue to stir until corn comes to a simmer. Simmer 4 minutes and remove from heat. Add salt and sherry, if desired. Reserve.

Saffron Hush Puppies

Preheat oven to 225 degrees. Allow saffron to bloom in hot water for 5 minutes. Combine all-purpose flour, corn flour, baking soda, salt, and pepper in a mixing bowl. In a separate bowl, beat egg with buttermilk, then add bloomed saffron, 1 tablespoon hot water, butter, and onions. Add wet mixture to dry mixture and combine, being careful not to overmix, as dough will toughen. In a heavy-bottomed medium saucepan, heat oil to 375 degrees. Drop tablespoon-sized portions of batter into oil and cook 3 minutes, turning once. Reserve in oven on a sheet tray lined with paper towels.

Shrimp

Set a 12-inch cast-iron skillet over high heat. Combine shrimp with salt and oil and add to skillet. Cook about 2 minutes per side until shrimp are pink and opaque.

To present

Set bottom of Panna Cotta ice tray in a shallow pan of hot water for 15 seconds. Invert tray to remove Panna Cotta. Set out 4 large plates and arrange Panna Cotta, warm Creamed Corn, hush puppies, and shrimp on each. Serve immediately with Biltmore Riesling. Make at the peak of fresh-corn season for best flavor.

Appalachian Sustainable Agriculture Project

306 West Haywood Street
Asheville, N.C. 28801
828-236-1282
www.asapconnections.org

The Appalachian Sustainable Agriculture Project is a not-for-profit corporation dedicated to helping create and expand local food markets in a manner "that will preserve our agricultural heritage, give everyone access to fresh, healthy food, and keep our farmers farming," according to the project's website.

The initiative began in the mid-1990s, when Charlie Jackson joined with a group of farmers, agricultural professionals, and community leaders in western North Carolina to help with the transition from tobacco as a primary crop. The Local Food Campaign eventually emerged as the best answer for creating new markets for farmers. It was formalized as the Appalachian Sustainable Agriculture Project in 2002. The federal tobacco quota system ended in 2004, wiping out price supports for tobacco. ASAP was and continues to be funded by a combination of sponsorships, donations, and grants. Some of the grant funding grew out of what is now known as "the tobacco settlement," the outcome of a lawsuit initiated by the attorneys general of 46 states. Tobacco companies agreed to pay more than $200 billion to the states over a period of 25 years.

Initially located in Madison County, ASAP has always been centered in the Asheville area. Realizing early on that the way food systems worked did not respect state lines, the organizers focused on a region within 100 miles of Asheville, defined by a shared history and geography. ASAP now covers

23 counties in the North Carolina mountains, in addition to counties in adjoining states.

Farms, restaurants, and retail markets can apply for "Appalachian Grown" certification, which identifies items produced under guidelines established by the organization. The "Appalachian Grown" identification assures consumers that they are buying food or farm products "grown or raised in our region by a local farmer," according to the project.

The ASAP website contrasts the concept of local food with the widespread distribution practices of the modern era: "On average . . . food today travels 1,500 miles from seed to plate. This distance translates into a loss of freshness and nutrition and into a loss of control over the way . . . food is produced. . . . If we no longer know our farmers, we have less control over the way our food is grown and over the kind of environmental and social impacts of food production. Localizing agriculture connects farmers and community members; it means that consumers are in direct contact with the farmers that grow their food or are only one or two steps removed."

ASAP provides promotional materials and assistance to its partners. The organization produces and distributes *The Local Food Guide*, a printed description of farms and other producers. The publication is available online as well as by visiting www.buyappalachian.org; a link to western North Carolina restaurants and bakeries affiliated with ASAP is also provided on that website. Another ASAP service is The Mixing Bowl, a farm-to-business trade directory for chefs and other food buyers; visit http://buyappalachian.org/mixingbowl. In addition, the organization provides educational programs about food and nutrition and assists school cafeterias with the acquisition of local produce. Farm visits for children and planting and harvesting of school gardens are also part of the ASAP initiative.

Judd Lohof

Judd Lohof
Photo by Paul M. Howey

Café Azalea

Four Seasons Plaza
1011 Tunnel Road
Asheville, N.C. 28805
828-299-3753
http://cafeazaleaasheville.com

The Chef

Judd Lohof was born in Ohio and raised in Florida. He began cooking while in college at Florida State in the early 1990s. After graduating with a degree in social studies, he moved to New Mexico and Washington, cooking food that "ran the gamut from insanely high-volume catering to fine dining to burgers at a Montana rodeo," he says. "I trained by showing up at work and getting screamed at by moody chef types. The idea is simple: figure out how not to get yelled at as quickly as possible, and do that same thing again every day. I learned from everyone I ever worked for or with—a lot of it being what not to do.

"Then one particular job got me interested enough in food to really care about what I was doing. It was in The Pollard Hotel in Red Lodge, Montana. The food was way over my head, and the menu changed pretty much daily. We served ostrich, liver mousse, charcuterie, cream-puff pastry—stuff mainstream restaurants just don't do. The chef was Bob Heenley. He taught me a lot of classical French technique—pan sauces, the brigade system, specific knife cuts, things one learns in culinary school nowadays. He was also very organized. Everything was written down to facilitate communication.

"Eventually, I guess my style coalesced out of distilling certain elements out of all these other people and forming a nucleus that I mirror. I am straightforward, honest, have varied interests, and am averse to pretense or flamboyance. My food is the same."

Before moving to Asheville, Judd worked for Scott Boswell at Stella! in New Orleans, named for the famous cry in Tennessee Williams's *A Streetcar Named Desire*. Chef Boswell was a James Beard Award nominee. Judd arrived in the North Carolina mountains in 2001. "I was looking for a progressive place, not too big, close to my family, with a dynamic farm-to-table food scene with a little live-and-let-live feel."

When not at Café Azalea, Judd likes to eat the kind of food he serves in his restaurant. "I generally do not cook at home. I go out to our garden and harvest some things, and my girlfriend cooks, although I am frequently in charge of cooking meats."

The Restaurant

Café Azalea seats about 45 patrons inside, plus 20 or more on the outdoor patio. The upscale interior features wine-colored faux stucco walls. Original art and photography are for sale gallery-style.

Chef Lohof describes Café Azalea as "a link in the chain of community well-being. We buy from members of the community, practice our craft as an exercise in value addition, and resell our products to others in the community. We spend extra money on recycled and compostable paper goods and organic and locally sourced ingredients, not only because they are tastier and healthier but also because these purchases benefit regular people in our community. We are different from a lot of restaurants in that we believe strongly in feeding people food that nourishes them, first and foremost.

"My philosophy centers on the integrity of food. We grow as much produce as we can in our yard. We hand-control most pests and all weeds, sow everything from seed, and spend what little free time we have cultivating vegetables and fruits, because then we can say with confidence to our customers, 'What you are eating represents a level of care that you will never find at a grocer or a chain restaurant. I grew that melon from a seed with my bare hands at the end of an 80-hour work week so that you could sit here, eat it, and leave a healthier, happier soul.'

"We also count on relationships with local food producers. We forged these relationships using the networking opportunities provided by the Appalachian Sustainable Agriculture Project," Chef Lohof says. "These days, we either get regular emails about product availability or random phone calls, such as the one I got the other day from a wild mushroom forager: 'You need any chicken of the woods today?' I use this information to write and rewrite menus every week. Peaceful Valley Farm supplies

Crooked Creek corn, which is used to make the meal based in Heirloom Corn Polenta.

"We are what we eat, and that is the reason there is so much obesity, so much hunger, so much malnutrition, so much angst. Sit down with some friends to a nice local lamb roast with fava beans, olives, Gorgonzola polenta, and a freshly baked boule and tell me what it was again that was so wrong with whatever. . . . You just can't do it. Good food makes you happy. Labor costs in a restaurant tend to stay in the community. We want that. And we want to be part of the foundation that supports area farms and other local artisans."

Café Azalea has been a finalist in the Best Dish North Carolina competition, sponsored by the North Carolina Department of Agriculture and *Our State* magazine. The competition recognizes original dishes utilizing ingredients from North Carolina.

The Recipe

Lentil Ragout with Tomato Coulis in Polenta Bowls
Serves 6

Polenta Bowls

>5 cups water
>1 cup cornmeal
>½ tablespoon fresh rosemary, chopped
>salt and pepper to taste
>pinch of sugar
>2 tablespoons olive oil

Tomato Coulis

>1 tablespoon olive oil
>½ yellow onion, chopped
>3 to 5 cloves garlic, chopped
>1 rib celery, chopped
>½ tablespoon tomato paste

Lentil Ragout with Tomato Coulis in Polenta Bowls
Photo by Paul M. Howey

½ cup dry white wine
2 pounds tomatoes, smoked or char-grilled, then chopped, liquid reserved
salt and pepper to taste

Lentil Ragout

    ½ pound shiitake mushrooms, tossed in olive oil and seasoned with salt and pepper
    ½ pound Brussels sprouts, tossed in olive oil and seasoned with salt and pepper
    1 medium onion, diced
    5 cloves garlic, minced
    1 carrot, diced
    2 ribs celery, diced
    1 tablespoon olive oil
    2 cups lentils, rinsed
    4 cups vegetable broth
    1 bay leaf

1 teaspoon or more curry powder
2 sprigs thyme
salt and pepper to taste

Preheat oven to 425 degrees. Bring water to a boil. Whisk in cornmeal. Add rosemary and sugar. Turn to a low simmer and cook 1 hour, stirring occasionally. Add small amounts of water as needed. Finished polenta should be creamy and thick. Salt and pepper to taste. Grease 6 coffee cups and the outside of 6 shot glasses with olive oil. Fill cups ⅔ full of polenta. Chill. When polenta is halfway set up, push shot glasses down into polenta, top side up, to form wells. Keep glasses down in polenta with pie weights or saucers. Continue to chill until polenta is firm.

Once polenta is cold and set, carefully remove shot glasses and invert coffee cups to release polenta baskets. Fry open side down in hot oil on medium-high just long enough to slightly darken the color. Finish in oven.

TOMATO COULIS

Heat olive oil and sauté onions, garlic, and celery until onions are translucent. Add tomato paste and continue cooking 2 to 3 minutes. Deglaze pan with wine. Add tomatoes and simmer 20 minutes. Purée mixture. Strain. Season sauce with salt and pepper. Add water to thin or cook a little longer to thicken.

LENTIL RAGOUT

Preheat oven to 425 degrees. Roast mushrooms 10 to 15 minutes in oven until browned. Remove and allow to cool. Chop into ½-inch pieces. Roast Brussels sprouts at 450 degrees for about 5 minutes until lightly browned but not softened. Remove from oven and set aside. Slice in half when cool enough to touch. Sauté onions, garlic, carrots, and celery in olive oil. Add lentils, broth, bay leaf, curry, and thyme. Season with salt and pepper. Cook until lentils are of desired doneness, adjusting moisture level and referring to directions on package. Once mixture is cooked, remove bay leaf and thyme stems. Toss mixture with roasted mushrooms and Brussels sprouts. Season to taste.

Place Polenta Bowls in center of plates. Distribute Lentil Ragout around bowls. Spoon Tomato Coulis into bowls.

Katie Button

Katie Button
Photo by
Peter Frank Edwards

Cúrate

11 Biltmore Avenue
Asheville, N.C. 28801
828-239-2946
http://cúratetapasbar.com/

The Chef

Katie Button was born in Conway and lived in Greenville, South Carolina, but grew up in Mountain Lakes, New Jersey. She started preparing meals for the family with her mother and eventually helping in her mother's catering business. "I was surrounded by excellent food and wonderful chefs when I was growing up," she says. "I just never considered cooking as a career path."

Her professional career began in academia. She graduated from Cornell with a B.S. in chemical engineering, then received a master's in biomedical engineering from L'École Centrale in Paris. She enrolled in the Ph.D. program in neuroscience administered by the National Institutes of Health in Bethesda, Maryland, and the Karolinska Institute in Stockholm, Sweden, and already had a lease on an apartment in Washington, D.C., when she discovered Café Atlántico, one of the restaurants owned by José Andrés. She had grown devoted to markets and cooking while living in Paris, and a career in restaurants seemed to be luring her. She withdrew from graduate school and went to work at Café Atlántico. "Looking back, I feel like fate had been giving me signs all along that this is where my passion lies, and that I should have been pursuing culinary arts all along," she says.

At Café Atlántico, she fell in love with restaurants, food, cooking, and Félix Meana, a former service manager from elBulli in Spain—arguably the best restaurant in the world, and certainly one of the most critically acclaimed. (Ferran Adrià's famous restaurant is now closed but is scheduled to reopen in 2014 as a think tank for food creations.) Katie subsequently became one of 40 out of 8,000 applicants selected for an internship at elBulli. She spent her initial three months there as the first American server in the restaurant's history, then entered a seven-month stage in the kitchen. During that formative period, she also worked with Johnny Iuzzini at Jean Georges in New York and at The Bazaar by José Andrés in Beverly Hills.

Katie thus cites two of the world's most illustrious contemporary chefs as her mentors. "José Andrés taught me the simplicity and clarity of traditional Spanish tapas and how to create a thriving restaurant group in the United States, and Ferran Adrià taught me how to organize and run a restaurant kitchen and manage a staff, as well as how to open up to new and unbelievable flavor combinations and techniques."

In January 2010, she returned to the United States, determined to open her own restaurant. She and her family investigated Raleigh, Chapel Hill, Winston-Salem, and Boone. But when they arrived in Asheville, they knew they had found the place they were seeking. "It had something to do with the wonderful sense of community and the vibrant downtown surrounded by these beautiful mountains that really won us over," Katie recalls.

At home, she cooks simply, "primarily because I am never at home. To be honest, on my days off of work, we eat out. We love to check out new restaurants and taste our way through the menu. Dining out is a passion of mine. When I do cook at home, it is something like an avocado and shallot salad drizzled in extra-virgin olive oil, or *pan con tomate* [Spanish tomato bread], topped with Manchego cheese slices and tuna in oil. Occasionally, I will poach some salmon in white wine and serve it with green beans steamed and tossed in olive oil and salt."

The Restaurant

Cúrate was reconstructed from Asheville's former bus depot, built in 1927. The interior features local paintings and sculptures. Seating along a 38-foot marble bar allows patrons to observe the open kitchen. Prices are moderate, the ambience casual.

"I remember the day before we were going to open, having a major emotional breakdown moment," Chef Button says. "Opening your first restaurant is like walking on stage in front of a huge audience, praying that you won't trip and fall flat on your face."

Katie married Félix Meana in early 2012. He is service and beverage director for Cúrate. Katie's mother, Elizabeth, is director of operations, and her father, Ted, is financial manager and handyman.

The kitchen staff works closely with local farms. Lettuces and micro greens come from Jolley Farms, tomatoes from Gaining Ground Farm, and eggplant and beets from Ivy Creek Family Farm. Smokin' J's Fiery Foods bought and planted Padron pepper seeds just for Cúrate. Ground beef, pork, and oxtails come from Brasstown Beef and Hickory Nut Gap Meats (see page 264). All honey comes from wild mountain apiaries.

Although open only since 2010, Cúrate has already garnered much media attention. *Mountain Xpress* published a feature article about Chef Button. Lisa Abend included Katie's internship at elBulli in her book *The Sorcerer's Apprentices*. She appears as well in the film *El Bulli: Cooking in Progress*. In spring 2012, Chef Button was named one of 30 semifinalists for the James Beard Foundation's Rising Star chef award.

The Recipes

Gambas al Ajillo
Serves 6

> 1½ pounds raw shrimp (about 32 shrimp, 26–30 size), peeled, deveined, and butterflied
> salt to taste
> ¾ cup mild or blended oil
> 6 cloves garlic, peeled and lightly smashed with the back of a knife
> 6 cloves garlic, sliced thin
> 6 dried arbol chili peppers, broken in half (or substitute pinch of chili pepper flakes)
> 6 bay leaves
> 1½ cups dry sherry wine
> toasted bread

Season shrimp liberally with salt and set aside. Heat oil in a large sauté pan over medium heat. Add whole garlic cloves and sauté until they just start to turn golden brown. Add sliced garlic and stir until it is fragrant and

Gambas al Ajillo
Photo by Peter Frank Edwards

a light golden brown also. Add chili peppers, bay leaves, and shrimp. Cook, stirring, until shrimp begin to turn pink but are not done. Add sherry and continue to heat until shrimp are just cooked through. Remove from heat. Using tongs, remove shrimp from pan and set aside. Return sauce to stovetop. Reduce slightly for 30 seconds and adjust seasoning if necessary. Remove from heat.

Divide shrimp among 6 small bowls. Garnish with 1 chili pepper, 1 bay leaf, and 1 whole garlic clove. Divide remaining sauce and sliced garlic among bowls. Serve immediately with toasted bread such as ciabatta to dip in sauce at bottom of bowls.

Gazpacho
Serves 6

1 cucumber, peeled
2½ cups chopped fresh ripe tomatoes
1 green bell pepper, seeded, stem and white membrane removed
⅓ cup firmly packed cubed white bread such as baguette, crust removed
2 tablespoons sherry vinegar
¼ cup sherry wine

Gazpacho
Photo by Peter Frank Edwards

1 clove garlic, peeled and chopped coarse
1 cup water
½ cup mild olive oil or blended oil
salt to taste
chopped cucumber, green pepper, and tomato for garnish

Combine cucumber, tomatoes, bell pepper, bread, vinegar, wine, garlic, and water in a food processor or blender and process in batches until smooth. Drizzle in olive oil a little at a time to create an emulsion. When thoroughly blended, pass mixture through a fine-meshed strainer and season with salt. Set aside in refrigerator to chill thoroughly before serving.

Pour chilled soup into bowls and garnish with a small quantity of finely chopped cucumber, green pepper, and tomato and a drizzle of extra-virgin olive oil.

Pimientos de Piquillo
Photo by Peter Frank Edwards

Pimientos de Piquillo
Serves 6

Peppers

18 whole canned piquillo peppers
(available from www.tienda.com)
¾ pound goat cheese
2 tablespoons extra-virgin olive
oil

Sauce

2 whole canned piquillo peppers
enough extra-virgin olive oil to
emulsify blended peppers
salt to taste

PEPPERS

Stuff each pepper with about 1 tablespoon goat cheese. Heat oil in a large nonstick sauté pan on medium-high. Sear peppers for 1 to 2 minutes on each side until cheese is just melted. Use a spatula to carefully remove peppers. Serve hot.

SAUCE

Blend peppers with a little bit of olive oil in a food processor until a smooth, loose sauce is achieved. Season with salt.

TO PRESENT

Spread sauce on each of 6 plates. Arrange 3 peppers on each plate next to sauce.

Jael Rattigan
*Photo provided
by French Broad
Chocolates*

French Broad Chocolate Lounge

10 South Lexington Avenue
Asheville, N.C. 28801
828-252-4181
www.frenchbroadchocolates.com

French Broad Chocolate Lounge is named after the river that
runs through Asheville. Owners Dan Rattigan—born in Honey Brook
in Pennsylvania's Amish country—and his wife, Jael—from Minneapolis, Minnesota—met in Minneapolis when Jael was attending business
school and Dan was in law school. They both dropped out to move to
Costa Rica and start a restaurant and a family. They called their restaurant Bread and Chocolate. One of their children was born in their
apartment, located above the restaurant. The nearest hospital was
about an hour away, so they planned a home birth with a midwife.
They closed the restaurant for one day to allow for an uninterrupted
birth process. Then Dan went downstairs into the restaurant kitchen,

Tumblers
Photo provided by French Broad Chocolates

where he prepared a beautiful tropical fruit salad for Jael.

They moved to Asheville around 2005 for two reasons: food and another baby. They love being a part of the local food culture. Dan has enjoyed cooking since he was a child. He worked in catering and baking while attending law school. Jael started making chocolates for friends and family in 2003 and fell in love with the process and the products. After experiencing cacao at its source in Costa Rica and working with local chocolate in their restaurant, they narrowed their focus to chocolate when they moved to Asheville. Both are self-taught, having learned their craft from textbooks, cookbooks, chef friends, online classes, the cacao farms of

Costa Rica, and culinary tours in the United States and Central America. Since they opened French Broad Chocolate Lounge in 2008, it has grown from a mom-and-pop shop to a full-scale operation with five pastry chefs and 30 employees.

French Broad Chocolate Lounge describes itself as "an inviting, high-end dessert café with a focus on chocolate." Value is central to the concept. "Even in a tough economy, people still feel the desire to treat themselves to luxury," according to the lounge's website. "They may not be able to afford a new car or even a four-star meal, but there's definitely room in the budget for a box of truffles or decadent brownies."

The lounge maintains a relationship with the local business community, buying its fruits and berries from Full Sun Farm and its free-range eggs from several farms in western North Carolina. It also acquires honey and milk locally. Dan and Jael pick herbs from their own backyard. Cacao, however, is a finicky tree that thrives only within a narrow range near the equator, so there is no such thing as a local source for their main ingredient. Most cacao is grown on farms smaller than five acres. The nature of the plant makes mechanized harvesting impossible; every pod must be removed by hand with a machete. Many chocolate manufacturers are showing leadership by protecting the interests of small farmers through such organizations as the World Cocoa Foundation and TransFair USA. So, although cacao is not local, the lounge manages to maintain its practice of working with small, family producers.

French Broad Chocolate Lounge has received much media coverage. Jael was photographed for the cover of the January/February 2009 issue of *Verve* magazine for a story about love and chocolate. The *Asheville Citizen-Times* has devoted two articles to the enterprise and the family's journey from Costa Rica to Asheville. *US Airways Magazine* called French Broad Chocolate Lounge the number-one indulgence in Asheville. *Mountain Xpress* has named it the top dessert destination in western North Carolina for the past three years. *WNC* magazine featured the lounge in its January/February 2008 edition. *Southern Living* included it in an article about holiday shopping in Asheville in December 2010 and listed the lounge among the "Best of the South" in February 2011.

Camp Boswell

Camp Boswell
Photo by Tanya Triber

The Junction

348 Depot Street
Asheville, N.C. 28801
828-225-3497
http://thejunctionasheville.com

The Chef

Camp Boswell, a Montgomery, Alabama, native, slung burgers and chicken fingers at a sports bar for his first job in a professional kitchen when he was in college at Auburn. But he had been cooking since he was a little kid. "My family is full of great home cooks," he says. "I've been cooking with my mom as far back as I can remember."

After about four years working in casual restaurants, he enrolled and eventually graduated from the culinary program at The Art Institute of Colorado in Denver. During that time, he also earned wine certification under a master sommelier at In Vino Veritas, a wine school. He then became a representative for a wholesale wine distributor, selling wines to fine-dining restaurants in the vicinity of Birmingham, Alabama. "Sales are just not my thing," he concluded after about three years. "I missed the kitchen."

Camp worked for Chris Hastings, a two-time James Beard Award nominee, at The Hot and Hot Fish Club in Birmingham. An offer to be sous chef at Rezaz brought him to Asheville. He then moved to Portland, Oregon, for a little over a year to help Alyssa Gregg open her restaurant, Spints. At that time, The Junction was in the planning stages. The owners summoned him back in early 2011, when the restaurant was nearly ready.

Chef Boswell summarizes his approach to creating dishes as "not trying to reinvent the wheel. I like to take good, fresh, seasonal, local ingredients and manipulate them a little bit to maximize their inherent flavor. I cook pretty simply. I like fresh flavors used smartly to complement each other. Less is more when it comes to cooking."

At home, he especially likes seafood. "I love to cook at home, but I seldom cook just for myself. I really enjoy cooking for other people."

The Restaurant

Owned by Charles and Tanya Triber, The Junction is located in the River Arts District, an up-and-coming section of Asheville. The restaurant's website describes it as "a neighborhood eatery serving simple food with a fine-dining twist. We offer a whole-foods, slow-foods approach. We brine our fried chicken, smoke our peaches, handcraft our soups, and visit tailgate markets weekly. We make our own bacon and corned beef, squeeze cases of citrus each week for cocktails, and work with other local, small businesses whenever possible. Meats are fully prepared in house and are free from antibiotics and hormones."

The restaurant is noted for its Southern tapas-style small plates. Other favorites include seasonal soups and salads and The Junction's signature burger, roasted root vegetable salad, and house charcuterie plate. Special emphasis goes to the bar, too. "Our lovely bar serves up local brews, affordable but sophisticated wines, and fabulous signature cocktails," Chef Boswell says. Sunday brunch service began in early 2012. A banquet room seating up to about 30 is available. Asheville residents and hotel guests can have food delivered from The Junction by using Westside Munchie Machine (http://westsidemunchiemachine.com). This service provides deliveries from other restaurants as well.

Chef Boswell spends every Wednesday and Saturday morning at area farmers' markets when vegetables are in season. "I just grab anything that looks good from any stand at the market," he says. The kitchen works in particular with Ten Mile Farm and Jake's Farm for produce and vegetables. It buys beef from Coastal Cattle on the North Carolina coast, through Southern Foods, a North Carolina wholesaler.

The Carolina Epicurean (http://carolinaepicurean.com), an excellent resource for both visitors and residents of the mountains, recommends The Junction.

Sweet Tea–Brined Fried Chicken
Photo by Tanya Triber

The Recipes

Sweet Tea–Brined Fried Chicken
Serves 4

Brine mixture
- 2 cups sugar
- 1 cup salt
- 2 quarts brewed tea
- 2 lemons, juiced
- 1 whole chicken, broken down into legs, thighs, and breasts

Batter mixture
- 2 cups flour
- ½ teaspoon pepper
- ½ teaspoon garlic powder
- 1 tablespoon salt
- 1 quart buttermilk
- 2 quarts canola oil

Add sugar and salt to tea and bring to a boil. Remove from heat and let cool to room temperature. Add lemon juice and squeezed lemons to brine. Cool completely in refrigerator. Once liquid is cool, submerge chicken pieces in brine and refrigerate 24 to 48 hours.

Combine flour, pepper, garlic powder, and salt. Whisk well to incorporate.

After chicken is fully marinated, remove from tea brine and cover with buttermilk. Allow to sit in buttermilk in refrigerator for 2 hours. Remove chicken from buttermilk, toss in flour mixture until completely coated, and shake off excess. Fill a large pot with canola oil and heat to 325 degrees. Fry chicken in batches until it reaches an internal temperature of 165 degrees.

Grilled Shrimp with Fried Green Tomatoes and Remoulade Sauce
Serves 3-4

Brine
- 2 cups champagne vinegar
- 2 cups water
- 2 cups sugar
- ¼ cup salt
- 2 tablespoons pickling spice

Fry mix
- 1 cup flour
- 1 cup corn flour
- 1 cup cornmeal
- 1 tablespoon salt
- 1 teaspoon pepper

Remoulade Sauce
>   1 pint mayonnaise
>   juice of ½ lemon
>   ½ cup finely chopped capers
>   ½ cup finely chopped cornichons
>   1 hard-boiled egg, chopped fine
>   ¼ cup chopped roasted red pepper
>   salt and pepper to taste

Fried Green Tomatoes
>   3 green tomatoes, cored and sliced ⅛ inch thick
>   2 cups buttermilk
>   canola oil
>   salt and pepper to taste

Grilled Shrimp
>   Olive or canola oil, enough to coat shrimp
>   12 large shrimp, peeled and deveined
>   salt and pepper to taste

BRINE

Combine all ingredients in a pot and bring to a boil. Cool to room temperature.

FRY MIX

Combine all ingredients. Whisk well to incorporate.

REMOULADE SAUCE

Combine all ingredients in a bowl. Mix well.

FRIED GREEN TOMATOES

Put tomatoes in a plastic container with a lid and cover with brine. Place tomatoes in refrigerator and allow to sit for 1 week or up to 1 month.

Remove tomatoes from brine, cover with buttermilk, and let sit for 5 to 10 minutes. Dredge tomatoes in fry mix, shake off excess, and fry in canola

Grilled Shrimp with Fried Green Tomatoes and Remoulade Sauce
Photo by Tanya Triber

oil at 350 degrees until golden brown. Remove from oil and place on paper towels to drain. Lightly season with salt and pepper.

GRILLED SHRIMP

Lightly oil shrimp and season with salt and pepper. Grill or sauté shrimp until pink and just cooked through.

TO PRESENT

Dab a small amount of Remoulade Sauce on a plate and lay tomatoes on top. Spoon more sauce on top of tomatoes and place shrimp on top.

William S. Dissen

William S. Dissen
*Photo provided by
The Market Place*

The Market Place

20 Wall Street
Asheville, N.C. 28801
828-252-4162
http://marketplace-restaurant.com

The Chef

William S. Dissen is originally from Charleston, West Virginia. At age 15, he started washing dishes at a country club in the area, then worked as a prep cook and eventually as a line cook.

After graduating from West Virginia University with a double major in English and French, he enrolled in the Culinary Institute of America in Hyde Park, New York, where he graduated with honors. He returned to West Virginia in the culinary apprenticeship program at The Greenbrier Resort. Working with Certified Master Chef Peter Timmins taught him the discipline of a refined kitchen.

From there, he moved to Charleston, South Carolina, where he worked under Donald Barickman of Magnolias and James Beard–nominated Craig Deihl of Cypress. As the sous chef at Cypress, William learned to manage a large kitchen team and to understand the importance of proper ordering and inventory. Sustainability was also an important goal. "We used whole animals and butchered them in order to utilize every part," he says. "Charcuterie was integral to this process as well."

William returned to formal education at the University of South Carolina, where he earned a master's in hospitality, restaurant, and tourism management. He moved to California in 2002 to work at the San Ysidro Ranch in Montecito, cooking under Chef Jamie West as a *poissonnier* (fish chef). There, he learned the importance of farm-to-table cuisine. The ranch had an organic orchard and garden, and Chef Dissen picked fresh produce daily for the kitchen. He also learned to use local and sustainable seafood and to "understand that making the right choice about what to order can affect our oceans and our planet."

While at the San Ysidro Ranch, he cooked with Julia Child at the Santa Barbara Food and Wine Festival. "I remember how tall she was and how charismatic and genuine she was," Chef Dissen recalls. "I will always remember the dish. We cooked Red-Wine-Braised Beef Short Ribs with Gorgonzola Polenta. Even as an older woman, she still floated around the kitchen and was gracious with the festival guests. It was an honor to have spent time with such an icon and legend."

Chef Dissen was recognized in *40 Chefs Under 40* by the Mother Nature Network in 2010 and was honored as a "Seafood Watch Ambassador" by the Monterey Bay Aquarium's Cooking for Solutions Gala.

He moved to Asheville during summer 2009. After traveling around the United States for work and school, he was looking for a place to settle down. "I grew up in the mountains of Appalachia in West Virginia, and moving here really felt like home," he says.

When not on duty, he likes to eat at local "hole in the wall" ethnic restaurants. "I want to walk into a place where I can't understand the language and have a meal made with great ingredients with techniques and recipes that I have never seen before," he says. "I am married to a beautiful Indian woman, so I eat a lot of spicy Indian cuisine."

The Restaurant

The Market Place has operated in Asheville for 32 years. Chef Dissen has owned it since 2009. The interior is painted in shades of gray and decorated with original, colorful, mostly abstract art. The ambience is fairly casual, the orientation being toward accessibility and affordability. A community table lines the center of the bar area. Tables are unclothed. Much of the cooking is done on a wood-fired grill and a rotisserie.

The Market Place is a farm-to-table restaurant. "We try to source all of our ingredients from within a hundred miles," Chef Dissen says. "We utilize the Appalachian Sustainable Agriculture Project [see page 198] as a resource to find artisanal farmers and unique ingredients for our menus." It is also a sustainable and "green" restaurant. Eight solar panels heat water. The space was recently renovated using recycled and local materials. And the staff uses green cleaning products and recycles and composts organic waste.

With regard to designing the menu, Chef Dissen vows that "my philosophy begins with farm-fresh ingredients. I look at it this way: my cuisine is always going to be best with fresh ingredients. For example, an ear of corn when ripe on the stalk is the freshest, sweetest, and most colorful when it is still part of a growing plant. As soon as the ear of corn is picked, it begins to convert its natural sugars to starches, losing its flavor, color, and, most importantly, taste. So farm-to-table is where it all begins. It is also about finding people who have a love for food because, just like my grandmother, cooking great food is always a labor of love. When we put our all into our work, it truly shines through. My style is simple cuisine with explosive flavors."

The Recipes

Coulotte Steak
Serves 4

Steak and marinade
- ½ cup extra-virgin olive oil, plus extra for grilling
- 2 tablespoons chopped basil
- 1 teaspoon minced garlic
- 1 teaspoon pepper
- 4 8-ounce coulotte steaks (preferably from Brasstown Beef or other local farm), trimmed
- salt and pepper to taste

Sweet potato chipotle hash
- 2 pounds sweet potatoes
- 2 tablespoons olive oil
- ¼ cup red onion, diced small
- ¼ cup chipotle peppers
- 2 tablespoons minced garlic
- 1 tablespoon lime juice
- 1 tablespoon butter
- salt and pepper to taste

Poached eggs
- 4 large eggs
- salt and pepper to taste

Coulotte Steak
Photo provided by The Market Place

Salsa verde

    10 tomatillos, husks removed
    1 white onion, diced medium
    1 tablespoon minced garlic
    2 jalapeño peppers, seeded
    2 scallions, sliced
    2 bunches cilantro, chopped
    2 to 3 tablespoons lime juice
    1 tablespoon sugar
    cayenne pepper to taste
    salt and pepper to taste

STEAK AND MARINADE

Combine ½ cup olive oil with basil, garlic, and pepper in a medium bowl. Mix thoroughly. Place steaks in bowl and toss to completely cover on both sides. Allow to marinate for at least ½ hour or overnight.

Preheat grill to medium-high. When grill comes to temperature, clean with a metal brush. Place oil on a clean towel and brush grill grates to lubricate. Season steaks liberally with salt and pepper and place on grill. Grill about 4 minutes. Turn over and grill an additional 3 to 5 minutes until medium-rare (internal temperature 145 degrees). Remove from grill and let rest 5 minutes. Slice against the grain and serve immediately.

SWEET POTATO CHIPOTLE HASH

Fill a medium pot with salted water. Add sweet potatoes and bring to a boil. Cook until fork-tender. Remove and allow to cool. Dice potatoes small. Reserve. Add olive oil to a medium sauté pan over medium-high heat. Add onions and cook until translucent. Stir in sweet potatoes and cook until they begin to caramelize. Stir in chipotle peppers, garlic, and lime juice. Cook until aromatic. Stir in butter and season with salt and pepper. Taste and reseason as necessary.

POACHED EGGS

Using an immersion circulator, bring a water bath to approximately 150 degrees (64 degrees Celsius). Place eggs in water bath and cook 45 minutes. Crack into a slotted spoon, season with salt and pepper, and serve immediately.

SALSA VERDE

Grill tomatillos to char outside flesh. Place in a pan and cover with plastic to steam. Pour off excess liquid. Use a paring knife to cut off any large stems. Add onions, garlic, jalapeños, scallions, and cilantro to a food processor and process until combined and diced medium. Add tomatillos, lime juice, sugar, cayenne, and salt and pepper. Pulse to blend ingredients. Taste and reseason as necessary.

TO PRESENT

Array slices of steak along 1 side of each plate. Dab salsa verde at ends of steak array. Place sweet potato chipotle hash in ramekin alongside steak array. Place egg on top of sweet potato hash.

Blueberry Semifreddo
Photo by John Batchelor

Blueberry Semifreddo with Lime Curd and Pistachio Brittle
Serves 8

Chef's Note

"Blueberry Semifreddo was inspired by a hike to Graveyard Fields along the Blue Ridge Parkway. Along the trail, there are thousands of wild blueberry bushes that are filled with fruit. At the end of a hot summer, I crave the refreshing taste of blueberries, and a semifreddo is a unique twist to a frozen dessert. The lime helps to accent the blueberries, while the Pistachio Brittle adds a nice crunch to the dish."

Lime Curd

    4 limes
    1½ cups sugar
    ¼ pound unsalted butter at room temperature
    4 extra-large eggs
    ⅛ teaspoon kosher salt

Blueberry Semifreddo

    5 large eggs, separated
    1 cup sugar, divided

⅓ cup blueberry purée
2 tablespoons finely zested lime peel
2 cups heavy cream

Pistachio Brittle
2 cups sugar
½ cup water
¼ pound unsalted butter
⅓ cup light corn syrup
½ teaspoon baking soda
13 ounces pistachios, shelled
sea salt to taste

1 cup fresh blueberries
8 edible flowers

LIME CURD

Zest limes, being careful to avoid white pith. Squeeze limes to acquire ½ cup juice. Put zest and sugar in a food processor and process until zest is finely chopped. Place butter and lime zest mixture in the bowl of an electric mixer and use paddle attachment to cream. Add eggs 1 at a time. Add lime juice and salt and mix until combined. Pour mixture into a small saucepan and simmer over low heat, constantly stirring, for about 10 minutes until thickened. Remove from heat and allow to cool.

BLUEBERRY SEMIFREDDO

Line a 9-by-5-by-3-inch loaf pan with 2 layers of plastic wrap, leaving overhang around all sides. Whisk together egg yolks, ½ cup of the sugar, blueberry purée, and lime zest in a medium metal bowl. Place bowl over a pot of simmering water and whisk constantly for about 3 minutes until mixture thickens and an instant-read thermometer shows 160 degrees. Beat cream in another large bowl until peaks form. Reserve. In another bowl, beat egg whites until soft peaks form. Gradually add remaining ½ cup sugar 1 tablespoon at a time. Beat egg white mixture until stiff but not dry. Fold egg white mixture into yolk mixture in 3 additions, followed by whipped cream. Stir until just incorporated. Spread Blueberry

Semifreddo mixture into loaf pan and fold plastic wrap over top to cover. Freeze overnight.

Pistachio Brittle

Combine sugar, water, butter, and corn syrup in a large saucepan and bring to a boil. Cook over medium-high heat, stirring occasionally, for about 10 minutes until sugar turns a deep amber caramel. Remove from heat and carefully stir in baking soda. Mixture will bubble. Carefully stir in pistachios, then spread mixture onto ½ sheet tray lined with a nonstick baking pan mat. Oil a rubber spatula and spread mixture smooth. Sprinkle with sea salt and allow to cool completely.

To present

Remove semifreddo from freezer and remove plastic wrap. Cut into 8 equal portions. Spread Lime Curd on bottom of rectangular plates. Place semifreddo on top. Dab Lime Curd on top of semifreddo. Break up Pistachio Brittle and scatter around and on top of semifreddo. Scatter fresh blueberries around plates and add an edible flower to each. Serve immediately.

Hominy Valley Farms

76 Hominy Valley Drive
Candler, N.C. 28715
www.hominyvalleyfarms.com

Frank and Jeanette Wilson met as students at North Carolina State University. With help from their young-adult sons, Anthony and Nathan, they own and operate Hominy Valley Farms.

As Jeanette's parents moved into retirement, she and Frank took over the farm and began selling cattle as finished beef. Frank had studied agriculture and managed other beef cattle farms. And Jeanette grew up on the farm, so animal husbandry was familiar to her as well. "Our learning curve came with deciding how to present our products and market them as meats to consumers and restaurants," the couple says on the farm's website. "Eventually, we decided to add pastured chickens, processed on the farm, and we will soon be adding pastured pork to our offerings."

The farm's varied terrain ranges from flood plains and hay ground to rolling hills and wooded mountainsides. Cattle are rotated among the pastures in order to better manage both animals and land. "Chickens 'graze' in the pastures, living in chicken tractors which are moved each day to fresh grass," according to the website. "Pigs greet us each day with dirt on their noses from doing what comes naturally. We do not implant our animals with growth hormones to make them grow faster, nor do we give them any antibiotics in their feed. They are fed an all-vegetable diet with no animal by-products and they spend all their days in pasture. . . . Eventually the yearlings chosen to finish as Hominy Valley Farms beef are given supplemental grain for several weeks to add the flavor our customers prefer. They are still free in our pastures, enjoying grass and hay and putting on their final layer of finish."

In addition to markets and restaurants, Hominy Valley sells directly to consumers. Patrons can special-order or buy just a couple of steaks. Sometimes as they make deliveries in Asheville, "it is amazing to realize that we are heading into some of the same neighborhoods and even some of the same stores where Jeanette's grandfather, Nathan Plemmons, was known for his excellent produce more than 75 years ago," the couple says.

233

Adam Hayes

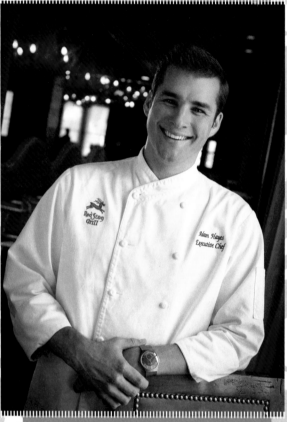

Adam Hayes
Photo provided by
Kessler Collection

Red Stag Grill at the Grand Bohemian Hotel

11 Boston Way
Asheville, N.C. 28803
828-398-5600
www.bohemianhotelasheville.com

The Chef

Adam Hayes, a Trinity, North Carolina, native, enjoys living in the mountains primarily because of the rich culture and the food scene. He is also drawn to the wide range of family activities and adventures and has found the people to be "just great."

He started cooking while attending the College of Charleston, "basically to stay alive," he says. "My friends and I would get together and do typical college stuff and cook out. We would experiment with different cuts of meat and see how crazy we could get with cooking methods. I learned a lot about what *not* to do in a professional kitchen!"

At the College of Charleston, Adam majored in "the science of intoxicology," he says. He left after two years and moved to the Greensboro–High Point area to cook at Ham's, a venerable sandwich place on N.C. 68. He began taking culinary classes at Guilford Technical Community College, met the woman who became his wife, and decided to be a chef. He graduated from the GTCC culinary arts program in three years, even though he was working full-time in various restaurants. "And here I am, 13 years later, executive chef of a great hotel and restaurant," he says.

Adam considers his time at Restaurant Pastiche in Greensboro his most formative experience. "This was my first true fine-dining restaurant. I saw duck and foie gras for the first time, made fresh mozzarella, made stocks and sauces from scratch. I worked with some great people there, and I loved every minute. Chef Mitchell Nicks was a great chef and teacher to me."

He moved to Charlotte to become a line cook at Mimosa Grill and was promoted to sous chef five months later. "I learned about casual fine dining with 350 seats—great food for so many people! Chef Jojo Alexander was my inspiration, and he taught me specifically about self-discipline. You have to have it in this business. Push yourself every day to do more, that's the goal!" Then he helped the same restaurant group open Arpa, a 50-seat Spanish tapas restaurant, where he was named *chef de cuisine*. "I was responsible for the kitchen on all levels and reported to Chef Tom

Condron directly," Adam says. "Chef Tom is the epitome of a passionate chef. He taught me to love what you do and do it the best that you can." When the company expanded again with Zink American Kitchen, Adam was the opening *chef de cuisine*, responsible for ordering and menu development.

Chef Hayes returned to Greensboro as *chef de cuisine* at Print Works Bistro in the Proximity Hotel, lauded in the *New York Times* architecture section as the greenest hotel in America. "Hotels are bigger than most people think," he says. "There are lots of moving parts. The Quaintance-Weaver Restaurant and Hotel group taught me a lot about leadership. In this business at this level, it's all about desired outcomes and your team helping you accomplish daily tasks. I have become a teacher!"

Chef Hayes moved into his first executive chef position at the Red Stag. He considers being a chef "a glamorous job, but with tons of work. It's not easy, but it's fun."

Outside the professional kitchen, Adam is a family man. "So it is usually home-cooked, simple, and delicious meals made with great ingredients. We do not waste food at home. You must not throw things away. We compost, make something out of what we have, and focus on preparing only what we need."

The Restaurant

The Grand Bohemian Hotel in Biltmore Village is a member of the Kessler Collection (www.kesslercollection.com), a family of uniquely designed, elegant, artistically inspired boutique properties. Other Kessler locations are in Florida, Georgia, Colorado, and New Mexico, each one organized around carefully selected art, music, and cultural influences personally acquired by the Kessler family. Eight Kessler Collection hotels are members of the Marriott Autograph Collection.

The Red Stag Grill, modeled after a European hunting lodge, features hand-hewn beams and tables, walnut flooring, and intimate lighting. "The antlers kind of tell the tale. We have some Austrian and German influences in the restaurant and on the menu," says Chef Hayes. The style "is simple and clean. I go for great ingredients and preparations that honor them. Less is more. We look for the best-quality meats and seafood, and we do not allow our vendors to send us anything that is less than perfect. Most of the suppliers love me for that, but some think I'm just an ass about quality, and they are right."

Chef Hayes calls local farms, researches what they have, sometimes criticizes their products, and studies their farming practices. "Just because it's local doesn't automatically mean it's the best," he warns. "Remember, quality comes first. Some farmers work for the money, and others work for the passion. I look for the passion, and that leads me to the quality products. I am a big supporter of 'Got to Be NC' [the North Carolina Department of Agriculture's farm-to-fork collaborative program]. I was born and raised in this state, and it has some of the best farms and artisan-made products in the country." Among the local providers the Red Stag employs are Looking Glass Creamery, Imladris Farms (see page 248), Lusty Monk, Goldfinch Gardens, Hickory Nut Gap Meats (see page 264), and Flying Cloud.

Weddings, rehearsal dinners, and large group meetings are easily accommodated at the Grand Bohemian. The property holds a Four Diamond rating from AAA and is a Diner's Choice winner from Open Table.

The Recipes

Sautéed Trout with Lemon-Thyme-Butter Pan Sauce
Serves 4

> 4 tablespoons olive oil
> 4 4- to 6-ounce trout fillets
> 4 tablespoons capers
> ½ cup white wine
> juice of 1 lemon
> 2 teaspoons finely chopped fresh thyme
> 6 tablespoons butter
> salt and pepper to taste

Trout
Photo provided by Kessler Collection

Heat olive oil in a 10-inch sauté pan until lightly smoking. Add fillets flesh side down and sear until golden brown. Try to avoid moving fillets, which should not stick once they brown. Flip fillets, trying to keep them whole. Cook about 2 minutes. Remove pan from heat and remove fillets. Return pan to medium-high heat. Add capers and wine. Deglaze pan by scraping with a wooden spoon. Reduce wine by ½. Add lemon juice and thyme. Remove pan from heat and slowly add butter, swirling pan until butter is incorporated. Use a whisk if necessary. This makes the pan sauce. Add salt and pepper.

To present, place fillets off-center on plates and ladle with sauce. Assemble favorite vegetables alongside.

Coq Au Vin with Plums
Serves 6 to 8

> 2 2½- to 3-pound chickens, quartered
> salt and pepper to taste
> 3 teaspoons freshly grated nutmeg, divided
> 5 or 6 slices thick-cut bacon, cut into large pieces
> 1 leek, sliced
> 1 medium parsnip, chopped coarse

Coq Au Vin with Plums
Photo provided by Kessler Collection

8 cloves garlic
¼ cup brandy
4 sprigs fresh thyme
4 bay leaves
4 plums, pitted and cut into wedges
1½ cups Chardonnay
14½-ounce can chicken broth
3 tablespoons vegetable oil
15 to 20 pearl onions, trimmed
1 pound mushrooms (chanterelles, cremini, or similar), whole or cut into
  bite-sized pieces
2 tablespoons arrowroot
2 tablespoons water
mashed potatoes

Preheat oven to 300 degrees. Season chicken pieces generously with salt and pepper and 2 teaspoons of the nutmeg. Set aside. In a Dutch oven, cook bacon over medium heat until crisp. Remove bacon with a slotted spoon and drain on paper towels. Brown chicken pieces in hot bacon drippings until golden brown. Remove chicken from Dutch oven. Drain all but 1 tablespoon drippings from Dutch oven. Add leeks, parsnips, and garlic to Dutch oven. Cook 4 minutes over medium heat until garlic is lightly browned. Remove Dutch oven from heat. Carefully add brandy and return to heat. Deglaze pan by stirring bottom with a wooden spoon to release any browned bits. Simmer until brandy glazes bottom of Dutch oven. Add thyme, bay leaves, and ½ of the plums. Add Chardonnay. Bring to a boil. Reduce heat and simmer, uncovered, until mixture is reduced by ⅓. Add chicken broth. Bring to a boil. Add chicken pieces.

Cover Dutch oven. Place in oven and bake 30 minutes or until chicken is no longer pink; internal temperature should be 180 degrees when an instant-read thermometer is inserted into the thickest part. Remove chicken from liquid and set aside. Strain braising liquid and discard solids. Skim fat from braising liquid. About 2½ cups liquid should remain.

Heat oil in Dutch oven. Cook pearl onions for 1 minute in a medium saucepan in enough boiling water to cover. Drain well. Cool onions slightly, then push onions from peels by squeezing root ends. Add onions to Dutch oven and cook about 6 minutes until browned. Add mushrooms and re-maining plums. Cook about 4 minutes until tender. Add braising liquid and remaining 1 teaspoon nutmeg. In a small bowl, combine arrowroot and water. Add mixture to Dutch oven. Cook and stir until mixture is slightly thickened and comes to a boil. Stir in bacon and chicken pieces and heat through. Season with salt and pepper. Serve with mashed potatoes.

Reza Setayesh

Reza Setayesh
Photo by Libby Williams

Rezaz

28 Hendersonville Road
Asheville, N.C. 28803
828-277-1510
www.rezaz.com

241

The Chef

The story behind Reza Setayesh and his restaurant is unique. Born in Tehran, Iran, in 1964, he moved with his family to Germany in the early 1970s. He traveled through much of Europe and North Africa before eventually landing in the United States by the end of the decade. He was working in Los Angeles, parking cars for luxury restaurants on Rodeo Drive, when a friend asked him, "What do you love doing?" The answer was immediate and obvious: cooking.

Reza started out at a deli but soon moved when a regular customer offered him a position at the restaurant the customer managed, the prestigious Pastelle. Reza worked there at night and at a German-California fusion restaurant during the day. He heard about a culinary school that was supposedly just as good as CIA or Johnson & Wales but much less expensive. When he asked for advice, his friends told him how nice *Nashville* was.

Reza arrived in Asheville in the summer of 1985 and completed the culinary program at Asheville-Buncombe Tech in two years. While there, he was a member of a culinary team that won a regional title. He interned at The Cloisters in Sea Island, Georgia, then went to work for the Marriott Corporation in Washington, D.C. Within six years, he rose to executive chef of two different Marriott hotels. In that role, he served myriad banquets, receptions, weddings, and other large-scale events in addition to overseeing the hotels' in-house restaurants. He jumped at the opportunity to return to Asheville as an instructor at his alma mater, A-B Tech. The next period in his professional life saw him as executive chef at restaurants in Waynesville and the Springdale Country Club near Asheville. But like so many young chefs, he aspired to his own restaurant. He opened Rezaz in 2002.

His approach to creating recipes and the menu at Rezaz evolved from his personal history. "I grew up eating seasonally," he says. "I cook the same way. I choose my ingredients based on a Mediterranean style of eating and cooking, and I build upon that tradition by adding unique twists."

When cooking for himself and family, Reza likes "to eat healthy, lots of vegetables," he says. "My choice of protein is seafood. I love lamb and duck as my red-meat choices. But I am open to try anything. I love ethnic, simple cooking. I can handle eating massive amounts of food on my culinary trips, which I take three or four times a year. I choose a destination and eat my way through the restaurants. This year, I have already done New York and San Francisco. I have a trip planned to London, and I am also scheduling a visit to Chicago."

The Restaurant

Rezaz quickly attracted a popular following. But in fall 2004, two hurricanes devastated western North Carolina, damaging property in the mountains much worse than on the coast. Biltmore Village was flooded. The water level inside Rezaz reached three feet, "ruining equipment, tables, chairs, floors, and electrical wiring," Reza recalls. "Only one thing survived: the answering machine." When Reza listened to the messages, they came from customers wishing for his return and offering their support. So he rebuilt—without the help of insurance—and reopened.

Reza utilizes Asheville's farmer-to-chef connections to create his own interpretations of Mediterranean-style dishes. The bar serves a casual small-plate menu. The Benedetto Room, in the back of the restaurant, is a private facility for groups of up to 24. An elaborate five-course tasting menu is provided for up to 12 guests at the Chef's Table in the kitchen, overseen directly by Reza. Menus can be custom-prepared. Patrons should call well in advance to arrange the Chef's Table. Catering is available as well.

Reza also owns and operates Piazza (4 Eastwood Village Boulevard, Asheville, N.C. 28803; 828-298-7224), a family-friendly wood-fired pizza restaurant.

Rezaz was the first restaurant to receive the "Best Customer Service" award from the Asheville Chamber of Commerce.

The Recipes

Potato and Spinach Rotolo
Serves 6 to 8

Rotolo
>2 pounds Idaho potatoes
>2 eggs plus 2 yolks
>2 teaspoons baking powder
>2⅔ cups all-purpose flour
>2 onions, diced small
>4 tablespoons butter
>32 ounces frozen spinach, thawed
>1 cup ricotta cheese
>2 cups Parmesan cheese
>1 teaspoon nutmeg
>salt and pepper to taste

Salsa rosso
>2 onions, diced small
>2 tablespoons diced garlic
>4 ounces extra-virgin olive oil
>2 carrots, peeled and diced small
>3 celery stalks, diced small
>2 red peppers, diced small
>1 cup (7 ounces) canned tomatoes
>2 sprigs rosemary, leaves stripped
>2 tablespoons fresh thyme
>6 tablespoons chopped parsley
>1 tablespoon chili flakes
>½ teaspoon cinnamon
>2 tablespoons sugar
>2 tablespoons red wine vinegar
>salt and pepper to taste

ROTOLO

Preheat oven to 375 degrees. Boil potatoes in skins. Peel and dice potatoes. In a large bowl, combine potatoes, eggs and extra yolks, baking

Potato and Spinach Rotolo
Photo by Steven Tingle

powder, and flour. Roll out into a 14-by-10-inch rectangle. Sauté onions in butter until translucent. Add spinach. Add next 3 ingredients and season with salt and pepper. Cover potato dough with this mixture. Roll into a log and cut into sections. Bake in oven until lightly browned.

Salsa rosso

Sauté onions and garlic in olive oil until translucent. Add carrots, celery, and red peppers and continue to sauté about 3 minutes. Add next 6 ingredients and cook for about 1 hour. Add sugar and vinegar and season with salt and pepper. Purée in a blender and adjust seasonings as needed.

To present

Pour ⅓ cup of salsa on each plate and serve 2 pieces of rotolo on top. Crusty bread and a nice, simple salad go well with this.

Reza Mezze
Serves 6 to 8

Mediterranean pimento cheese

    1 cup green olives
    ⅔ cup walnuts, toasted
    1 red pepper, roasted and peeled
    ½ cup chopped parsley
    ¼ cup diced scallions
    2 tablespoons olive oil
    2 tablespoons pomegranate syrup
    1 tablespoon lemon juice
    ½ teaspoon cumin
    ½ teaspoon chili powder
    pinch of sugar
    4 ounces feta cheese, crumbled
    salt and pepper to taste

Tzatziki sauce

    32 ounces yogurt
    2 cucumbers, peeled, shredded, salted, and squeezed of excess moisture
    4 tablespoons chopped mint
    1 teaspoon cinnamon
    2 teaspoons chopped garlic
    2 teaspoons ground cumin
    2 tablespoons salt
    2 teaspoons pepper
    ¼ cup lemon juice

Summer eggplant dip

    4 onions, diced small
    1 cup minced garlic
    ½ cup minced ginger
    2 bunches cilantro, chopped
    2 bunches mint, chopped
    4 tablespoons tagine spice
    4 tablespoons ground coriander
    4 tablespoons ground cumin
    12 eggplants, diced medium
    12 tomatoes, diced medium

Reza Mezze
Photo by Libby Williams

16 ounces yogurt
salt and pepper to taste

pita bread
romaine lettuce
savoy cabbage

Mediterranean pimento cheese

Place first 3 ingredients in a blender and pulse to combine. Add remaining ingredients except for cheese and salt and pepper. Pulse to combine. Place mixture in a bowl. Fold in cheese and adjust seasonings.

Tzatziki sauce

Mix all ingredients together. Adjust seasonings as needed.

Summer eggplant dip

Sweat onions, garlic, and ginger together in a sauté pan. Add next 5 ingredients. Add eggplant and tomatoes. Cook slowly until eggplant falls apart. Keep covered while cooking. Cool and purée. Fold in yogurt and season as needed.

To present

Serve with warm pita bread and wedges of romaine and savoy cabbage for your gluten-free guests.

Imladris Farm

45 Little Pond Road
Fairview, N.C. 28730
828-628-9377
www.imladrisfarm.com

Andy Harrill represents the seventh generation to work his family's land. He is 10 years old and has been operating his own business—a free-range egg operation—for three years. He gets up early every morning, collects eggs, and feeds the chickens before school. In the afternoons, he cleans the henhouse, gathers in the residents, and locks them up for the night to protect them from predators. On Saturdays, he sells eggs at the North Asheville Tailgate Market.

Walter Harrill's great-grandparents originally owned the land. Previous generations had worked a family farm of 50 to 150 acres in an essentially subsistence mode, as was typical of Appalachian families a few generations ago. They labored part-time to earn cash to pay doctor bills and cover other necessities that required money. At least one family member generated a little additional revenue by following another North Carolina mountain tradition: bootlegging.

Walter and his wife, Wendy, both trained as medical technologists. They moved back to the mountains around 2000 not to farm but because land was available near where Walter's family already owned the farm. Then they started looking at the land in the context of a family vegetable garden and fruit farm. After about a year, they realized they were producing more fruit than they could consume, so

Photos provided
by Imladris Farm

they started selling it. Gradually, they began to realize they liked farming better than their day jobs.

According to Walter, he and Wendy learned to farm "by screwing up and doing it over. Very little of what we do is done the way commercial agriculture does it. It's more like the way things were done 200 years ago. Instead of buying fertilizer, for example, we raise rabbits for meat and for fertilizer. We let the goats prune the raspberries instead of using mechanized methods. Chickens following the goats eat up a lot of parasites, so we don't have to spray for bugs. We help cut our neighbor's corn in return for stalks that will feed the goats."

The primary products from Imladris Farm are a line of gourmet blueberry, raspberry, and blackberry jams, plus apple butter. They are sold in Whole Foods, Earth Fare, and Ingles supermarkets and about two dozen restaurants. Products can also be ordered directly from the website. In addition, the farm produces rabbit meat and pasture-raised goat meat.

Walter remarks that the family "doesn't necessarily eat organic always, but we try to eat local. The problem with sustainable agriculture is the people who are producing really good products often can't afford them for themselves. So we barter our goods a lot with other farms."

249

Randy Dunn

Randy Dunn
*Photo by Biltmore
Farms Hotels*

Roux

Hilton Asheville Biltmore Park
43 Town Square Boulevard
Asheville, N.C. 28803
828-209-2715
www.rouxasheville.com

The Chef

Randy Dunn is from Sparta, Tennessee. He moved to the North Carolina mountains to open Roux. He says he loves "the eclectic vibe and the connection with the mountains, farmers, and farmers' markets" in Asheville and the surrounding area.

He began cooking at about age eight, stirring the pot during jelly making while standing on a chair by the stove. He became his family's official dressing taster at Thanksgiving dinner. Randy cites his mother and grandmother as his earliest and strongest influences. He says he always knew he wanted to please people with his food. Although his education after high school began in civil engineering at Tennessee Tech, he decided to pursue a culinary program shortly before graduation and transferred to Johnson & Wales in Charleston, South Carolina.

His early experiences included making and delivering pizzas at a Pizza Inn, which taught him to work on someone else's schedule. Then he worked at a KFC. Learning management skills while attending Tennessee Tech was another important aspect of his early development. He cooked during the summer at Young Life Camps, feeding 350 people three family-style meals per day.

After culinary school, he cooked at the Carolina Inn in Chapel Hill, where he was able to focus on creativity and use his management skills. He climbed quickly to sous chef, then banquet chef. The restaurant achieved a Four Diamond rating from AAA. He then moved to Cambridge, Massachusetts, to open The Hotel at MIT (now Le Méridien Cambridge). Randy has also served as executive chef at the Doubletree Hotel in Detroit and as executive chef at the Birmingham Marriott. But he ultimately decided he wanted something smaller—more in the boutique mode—so he was strongly attracted to the Hilton Asheville Biltmore Park.

Fall is Randy's favorite season. Outside the professional kitchen, he likes to cook squash and anything slow-roasted, served with savory conserves.

The Restaurant

Roux takes its name from the key element in three classic French mother sauces, a basic starting point in much cooking. Chef Dunn terms the restaurant's cuisine "inspired Southern." Every dish starts with the best ingredients. "Take your time, build layers, and let the food speak for itself," he advises. "Don't underestimate *simple*."

Chef Dunn tells a story about one of his first encounters with a local vendor in Asheville. "I met a lady named Claire of Claire's ABC Preserves in Fletcher. We met here in Biltmore Park at what was then a very small farmers' market. She sells jams and preserves. I purchased her apricot-jalapeño jam and loved it so much we started putting it on our Hot Turkey Club, and we make a sauce out of it for our cheesecake."

Restaurant personnel shop at the Biltmore Park Town Square Farmers' Market on Wednesday afternoons to prepare specials for the weekend. Roux has formed partnerships with local vendors Three Graces Dairy, Sunburst Trout Farm (see page 291), Cane Creek Valley Organics, Blue Ridge Bio Fuels, and City Market South. The restaurant is an active member of the Appalachian Sustainable Agriculture Project (see page 198). Staff members recycle cooking oil to make bio fuel, use solar hot water, recycle all glass, plastic, and paper, and use natural filtered water to eliminate the use of plastic products.

The Hilton Asheville Biltmore Park has received a Four Diamond rating from AAA. It is a LEED-certified Silver property. A day spa provides services on-site. Weddings and large group meetings are readily accommodated in private banquet rooms, ballrooms, and conference rooms.

Mushroom Bisque
Photo by Biltmore Farms Hotels

The Recipes

Mushroom Bisque

Serves 6 to 8 as a main course or 10 to 12 as a first course

6 to 8 baguettes (10 to 12, if serving as a main course)
½ cup butter
1 medium onion, diced
1 to 1½ pounds fresh assorted mushrooms (such as portobello, shiitake, and cremini), diced small
salt and pepper to taste
½ cup sherry, plus extra for serving
½ cup flour
1 quart whole milk
1 pint heavy cream
1 to 2 cups mushroom or chicken stock

Slice and grill or toast baguettes. Set aside. Heat a large stockpot over medium-high heat and melt butter. Add onions and sauté 2 to 3 minutes. Add mushrooms, season with salt and pepper, and sauté 6 to 8 minutes until soft. Add sherry and cook about 2 more minutes. Sprinkle flour over mushroom mixture and stir to make a roux. Cook for 3 to 4 minutes while stirring. Add milk, heavy cream, and stock. Bring to a simmer for about 5 minutes while stirring. Reduce heat to low and stir occasionally for about

30 minutes. Adjust seasonings with additional salt and pepper.

Serve in warm soup bowls or cups. Garnish with grilled baguettes and splashes of sherry.

BBQ Salmon
Serves 4

Dry rub

    1 cup celery seed
    ½ cup paprika
    ½ cup ground nutmeg
    ½ cup chili powder
    ½ cup garlic powder
    ½ cup onion salt
    1 cup dried marjoram
    ½ cup kosher salt
    ¾ cup light brown sugar
    ½ cup pepper

Salmon

    2 tablespoons olive oil
    4 6-ounce portions salmon

BBQ Salmon
Photo by Biltmore Farms Hotels

DRY RUB

Combine all ingredients in a large bowl, making sure to break up brown sugar. Store in an airtight container. Because of sugar's moisture, it will clump over time. Just break it up before next use. Mixture will keep on the shelf for 8 to 10 months. Dry rub is great on any meat or vegetable.

SALMON

Heat a large sauté pan over medium-high heat and add oil. Make sure to use a pan large enough to prevent temperature from dropping when all 4 pieces of salmon are added. Pat salmon dry, then dredge in about 4 table-spoons dry rub to coat. Place in pan rub side down. Cook 3 to 4 minutes per side, depending on thickness.

Serve with your favorite side dishes or on any good salad.

Bistro Meat Loaf

Serves 8 to 10

2 large eggs
1 cup panko breadcrumbs
1 teaspoon salt
1 teaspoon pepper
1½ pounds lean ground beef
1½ pounds lean ground pork
1 tablespoon olive oil
1 large or 2 small yellow onions, diced small
½ cup thinly sliced garlic
1½ teaspoons dried thyme
¼ cup red wine vinegar
4 Roma tomatoes, sliced

Bistro Meat Loaf
Photo by Biltmore Farms Hotels

Preheat oven to 350 degrees. Prepare two 8-by-4-inch loaf pans by spraying with cooking spray. Set aside. In a large mixing bowl, beat eggs, breadcrumbs, salt, and pepper. In a separate bowl, combine beef and pork. Mix with hands until well combined, then add egg mixture. In a large sauté pan, heat oil and cook onions, garlic, and thyme for 3 to 4 minutes over medium-high heat. Do not brown; cook just until onions are translucent. Let cool slightly, then add to meat mixture. Add vinegar and mix well. Divide mixture in half and pack each half into a loaf pan. Or you can free-form the loaves and bake them in a 9-by-13-inch cake pan. Top each loaf with tomato slices and season with a pinch of salt. Bake in oven for 60 to 70 minutes, depending on thickness of loaves. Test with a meat thermometer; cook to a minimum internal temperature of 170 degrees. Let rest for 5 to 15 minutes to retain juices. Slice into portions and serve hot.

Conserves and savory jams go well with this recipe. Roux serves it with red onion marmalade and mashed potatoes.

Hendersonville

Jesse Roque

Jesse Roque
*Photo provided by
Never Blue*

Never Blue
on Main

119 South Main Street
Hendersonville, N.C. 28792
828-693-4646
http://theneverblue.com

Blue
Gypsy

101 Main Street
Saluda, N.C. 28773
828-693-4646

257

The Chef

Jesse Roque grew up in south Florida, where her grandfather was an inventor, her father was a biochemist, and her mother was a professional sculptor and artist. The family dynamic centered on creativity and invention. She and her brother were always encouraged to make things, whether it was food or crafts. "We didn't go out and buy it, we made it," she recalls.

She moved to western North Carolina in 2006. Her mother, Pamela Cosner, had already relocated to the area because of its welcoming environment for artists. Pamela encouraged Jesse and her husband, Edson, to join her. Jesse remembers the invitation: "One visit later, we were on our way. We found a spot on Main Street in downtown Hendersonville and initially thought we would have an art gallery and coffee shop. Before long—I couldn't help it—we transformed our space into a full-blown restaurant, but the art still stayed. To this day, my mom's art adorns the carpeted walls of Never Blue."

Jesse has been cooking since age five or six—"as soon as I could find my way around a kitchen," she says. "My first dish was a cheesecake. My mom let me do that because I didn't have to actually cook anything, and she thought I'd be safe."

Jesse intended to be a ballet dancer. "When I realized I couldn't do that forever, I started bouncing around trying to figure out what to do. I began waiting tables and working in restaurants. When the chefs told me I couldn't come into the kitchen, much less run a kitchen, unless I was a guy, my path became really clear. No way would I stand for that!" She researched culinary programs and found that Johnson & Wales was opening a campus in Charleston, South Carolina. She attended the school from 1992 to 1994, then moved into an externship in the pastry department at the Fontainebleau Hilton in Miami Beach. She continued her career in several well-known restaurants, including the Charleston Grill.

"Some of my most interesting and more heated moments in the kitchen were working in a very small, very hot French restaurant, Le Festival in Coral Gables, Florida, where I made soufflés from the time I arrived until the time I left each night," she recalls. "I was the only female and non-French person in the kitchen—quite an experience! To say it was hot would be an understatement. And the treatment was much like what happens in any professional kitchen—tough. It was so hot in that kitchen, I often made the soufflés while wearing a bikini. It was Florida, after all, and I was a few pounds lighter. I had no money and no car, so I rode my bike to get there every day. The experience had an unexpected consequence: to this day, I really don't like to eat soufflés."

She met Edson in St. Louis at Yia Yia's Eurobistro, when she trained him to be her sous chef. "We worked really well together—so well, in fact, that we ended up getting married, having two kids, three restaurants, a few dogs, and a donkey, and we're still together! I may have trained him and taught him most of what he knows, but now he runs circles around me in the kitchen and has turned out to be an amazing chef in his own right!"

Jesse considers her home cooking "about as boring as you get! I just want someone to cook for me. My publicist made a squash casserole from her garden this past summer, and I ate the whole thing. She thought I wouldn't like it. I loved it! Good, basic foods are what make me happy. My husband usually does the cooking at home."

The Restaurants

The Never Blue restaurants feature a style of cooking that Chef Roque calls "Low-Mex," a blend of Low Country South Carolina cuisine with Mexican tradition. "You can really see it in my Shrimp and Grits and in my Tacos Cubano," she says. "The Low Country influence grows out of my time in Charleston, and the Mexican and Latin influence comes from my upbringing in south Florida and being married to a Mexican. . . . I use a lot of flavors, and I like to put unexpected combinations together, but not in a weird, out-there sort of way. I don't want my food to be unattainable or intimidating. It has to taste good, more than anything else!"

She saves her most creative impulses for pastries. "As a trained pastry chef, I also enjoy creating desserts that blow my guests away. In the desserts list, my specialties are homemade ice creams and eclectic bread puddings. I don't take myself too seriously, though, and I really enjoy reinventing favorite dishes. I also have a drink menu that people love. The names and the tastes are unique, yet very pleasing. I work seasonally to create all of my menu items, from tapas and entrées to desserts and drinks. The menu changes to reflect the season and local ingredients whenever possible."

The restaurant in Hendersonville has a small-plate focus. But it's "tapas done my way, not necessarily traditional Spanish tapas," Jesse says. "My dishes have an underlying element of fun and adventure. I like for my guests to try a little bit of everything and enjoy the flavors.

"Aesthetically, my restaurants have bright, bold colors. . . . My husband and I usually do most of the construction work ourselves, and my mother applies a mosaic to the bar; we have them in each of our restaurants. The atmosphere is a bit irreverent. This is a feeling that my regulars identify with and new folks are drawn to."

Food for both Never Blue and Blue Gypsy is prepared at Never Blue in Hendersonville. The kitchen uses local foods as much as possible. Kirby Johnson Farms in Henderson County supplies heirloom tomatoes all summer and into early fall. The Johnson family devotes entire rows to tomatoes, cucumbers, and peppers for Never Blue.

Chef Roque was the first female to compete in the Western North Carolina Chef's Challenge and will be entering again in 2012.

The Recipes

Devils on Horseback
Serves 2

Chef's Note
"My mom used to make these for dinner parties. My brother and I would sneak in and eat them when she wasn't looking. I

Devils on Horseback
Photo provided by Never Blue

have varied her recipe, in that I don't stuff the dates like she did—she always went to a lot of trouble! Instead, I put the good stuff on top, once the dates and prosciutto are nice and warm and crispy. If I'm feeling really wild, I'll drizzle them with local honey."

12 medjool dates, pitted
6 thin slices prosciutto, cut down the middle
2 8-inch skewers
¼ cup goat cheese, crumbled
¼ cup salted Marcona almonds, chopped

Preheat oven to 425 degrees. Wrap each date with ½ piece of prosciutto. Skewer 6 dates on each skewer. Place skewers on a baking sheet lined with parchment and bake for 12 to 15 minutes until prosciutto is slightly crisp. Remove from oven, place on plates, and sprinkle with goat cheese and almonds. Serve hot.

Tacos Cubano
Yields 2 entrée portions or 4 tapas portions

Chef's Note
"I created Tacos Cubano as a compromise for my husband. We both love tacos. I grew up eating more Cuban-style foods; he, of course, grew up with a Mexican influence. The mojo marinade is the Cuban influence; the rest is a nod to his upbringing. It's as simple as you can get, but it's also a dish that never comes off our menu. Our customers would have a revolt."

Mojo marinade
1 cup sour orange juice, or juices from 1 lemon, 1 lime, and 1 orange to total 1 cup
2 teaspoons ground cumin
2 teaspoons ground coriander
3 cloves garlic, minced fine
½ cup olive oil
kosher salt to taste

Tacos Cubano
Photo provided by Never Blue

Cilantro-lime crema

    ½ cup Mexican-style table cream (available at Mexican grocers or
      Walmart)
    ½ cup mayonnaise
    2 teaspoons ground coriander
    1 teaspoon white pepper
    ¼ cup finely chopped cilantro
    zest and juice of 1 lime

Chicken

    8-ounce skinless, boneless chicken breast
    1 small Spanish white onion
    4 6-inch flour tortillas
    ¼ cup chopped cilantro
    lime wedges (optional)

MOJO MARINADE

Combine all ingredients in a bowl. Mix. Store in a nonreactive container (glass, ceramic, or stainless steel) in refrigerator for up to 1 week.

CILANTRO-LIME CREMA

Combine all ingredients in a nonreactive bowl. Refrigerate.

CHICKEN

Cut chicken into bite-sized chunks. Slice onion in half and julienne into thin strips. Place chicken and onion in bowl and toss together. Cover with mojo marinade. Cover and refrigerate for 2 to 4 hours or overnight.

After chicken has marinated, heat a skillet on medium-high. Remove onions and chicken from marinade and place in skillet. Sauté 4 to 5 minutes until chicken is brown and onions start to caramelize. Toast tortillas on a comal (a Mexican flat pan available at Mexican groceries or Walmart), in the microwave, or in another dry skillet. Lay tortillas out flat. Divide chicken mixture evenly onto tortillas and garnish with cilantro, cilantro-lime crema, and lime wedges, if desired.

Hickory Nut Gap Meats

57 Sugar Hollow Road
Fairview, N.C. 28730
828-628-1027
www.hickorynutgapfarm.com

Hickory Nut Gap Meats is located about 20 minutes southeast of Asheville, roughly halfway to Chimney Rock. Owners Jamie and Amy Ager have three children. Jamie represents the fourth generation to operate the family farm. His great-grandfather moved to western North Carolina in 1916, bought a stagecoach station, and renamed it Hickory Nut Gap. He helped found the Farmers' Federation in 1920. The farm currently has six employees. Members of the extended family own surrounding land, which, along with the farm, has been placed in a conservation easement with the Southern Appalachian Highlands Conservancy, ensuring that it will remain undeveloped or be used for agriculture.

Jamie Ager describes how the family approaches its meat business: "Growing up on the farm, I learned how to interact with animals from a young age. Amy and I both graduated from Warren Wilson College in 2000 with degrees in environmental studies, concentrating on sustainable agriculture." About a year after graduation, they started raising 100 percent grass-fed beef and all-natural, pasture-grown hogs, chickens, goats, and turkeys. "When we decided to raise a different product from mainstream beef and pork, we realized we needed to create a brand that represents that difference in the marketplace." The farm's animals are raised without growth hormones. Although they receive appropriate veterinary monitoring, and although careful health records are maintained as part of a protocol, the animals never receive non-therapeutic antibiotics. The open, spacious, naturally clean environment makes them unnecessary. Animals that become sick are treated but do not enter the food supply. No grains, animal by-products, fish by-products, corn silage, or food waste is incorporated into the animals' food. Humane practices are maintained throughout the animals' lives. Low-stress transportation is mandated, and electric prods are prohibited.

The farm store on the property, open year-round, sells various cuts of beef and pork, several varieties of sausage and bratwurst, chicken, turkey, and free-range eggs. Fruits and vegetables, among them blueberries, blackberries, asparagus, raspberries, and black raspberries, are available in the summer. Customers can also place website orders. Tours of the farm are available by prior arrangement. A shed may be rented for children's parties. The farm can provide pony rides and allows appropriate interaction with animals.

Because of the area's strong interest in natural foods, the Agers consider themselves fortunate to live close to Asheville.

Rob Keener

Rob Keener
*Photo provided by
Rob Keener*

Square 1 Bistro

111 South Main Street
Hendersonville, N.C. 28792
828-698-5598
www.square1bistro.com

The Chef

Rob Keener, a Hickory, North Carolina, native, has lived in the mountains or the foothills almost all his life. "This is my home. There is no place like it on earth," he says. "Great people, culture, and plenty to do outside—climbing, mountain biking, kayaking."

Outdoor activities almost caught up with him once. "I was mountain biking in Mills River in January, after a big ice storm, and I got too far into the woods," he recalls. "There were trees everywhere. I was at the point of no return—it would take as long to go back as to keep going—and I was running very late because I had to prepare a special beer dinner at the restaurant that night. I barely made it to the restaurant in time to cook. No one knew the difference, but underneath my chef togs, my legs were all cut up, and I was sore for days!"

He started in food service at the Hickory Furniture Mart when he was 13. "It's in my blood," he says. Rob worked with several talented chefs while attending North Carolina State University in Raleigh before moving to Vail, Colorado. He took classes at the French Culinary Institute in Manhattan. But a lot of what he knows came from colleagues and from personal experience. "I worked for a lot of CIA [Culinary Institute of America] and JW [Johnson & Wales] chefs who helped shape my style, but traveling is what really exposed me to different foods and techniques." Rob's travels are varied. He has lived or visited extensively in Colorado, Wyoming, California, Oregon, Western Europe, and South America. Although each has influenced his cooking style, the underlying Southern cuisine shines through. "I've learned that people like my food, and [Southern] is an easy style that's approachable and always focuses on local ingredients."

He opened Square 1 in 2011. Before that, he was the executive chef at Flight Wood Grill.

When cooking for himself or friends and family, Rob likes casual Mexican and grilling outdoors. "I love tacos. I cook carnitas and giant steaks. I'm really into the grill and all the cool stuff you can do with slow cookers as well."

The Restaurant

Square 1 is located near Flat Rock's historic theater. A partially reconstructed brick wall from a downtown structure lines one side, while a full-service bar travels partway down the other. The restaurant is open every day for breakfast, lunch, and dinner; brunch is offered on Saturday and Sunday. Chef Keener considers the style "upscale casual dining." Live music is often provided on weekends.

Square 1 "is all about fresh food," he says. "Portions of the menu change daily, as we work with local farmers and producers. Local ingredients are the foundation, and we just build from there to bring products to the table. My style is regional cuisine with the focus on fresh, local ingredients. I love ethnic food, so a lot of cool stuff finds its way to the plate when we get going."

The kitchen works with Hickory Nut Gap Meats (see page 264), Apple Brandy Beef (see page 17), the Appalachian Sustainable Agriculture Project (see page 198), and especially Mountain Foods, a vegetable grower in Swannanoa. "The Local Food Guide is our bible," Chef Keener says.

Even though the restaurant is relatively new, Chef Keener has been a guest several times on the "Carolina Kitchen" segment on WLOS-TV, Asheville's ABC affiliate.

The Recipes

Beet and Spinach Salad
Serves 4

> 8 slices bacon (omit for vegetarian)
> 2 large beets, gold if available
> 2 tablespoons butter
> 1 pound spinach
> sesame dressing (available in most grocery stores)
> 8 ounces feta cheese, crumbled
> 1 red pepper, sliced thin

Beet and Spinach Salad
Photo by Rob Keener

Cook bacon until crisp. Peel beets and slice about ⅛ inch thick. Sauté in butter 1 minute on each side. Divide spinach among 4 bowls. Drizzle with dressing and top with feta, peppers, bacon, and beets.

Scallops Pasta
Serves 4

> 1 pound angel hair pasta
> 2 cups spinach
> 2 cups heavy cream
> ½ pound Gorgonzola or domestic blue cheese, crumbled
> 12 to 16 jumbo diver scallops
> 4 tablespoons fresh basil, chopped

Cook pasta until al dente, following package directions. Reserve. Simmer spinach, cream, and cheese in a saucepan until cheese melts and spinach becomes tender. Sear scallops on each side until golden brown; this is most simply accomplished in an oiled skillet or sauté pan on high heat. Place noodles in saucepan with spinach mixture and combine thoroughly. Divide pasta among 4 plates, top with scallops, and garnish with basil.

New York Strip Steaks with Homemade Steak Sauce
Serves 4

> 4 cups ketchup
> 1 tablespoon white wine vinegar
> 1 teaspoon cumin
> 1 teaspoon oregano
> 1 teaspoon garlic powder
> 1 teaspoon brown sugar
> 1 teaspoon hot sauce
> ¼ cup Worcestershire sauce
> 1 teaspoon horseradish
> 4 12-ounce New York strip steaks
> 1 pound small green beans, ends and strings removed
> 1 bell pepper, sliced, seeds and white pith trimmed out
> 2 tablespoons oil
> salt and pepper to taste

Combine first 9 ingredients in a medium saucepan. Simmer about 5 minutes until sauce becomes a thick liquid. If using an iron skillet, heat very hot, then spray with nonstick spray just before adding steaks. If using a grill, preheat to high and spray with nonstick spray just before adding steaks, or soak a cloth in grapeseed or canola oil, hold with tongs, and wipe grill just before adding steaks. When steaks reach desired degree of doneness, turn over. Insert a meat thermometer and continue to cook until internal temperature reaches 145 degrees for medium-rare. While steaks are cooking, sauté beans and peppers in oil until al dente. Season with salt and pepper.

To present, place steaks on heated plates and serve with steak sauce. Place beans and peppers to the side.

Flat Rock

Peter Fassbender

Peter Fassbender
*Photo by Season's
at Highland
Lake Inn*

Season's at Highland Lake Inn

86 Lily Pad Lane
Flat Rock, N.C. 28731
828-696-9094 (restaurant) or
800-635-5101 (inn)
www.hlinn.com

The Chef

Peter Fassbender was born in Punta Arenas, Chile, in 1969. He lived in Chile, Brazil, Argentina, and California through his teens. After high school, he went to Texas A&M to study industrial engineering but returned to Chile after a year to pursue the culinary arts. He received a business management and international chef's degree from Instituto de los Andes in Lima, Peru. He then continued his culinary studies by cooking under master chefs in Chile, Italy, and France before relocating to the United States, where he has lived and worked since 2001. Peter moved to the North Carolina mountains around 2005 after spending some vacation time in the area. "This area reminded me a lot of southern Chile," he says. "It was love at first sight. I knew then that this is the place I wanted to call home."

He started cooking when he was 12 years old. "I used to make breakfast for my parents during the weekend," he recalls. "I moved around a lot with family, and we used to go out to eat on weekends in the different countries we had the fortune of living in. So the relationship between different cultures and their cuisine has always fascinated me. When I was attending engineering school, I used to invite friends over to eat, and more than once they told me I was a good cook for an engineer. A few years later, I realized I enjoyed cooking more than I enjoyed engineering. When I went to Lima, Peru, I found one of the world's richest gastronomic cultures."

During his culinary training in Peru, he attended classes in the morning, then worked at night in a bistro-style restaurant that belonged to a famous Peruvian restaurateur, Gaston Acurio, who studied at Le Cordon Bleu in Paris and told his protégé how influential that had been. After his two years in Chile, Peter decided to move to Paris to attend Le Cordon Bleu himself. "It was one of the most important decisions I made in my life," he says. "I realized that I knew nothing about cuisine. I learned that I could apply the French techniques developed by Escoffier to any regional cuisine."

Peter received a double degree in cuisine and pastry, graduating first in his class at Le Cordon Bleu. He promptly received three job offers in the

United States. "What fascinates me about American cuisine is the lack of boundaries," he says. "I find that very appealing. This is the world capital of fusion cuisine, and Americans have been doing this for centuries. I have always been fascinated by the close relationship I have seen between local flavors and local culture. Southern food is no exception. Southern hospitality is reflected in the soul that goes into the food."

Peter enjoys the camaraderie of the kitchen, as well as the practical joking. "We love playing jokes on interns. They try so hard to please. They will do anything for you, no questions asked. One time, we had an intern chop flour for us for two straight hours. Needless to say, this is an absolutely pointless task. Another time, I told an intern to go to the pantry and grab me two bottles of evaporated water. It took him 30 minutes to build up the courage to come ask me what that was. Such a thing does not exist, of course."

At home, Chef Fassbender enjoys seafood for its versatility. He is also fond of simple, wholesome foods such as spare ribs, barbecued pork, fried chicken, ceviche, and pasta dishes.

The Restaurant

The name of the restaurant, Season's, reflects its core concept of working with seasonal, sustainable, fresh local ingredients. The restaurant maintains its own organic garden, utilizing a drip irrigation system from the property's 40-acre lake. "All product deteriorates in the transportation process, and being able to utilize produce from only a few feet away has a tremendous impact on the quality of the dish," Chef Fassbender says. "That, together with a well-defined, polished technique, creates a wonderful outcome. We also believe that using a sustainable product is important for the environment and allows for future generations to enjoy what we have."

The restaurant is an avid participant in the Appalachian Sustainable Agricultural Project (see page 198), which helps staff members purchase ingredients from local farmers. "Most of our menu items feature staples of the area," Chef Fassbender says. "Season's is truly a garden-to-your-plate restaurant. Season's also participates in the sustainable seafood program to ensure that the seafood we purchase is not [the product of] environmentally destructive seafood harvesting."

Highland Lake Inn offers cooking classes throughout the year to educate guests about how to grow, harvest, and cook vegetables, fresh herbs, and flowers.

Season's of Highland Lake Inn has received awards from *Wine Spectator* for the past 10 years and has been featured many times in *Southern Living*, *Our State*, *Organic Style*, and *Country Gardens* magazines. UNC-TV profiled the inn and restaurant on *North Carolina Weekend*. The property has the facilities to accommodate weddings, retreats, and other special events.

The Recipes

Applewood-Bacon-Wrapped Carolina Bison Meat Loaf
Serves 15

Chef's Note
"The Bison Meat Loaf is actually a creation of our sous chef, Matthew Lineback. It is his take on an old-time childhood favorite. Due to the abundant production of bison in this area, it only made sense to give it a twist and do this meat loaf in particular with bison and bison sausage. This is one of our most popular dishes. The combination with garden herb pesto and grainy mustard jus makes this once-simple dish a much more refined version with a subtle, yet complex, plethora of flavors."

Meat loaf
½ pound pancetta, diced medium
1 cup minced celery
1½ carrots, diced medium

1 large yellow onion, diced medium
1 yellow bell pepper, diced medium
1 red bell pepper, diced medium
1 green bell pepper, diced medium
½ tablespoon minced garlic
3 tablespoons minced fresh herbs of choice
1 tablespoon dried oregano
5 eggs
1 pint heavy cream
5 cups panko breadcrumbs
5 pounds ground bison
1 pound bison sausage
salt and pepper to taste
bacon, 8 strips or more for wrapping as needed

Mustard jus

2 cups beef demi-glace
½ cup barbecue sauce
1½ tablespoons whole-grain mustard

Yukon mash

15 large potatoes
1 stick butter
1 cup heavy cream
salt and pepper to taste

asparagus, carrots, or other vegetables of choice for garnish

Meat loaf

Preheat oven to 380 degrees. Render pancetta in a large pan until crispy. Add vegetables, garlic, and herbs and sauté until tender, then cool on a sheet pan. Mix together eggs, cream, and breadcrumbs in a bowl. Refrigerate. Mix together ground bison, sausage, vegetables, and breadcrumb mixture. Season with salt and pepper. Wrap mixture with bacon and put in a mold. Bake for 1 hour. Let rest 15 minutes before serving.

Bison Meat Loaf
Photo provided by Season's at Highland Lake Inn

MUSTARD JUS

Bring all ingredients to a slow simmer in a saucepan until reduced to a paste and nearly dry.

YUKON MASH

Cook potatoes in water until done. Strain. Mix in remaining ingredients.

TO SERVE

Slice meatloaf into ¾- to 1-inch-thick serving size. Place in center of plate. Flank with vegetables.

Sunburst Trout with Grits Cakes
Serves 6

Chef's Note

"Both the bison and trout dishes reflect not only our philosophy of sustainability, but they represent Appalachian fare very well. We have an amazing purveyor for trout [Sunburst Trout Farm, see page 291]. And for this particular dish, we also wanted to highlight the use of goat cheese—we use Pyrwood Dairy—which is also a very popular product in the area. The goat cheese with the organic grits gives this dish a wholesome feel, and the acidity of the cheese pairs wonderfully with the trout. Tasso ham gravy binds it all together and adds that different layer of flavor to the dish."

Farm-Raised Sunburst Trout
Photo provided by Season's at Highland Lake Inn

6 6-ounce trout fillets
salt and pepper to taste
2 cups yellow stone-ground grits
3 cups whole milk, divided
1 cup water
½ cup butter
½ cup goat cheese
1 egg
Flour, enough to dredge grits cakes
panko breadcrumbs, enough to dredge grits cakes
1 pound tasso ham, diced small
1 large onion, minced
2 tablespoons minced garlic
1 green pepper, chopped
¼ cup red wine
4 cups chicken stock
1 quart heavy cream
canola oil
sautéed asparagus and grape tomatoes for garnish

Clean fillets. Season with salt and pepper and set aside. Make grits cakes by combining grits, 2 cups of the milk, water, butter, and goat cheese. Cook at a soft boil until grits are soft. Pour into a tray and let cool. Cut into circles. Combine remaining 1 cup milk and egg to make an egg wash. Pass cakes through flour, egg wash, and finally panko breadcrumbs. Set aside. For the gravy, sauté tasso ham, onions, garlic, and green peppers. Deglaze pan with chicken stock and red wine. Reduce by ½. Incorporate heavy cream and reduce by ½. Deep-fry grits cakes approximately 2 minutes per side, until browned. Lightly coat a sauté pan with canola oil and sauté trout 2 to 3 minutes on service side, then flip skin side down and sauté another 2 minutes.

To Present

Place grits cakes in center of plates. Drizzle with gravy, cover with trout, and decorate with sautéed asparagus and grape tomatoes.

Saluda

Marianne Blazar

The Orchard Inn

100 Orchard Inn Lane (U.S. 176)
P.O. Box 128
Saluda, N.C. 28773
800-581-3800 or 828-749-5471
www.orchardinn.com

The Chef

Marianne Blazar was born in Vienna, Austria. She refers to herself as "an old Austrian mountain goat. I always loved living in the mountains—the air, the climate, the lifestyle, the people. This area reminds me a lot of my home country—natural living in a wonderful environment with friendly people."

She started cooking with her grandmother in Vienna when she was five years old. "Grandmother taught me not only some basics, but also the appreciation of every morsel of food," she says. In Austria, "in my time, anyway—don't ask how long ago that was—every school also had a house-hold course, and I always took cooking lessons."

Her husband, Marc, has been a professional photographer for the last 20 years. They have traveled the world. "Seeking out fabulous food was one of our perks and passions," Marianne says. They have climbed Mount Kilimanjaro, wandered the streets of Paris, and gone on safari in Africa, among myriad other experiences.

The Blazars operated a charter boat in the Virgin Islands in the late 1970s and early 1980s. "That was my first encounter with professional food service, and I loved it," recalls Marianne. "Cooking on the sailboat was a good lesson, since not all food was available on the islands all the time. That's when I really learned to improve and work around recipes, using what was on hand." Cookbook collections from all over the world guided her. One of the keys to her development? "Reading, reading, reading," she says. Despite the rigors, she maintained a sense of humor. "On my sailboat, I used to cook turkey once a week, telling my guests it was pelican, a Caribbean specialty! Amazing how it did not really taste fishy, given the fact that we watched those pelicans all day long eating fish. In the end, I would tell them the truth, but I always had them going for quite a while."

Marianne describes her style as "simple cooking with great ingredients and lots of fantasy." She changes recipes—even the standards—according to the season and the availability of goods at the nearby farmers' market.

At home, she prepares Austrian comfort food—roesti, strudels, pasta, and lots of salads in the summer. And she loves to cook desserts. "I always fear that I would lose my Austrian heritage if I don't eat dessert every day," she says.

The Restaurant

The Orchard Inn was built by Southern Railway's Brotherhood of Clerks in 1926 as a summer getaway for railroad employees and their families. Porches surround all four sides. Two separate cottages were constructed near the inn around the same time. The property passed into private ownership in the mid-1960s. A decade later, it returned to its role as an inn, first as The White Stag and later as The Wayside Inn. It then became a restaurant named the Railroad House. In 1981, the property closed and the furniture and fixtures were sold at auction. Later that year, Ken and Ann Hough purchased the property, renovated it, and opened The Orchard Inn. Two other families managed the inn over about a 25-year period. Marc and Marianne Blazar purchased it in November 2010.

The fine-dining restaurant serves a set menu of four courses, usually from Thursday evening to Sunday evening. Chef Blazar changes the menu daily. Although the ambience is not formal, jackets are suggested for gentlemen. Marc is the host and wine manager. He also helps out in the kitchen. He cooks macrobiotic on demand and specializes in what he calls "stunning vegetable dishes," having been a vegetarian before marrying Marianne. He also prepares homemade granola, which is served for breakfast. The inn often hosts weddings, receptions, and other group events.

The Blazars work with a local farmers' cooperative during winter and buy at the local farmers' market and from neighboring farmers during summer. Eggs come from a neighbor's chicken farm. "He keeps his chickens free-range and happy," Chef Blazar says.

Since the Blazars took over the inn, many guests have written favorable reviews on TripAdvisor. The inn has also received positive attention from *Town* magazine. The Orchard Inn is a member of the Select Registry of Distinguished Inns of North America. The property is listed on the National Register of Historic Places as the Railway Clerks' Mountain Home.

The Recipes

Warrior Mountain Eggs
Serves 1 or 2

Author's Note

The dining room at The Orchard Inn looks out over the Warrior Mountain range, where "Eggman" Jay Summey lives. He delivers fresh, organic free-range eggs every Friday morning.

Tartar sauce
½ cup mayonnaise
½ teaspoon Dijon mustard
1 teaspoon capers
1 small dill pickle, chopped
salt and pepper to taste

Warrior
Mountain Eggs
*Photo by Marc Blazar
Photography*

Eggs

½ red, yellow, or orange sweet baby pepper (mixing colors looks nice)
2 tablespoons olive oil
1 teaspoon butter
2 eggs
1 teaspoon white wine vinegar

Wilted spinach

1½ teaspoons olive oil
½ cup fresh spinach
pinch of cumin
salt to taste

1 English muffin, slightly toasted

TARTAR SAUCE

This can be made a day ahead. Combine first 4 ingredients in a blender and blend for 30 seconds. Season with salt and pepper.

EGGS

Chop peppers and sauté for 2 minutes in olive oil and butter. Poach eggs by adding vinegar to 4 cups salted water and bringing to a boil. Crack eggs into a teacup, remove all shell pieces, and make sure yolks are not broken. Carefully transfer eggs into water. Let boil up once, switch off heat, and cover pot for 4 minutes. Remove eggs with a slotted spoon and cut off any excess white to make eggs look nice and neat.

WILTED SPINACH

Heat olive oil, quickly toss spinach, and season slightly with cumin and salt.

TO PRESENT

Place toasted muffin on a plate, heap spinach on top of muffin halves, add poached eggs, top eggs with tartar sauce, and sprinkle sautéed baby peppers on top. Fruit and home fries go well with this dish.

Veal San Marco
Photo by Marc Blazar
Photography

Veal San Marco
Serves 6

Chef's Note

"I created this dish for my husband, Marc, alias Marco, his professional name in his role as a photographer. It contains all his favorite ingredients, and we love Venice, so 'San Marco' just came to me when I named the dish."

Mushroom sauce

10 white mushrooms (substitute 1 large Portobello or 5 baby portobellos), sliced
½ purple onion, sliced
½ stick butter
¼ cup red wine
salt and pepper to taste
1 cup beef broth
1 can (14.5 ounces) artichoke hearts
1 cup heavy cream
1 cup fresh spinach leaves

Risotto

½ cup chopped onion
1 stick butter
1½ cups Arborio rice
4 cups chicken broth or water

snippet of fresh saffron
salt and pepper to taste

Veal cutlets
½ cup flour
salt and pepper to taste
6 6- to 8-ounce veal cutlets
¼ cup olive oil

Mushroom sauce

Sauté mushrooms and onions in butter until slightly brown. Add wine and deglaze pan, scraping with a wooden spoon. Add salt and pepper and sauté another 2 minutes. Add broth and reduce by ½. Add artichoke hearts. Add heavy cream. Simmer 3 to 5 minutes until mixture begins to thicken. If you cut up artichokes, mixture will be thicker, so do not simmer as long. Fold in spinach just before serving.

Risotto

Sauté onions in butter until glassy. Add rice, stirring constantly. Slowly add chicken broth or water while stirring. Add saffron. Season with salt and pepper. Stir and keep warm.

Veal cutlets

Mix flour with salt and pepper in a shallow dish. Rinse and dry cutlets, then slightly coat them in flour mix. Heat olive oil on medium heat and pan-fry cutlets about 2 minutes on 1 side and 1 minute on other side. Place in a 250-degree oven and bake 8 minutes before serving. Do not overcook.

To present

Spoon risotto on center of plates. Place cutlets on top of risotto, letting them hang just a little to the side. Cover cutlets with mushroom sauce; if you did not cut up artichokes, take care to ensure that each person gets at least 1 whole artichoke. Serve with your favorite vegetables on the other side of the plate. The Orchard Inn suggests roasted mini peppers and fresh asparagus to add color.

Waynesville

Keith Davis

Keith Davis
*Photo provided by
The Swag*

The Swag
Country Inn

2300 Swag Road
Waynesville, N.C. 28785
800-789-7672
www.theswag.com

The Chef

Growing up, Rocky Mount, North Carolina, native Keith Davis found the eastern North Carolina summers almost unbearable, due to the heat and humidity. In 1994, he decided to live in the Boone–Blowing Rock area. He and his wife moved to Waynesville in 2003, after the birth of their first son. Keith says he has always loved the mountains. He and his wife enjoy the outdoor activities, scenery, and weather.

Keith started cooking with his grandparents when he was a child. After working in several different fields, he decided on a career in food because it simply never seemed like work. "I've just always enjoyed being in the kitchen," he says. He graduated from the culinary program at Asheville-Buncombe Technical Community College.

He credits "a lot of well-trained chefs" with helping him develop his knowledge and skills. As his career progressed, he cooked at Chetola Resort and the Meadowbrook Inn in Blowing Rock, Black Diamond in Banner Elk, and Lomo Grill, Wild Fire, and The Sweet Onion in the Waynesville area. "All of these places offered a chance to gain different knowledge and experiences in their own right," he says. Before arriving at The Swag, he was executive chef at Maggie Valley Club and Resort.

Keith's style starts with as many high-quality local ingredients as possible, in preparations that place the natural flavor and appearance of the ingredients in the forefront. He loves cooking on the grill at home. "It doesn't matter what it is, as long as I'm able to be with my family and share my passion of food with them," he says.

The Restaurant

In mountain parlance, a swag is a dip—sometimes in the back of a horse, or perhaps a valley between two peaks. The Swag Country Inn, about 50 miles from Asheville, is located outside Waynesville on a dip at 5,000 feet in elevation between two ridges. The property covers approximately 250 acres of secluded mountaintop land bordered by Great Smoky Mountains National Park. Innkeepers Dan and Deener Matthews bought it in 1969 and built what is now the lodge the following year as a private home. The construction incorporated several existing buildings that were relocated to the property, among them the former Lonesome Valley Primitive Baptist Church. For 10 years, Deener Matthews ran weekend retreats for church groups before opening the inn in 1982. Dan served Southern Episcopal missions and churches prior to being called to Trinity Church on Wall Street in New York in 1987. After 17 years there, he is now rector emeritus.

Guests usually spend their entire visit on the grounds, away from crowds, enjoying the serenity of the mountain views. The 14 rooms and private cabins, constructed of 18th- and 19th-century hand-hewn logs and local fieldstone, are decorated with handmade quilts, woven rugs, early-American rustic antiques, and original artwork. Most rooms have private balconies, wood-burning fireplaces, and walls of stone, brick, or logs. Weddings, private parties, and large group retreats are hosted at the inn. The entire property can be reserved with sufficient notice—the farther in advance, the better. Special events with authors, songwriters and singers, naturalists (especially bird experts), photographers, and storytellers with links to the mountains are usually provided at no extra charge. Check the website for specifics.

Room rates include all meals. A breakfast buffet is offered in the morning; brunch is served on Sunday. Picnic lunches are packed for midday. Evening meals are open to non-guests by reservation only. The ambience at dinner is elegant, yet informal and relaxed. A four-course meal is served by candlelight. Thursday evenings are devoted to a barbecue cookout, with service on the porch.

Chef Davis believes in supporting the community and utilizing nearby sources. He is a member of the Appalachian Sustainable Agriculture Project (see page 198), which coordinates communication between restaurants and local farms.

The Swag has received many awards and honors. *Condé Nast Traveler* readers voted The Swag number five among small hotels in the United States and cited it as one of the top hundred small hotels in the world.

National Geographic has published several articles about the inn. Other articles have appeared in *Our State, WNC, Atlanta*, and *Blue Ridge Country*.

At the time of this writing, Haywood County was "dry," meaning that no alcohol is served in restaurants. Guests are, however, allowed to bring their own. Check to ascertain the current status when you make reservations at The Swag.

The Recipes

Roasted Butternut Squash Soup
Serves 4

> 2 large butternut squash
> 2 tablespoons extra-virgin olive oil, plus extra for rubbing
> ½ cup onion, diced ¼ inch
> ¼ cup celery, diced ¼ inch
> ¼ cup carrot, diced ¼ inch
> 1 stick cinnamon
> salt and pepper to taste
> 4 cups chicken or vegetable broth
> ½ teaspoon ground coriander, toasted
> 2 tablespoons butter (optional)
> ½ cup half-and-half, if desired

Preheat oven to 375 degrees. Slice squash lengthwise and remove seeds. Rub squash halves with olive oil. Place squash cut sides up on a sheet pan and roast 30 to 40 minutes until golden and soft. Spoon squash out of shells and reserve. Heat 2 tablespoons olive oil in a large saucepan over medium heat until hot. Add onions, celery, carrots, and cinnamon stick. Add butter if desired. Sauté about 10 minutes until soft but not brown. Season with salt and pepper. Add broth and coriander. Bring to a boil, then reduce heat and simmer 4 minutes. Stir in reserved squash until smooth. Simmer gently about 30 minutes to blend flavors. Discard cinnamon stick. Purée

Roasted Butternut Squash Soup
Photo provided by The Swag

using an immersion blender or regular blender until smooth. Return to pan and reheat gently. Add half-and-half, if desired. Adjust salt and pepper.

Braised Beef Short Ribs with Wild Barley and Root Vegetables
Serves 2 to 4

2 to 4 short ribs
salt and freshly cracked pepper to taste
4 cloves peeled garlic, divided
2 cups celery, diced medium, divided
2 cups yellow onion, diced medium
2 cups carrots, peeled and diced medium
4 cups beef broth
1 cup barley
2 sweet potatoes, peeled and diced medium

Braised Beef Short Ribs
Photo provided by The Swag

1 turnip, peeled and diced medium
1 rutabaga, peeled and diced medium
oil
pinch of dried herbs (oregano, rosemary, or Italian seasoning)

Preheat oven to 300 degrees. Season ribs with salt and pepper. Place ribs in a hot pan and sear 3 to 4 minutes until all sides are golden brown. Remove from pan and place in an ovenproof dish. Add 2 cloves of the garlic, 1 cup of the celery, onions, and carrots. Pour enough broth over ribs and vegetables to cover. Seal tightly with aluminum foil and bake 4 to 6 hours until meat falls off the bone when touched.

Combine barley with remaining 2 cloves garlic and remaining 1 cup celery, onions, and carrots in a saucepan. Cover with remaining broth. Be sure liquid is a few inches above barley; add water if necessary. Cook for 30 minutes, stirring occasionally. Toss sweet potatoes, turnips, and rutabagas in oil to coat, then lay them out on a baking pan. Roast 25 to 30 minutes until soft. Remove from pan and reserve.

Once ribs are done, remove from dish and strain cooking liquid. Put liquid in a sauté pan and reduce over high heat until thick. In a separate pan, sauté vegetables with oil and dried herbs until hot.

To Present

Place a scoop of barley on each plate, then top with short ribs. Place root vegetables alongside and garnish with reduced sauce.

Sunburst Trout Farm

128 Raceway Place
Canton, N.C. 28716
800-673-3051 or 828-648-3010
www.sunbursttrout.com

Retail market:
133 Montgomery Street
Waynesville, N.C. 28786

When veteran Dick Jennings returned home after World War II, his father warned him to get out of the mountains because he would never be able to make a good living there. Dick subsequently went to Yale, where he was an honor student, but came back home and established what became the first commercial trout farm in the South. It continues to operate under the third generation of Jennings family ownership.

All Sunburst products are raised without the use of hormones, antibiotics, or animal by-products. Ongoing lab testing ensures that fish are free of PCBs, mercury, pesticides, and other contaminants often found in some species of farmed seafood. Trout are netted alive and preserved at 36 degrees within one hour.

Sunburst supplies many of the better restaurants in North Carolina, especially those located in the mountains. In addition to its wholesale business, it sells directly to consumers from its website, from its retail store in Waynesville, and at tailgate and farmers' markets.

Sunburst employs an in-house chef, Charles Hudson, who develops value-added products, creates recipes, cooks samples, provides demonstrations at markets, and in general finds ways to showcase Sunburst's products, which include trout sausage, trout caviar, simple red fillets, and fillets that have been smoked, pepper crusted, or marinated with bourbon, ginger, or lime.

Charles got to know members of the Jennings family through catering. He wanted to learn how to make caviar, so he asked to work part-time during caviar season. "I enjoyed it so much, I approached the CEO about coming to work full-time as the research and development chef," he says. "This was back in 2006. I have been here ever since."

He is an Asheville native who has also lived in Virginia, Colorado, and Florida. But every time he left the North Carolina mountains, something drew him back. "So, finally, I just decided to stay put," he recalls. He enjoys the seasons, the people, and the variety of outdoor activities in the area, especially skiing, gardening, soccer, hiking, and biking. Professionally, he is attracted by the availability of ingredients and food products.

Charles developed a love of food at a young age. "I have been handling food since I was four or five years old," he says. "I remember digging potatoes and snapping beans for my grandmother. I was fascinated by what was going on in the kitchen during holiday meals at her house. There were usually 15 to 20 people at these functions. I was always amazed at how she could bring the whole meal together for so many people at once. I enjoyed her green beans the most of all. I would still be eating them while the table was being cleared and dessert was brought out."

Charles Hudson has cooked in some of western North Carolina's best restaurants. He interned at Morels in Banner Elk and worked at Deerpark on the Biltmore Estate, 23 Page, and Gabrielle's at Richmond Hill in Asheville. He especially recalls his time at 23 Page. "It was really my first exposure to fine dining and haute cuisine," he says. "The first time I tasted goat cheese. The first time I roasted a pepper. I can still feel the heat of the kitchen."

Sunburst Trout Farms has been featured in multiple publications, including *Wine Spectator, Gourmet, Bon Appétit, Business North Carolina*, and *Forbes*. It received the International Sustainability Award from the Seafood Choices Alliance in 2008 and was named the 2009 Business of the Year by the Haywood County Chamber of Commerce.

Cashiers

Sean Ruddy

Sean Ruddy
*Photo by
Theodore Flagg*

High Hampton Inn
and Country Club

1525 N.C. 107 South
Cashiers, N.C. 28717
828-743-2411
www.highhamptoninn.com

The Chef

Sean Ruddy was born in New York City, became a Florida transplant in his youth, then relocated to the North Carolina mountains when a job opportunity arose at Wildcat Cliffs Country Club in Highlands.

He started cooking at the age of eight when he fixed snacks for his mother, a single parent, so she would have something to eat when she got home from work. One of his favorite childhood memories is hearing her bragging to her friends about the English muffin pizzas he made for her, using ketchup, onions, and some Parmesan cheese.

Sean started working part-time in restaurants when he was about 15. After high school, he went to the Florida Culinary Institute in West Palm Beach, graduating in 1995. Following a few subsequent jobs, he was offered a position in the Cayman Islands, so "off I went for a few months to the wealthy little island, where I had to find my own niche in Caribbean cooking," he recalls. "Caribbean cooking is a mix of many different cultures—Indian, Asian, and South American—so I learned from the locals about using the fresh local ingredients and spices."

Chef Ruddy later completed studies in food and wine pairing at the Culinary Institute of America in St. Helena, California. "I feel that any great dish should be paired properly with a great wine, so as to complement each other utilizing the balance between fats and acids," he says.

When he describes his style, he hearkens back to the Caribbean. "I think that experience was one that I use today. Even though I cook mostly 'New Southern' cuisine now, you will sometimes find a Caribbean spice or two in some of my dishes." He starts with the best and freshest ingredients he can find. "Keep it local and simple, yet well seasoned," he advises. "I like Low Country cooking, Cajun and Creole."

He hit the proverbial "big leagues" in the mountains when he was named executive chef at the Greystone Inn in Lake Toxaway, North Carolina. During his tenure, the inn was named one of the top 15 places to stay in the United States by *Condé Nast Traveler*. It was also awarded a AAA Four Diamond award every year he was there.

In 2008, Sean became the executive chef at High Hampton Inn and Country Club, where he continues to cook Southern favorites with a twist. "I like taking different styles of cooking from all different regions and bringing it south," he says. "Cooking is an act of love, and it requires a special touch to make it appealing to everyone."

Chef Ruddy provides this advice for anyone who aspires to be a chef: "If you are considering this career, keep in mind you will work harder than you ever have. You will work every weekend and holiday, even when your family is celebrating Thanksgiving, Christmas, New Year's Eve, Valentine's Day, the Fourth of July, or any other holiday. You will work long, hot hours on your feet. But when a guest tells you, 'That was the best meal I have ever eaten in my life,' it makes it all worthwhile. And no matter how much training and experience you have, keep this in mind: you're only as good as the last meal you served."

When Sean cooks for himself and his family, he likes comfort food. "Let me braise a lamb shank or some short ribs for about four hours and then sit down with a nice glass of Pinot Noir," he says.

The Inn and Restaurant

Wade Hampton III, who owned this land in the 1800s, was one of the wealthiest men in the South. He opposed secession but devoted part of his fortune to raising and equipping a cavalry regiment for the Confederacy, rising to the rank of major general during the Civil War. Combat led to the death of his son and other family members, as well as the loss of family wealth. He nevertheless served as governor of South Carolina and as United States senator during Reconstruction.

After the last members of a later generation of the Hampton family died without heirs in 1922, E. L. McKee of Sylva, North Carolina, bought the property. The McKee family constructed a two-story inn, but fire destroyed it in 1932. A larger three-story inn with chestnut-bark siding was constructed over the next year, providing employment for 20 men during the Depression. Descendants of the McKee family continue to own and operate the inn, along with several other enterprises in the area.

The resort sprawls across 1,400 acres, including mountain lakes and streams for swimming, boating, and fishing. Guests have opportunities for golf, tennis, and spa services. The inn was constructed in the Adirondack shingle style. The website describes the ambience as "sanctuary-like." The rooms have no electronic "intrusions," although television and modern communications are available in the lobby and public areas. Lodging is provided in more than a hundred wood-walled rooms, suites, and cottages.

Men are required to wear jackets for dinner, except on the occasional casual evening. The kitchen staff shops local fresh markets to buy cheeses and other goods. Vegetables come from the Cashiers Farmers Market, which uses local growers, so the inn's tomatoes, berries, and melons are always "the freshest and best you can get," according to Chef Ruddy. The dining room is famous for its fried chicken and fresh mountain trout. Tapas selections are offered in the Rock Mountain Tavern.

High Hampton Inn and Country Club provides special programs to entertain children in summer. The property is listed on the National Register of Historic Places. *Tampa Bay* magazine remarked, "The slow-paced, homey comforts and cheerful personnel make every moment here a pleasure."

Chef Ruddy has been featured in the *Knoxville News Sentinel*. He has hosted 12 episodes of "Carolina Kitchen" on the Asheville ABC television affiliate. The High Hampton Inn has been showcased on WUNC-TV and on WSPA in Greenville, South Carolina. Among others, *Atlanta, Birmingham, Knoxville, Garden & Gun, WNC*, and *Our State* magazines have published articles about the inn.

Chicken Saltimbocca Southern-Style
Photo by Theodore Flagg

The Recipe

Chicken Saltimbocca Southern-Style
Serves 4

Chef's Note

"This recipe gives me a chance to utilize some fantastic local ingredients. I have taken a classic dish and put a taste of the South in it. The goat cheese that I use is from a small farmstead dairy named Three Graces Dairy in Marshall, just north of Asheville. I usually go to the outdoor fresh market to get this luscious delight. The other twist in the dish is the local country ham. I love when the fresh crowder peas (also known as field peas) come into season early in the summer, and they can be readily available at most any good local fresh market. Make sure you get them shelled to spare yourself the agony of shelling them. The apricot glaze is a nice contrast to the crunchy outside of the chicken and the saltiness of the country ham and the creaminess of the goat cheese. This recipe is really pretty easy to make, and you can start the peas earlier in the day and prepare the chicken breasts in advance and have them ready for the oven stage of the recipe 20 minutes before you are ready to serve."

Crowder peas and green beans

Chef's Note

"Some ham hocks are saltier than others, so I do not recommend adding salt until the flavor of the ham hock has incorporated with the peas."

4 cups freshly shelled crowder peas
1 slice hickory-smoked bacon, diced
½ sweet Vidalia onion, diced
1 cup green beans, trimmed and cut into small pieces
1 smoked ham hock
1 quart chicken or ham stock
salt and pepper to taste

Chicken

4 boneless, skinless chicken breasts, trimmed
4 fresh sage leaves
4 ounces goat cheese
4-ounce slice country ham, diced fine
1 egg
4 tablespoons cool water
1 cup all-purpose flour
½ teaspoon salt
1 teaspoon freshly ground pepper
2 cups panko breadcrumbs
2 cups canola oil

    2 tablespoons softened butter, divided
    1 shallot, minced fine
    4 dried apricot halves, sliced in small pieces
    ¼ cup brandy
    ¼ cup apricot preserves
    ¼ cup water

CROWDER PEAS AND GREEN BEANS

Soak peas overnight in water in refrigerator.

In a medium-sized saucepan over medium-low heat, cook bacon until it starts to render. Add onions and cook until onions become translucent. Add peas, green beans, ham hock, and stock and bring to a boil. Turn down to a simmer and cook for 1 to 2 hours on low heat until peas become soft. Remove ham hock, let cool, and remove meat from bone. Chop up meat and add it to peas. Adjust seasonings. Drain and serve.

CHICKEN

Place chicken breasts between sheets of wax paper or plastic film and gently pound until thinner and even in thickness. Place 1 sage leaf on inside part of each breast. Combine goat cheese and country ham and place about 2 tablespoons of mixture in center of each breast. Beat egg, add cool water, and beat together. In a separate bowl, season flour with salt and pepper. Set up 3 different bowls for breading—1 with breadcrumbs, 1 with flour, and 1 with egg wash. Gently roll chicken over goat cheese mixture like a cigar; fold the ends in before completely rolling over. Insert toothpicks to hold breasts together. Heat oil in an iron skillet over medium heat. At the same time, preheat oven to 350 degrees. Allow oil to reach about 350 degrees. Place rolled chicken first in flour, coating evenly, then in egg wash, then in breadcrumbs. Carefully place each breast in hot oil and brown evenly on all sides. When golden brown, place chicken on paper towels to drain, then place on a sheet pan in the oven for about 20 minutes. Use a meat thermometer to make sure internal temperature reaches 165 degrees.

Apricot glaze

In a small saucepan, melt 1 tablespoon of the butter and cook shallots over medium-low heat until they just begin to brown. Add apricot pieces and brandy away from heat. Let brandy cook off for 2 to 3 minutes. Add preserves and water. Let simmer a few minutes more. Add remaining 1 tablespoon butter and whisk in away from heat. Brush over chicken.

To present

Remove toothpicks from chicken. Slice chicken ¾-1-inch thick. Arrange four slices along the side of the plate. Be sure apricot glaze has been generously applied. Ladle peas and beans along center of plate. Garnish with colorful fruit or heirloom tomato slices.

Travis Boswell

Travis Boswell
Photo by
SCB Photography

The Orchard

905 N.C. 107 South
Cashiers, N.C. 28717
828-743-7614
www.theorchardcashiers.com

The Chef

Travis Boswell was born in Miami, Florida. His family moved to Cashiers when he was nine. The Boswells wanted a lifestyle change and bought the Oakmont Lodge. When Travis was 18, his father built and opened the White Goose Café on the lodge property.

Travis enjoys the beauty of the mountains. "On my day off, I love to go trail running with my dogs on one of the many mountain trails in the area, or spend the day on beautiful Lake Glenville with my family and friends," he says. "During the summer months, I love to take my children on mushroom hunts. Both my son and daughter have been going with me since they could fit in the backpack carrier and walk around. They both could spot and identify a chanterelle mushroom by the age of two and a half. A good day for me is finding four or five pounds of chanterelles with the children, then coming home and sautéing them for a topping on their hot dogs."

Travis's mother passed away when he was 11, after which his father assumed the role of cooking for the family. "I learned a lot from him," Travis says. "We would take turns cooking dinner. I always enjoyed cooking at home, and when the White Goose opened, it was natural to work there in the kitchen when needed. Of course, with a restaurant kitchen, food and equipment at my disposal, literally in my front yard, it was easy to take what I had learned at home and experiment and create new dishes for the restaurant. I took the foundation of what I had learned at the White Goose and used it in The Orchard's kitchen. It is there where creativity and experience came together. When that happens, a memorable, enjoyable meal is hopefully created for the guests."

He completed his formal education at UNC–Chapel Hill, graduating with a business degree and a concentration in marketing. The year afterward, he moved to Charleston, South Carolina, for a sales job. "I fell in love with the city, its food, and the Low Country lifestyle," he says. "I loved to go to the fish and vegetable markets on weekends and cook dinner for friends. It was there that I developed a fondness for Southern cuisine." His culinary education has been self-directed. "I read a lot of cookbooks and cooking magazines, watch a lot of Food Network TV shows. They were and still are great sources for not only learning, but to get ideas. I can't say I would follow a lot of the recipes I see, but they do give me ideas about doing new things." He adds, "Over the years, I have had some great cooks and chefs work with me in the kitchen. When you work with each other on a daily basis, you bounce ideas off one another, and you learn from that."

On the home front, Travis says his wife is "in love with risotto cakes I make, topped with a protein of choice and a roasted tomato and onion sauce, so I end up making a lot of that."

The Restaurant

The Orchard is housed in a hundred-year-old farmhouse. The ambience features "rustic elegance with mountain charm," according to the restaurant. The staff seeks to provide "quality, consistent, approachable food and service experiences." Most dishes grow out of Southern traditions. The set menu does not change often. "We have found what works, as far as what our customers like, and we fine-tune it from time to time," Chef Boswell says. "But the Sautéed Trout, the Orchard Chicken, or other regular menu items will taste the same every time somebody orders them. I think this is a key factor for any restaurant to be successful in the long term. People have favorite dishes, and that is why they come. I provide menu variety in our evening specials.

"I try to make sure that everything I cook is something I would enjoy eating. I remember the first year we opened The Orchard, one of the cooks (who did go to culinary school) asked me about a soup I was making. He said, 'What would make it better?' Years later, I still ask myself that about everything I make: 'What can I do to make this better?' What separates a good cook from a bad cook is knowing what it takes to make a dish better—not just knowing what it is, but also being able to execute that task."

The Orchard buys from local farmers and uses ingredients from the area whenever they are available. Among the farms it works with on a regular basis are Carolina Mountain Trout Farm, Sunburst Trout Farm (see page 291), Jolly Farms, and Dark Cove Farms. Other regional ingredients routinely incorporated are chicken from Ashley Farms, grits from Anson Mills and Adluh Mills, breader from House of Autry Seafood, and quail from Plantation Quail. But Chef Boswell adds, "I am not a die-hard local-food-or-nothing type of chef. I guess my business school background tells me that at the end of the day, the restaurant is still a business that needs to make a profit to survive. Don't get me wrong, I would rather use the local or regional small farmer, and I do for many items on our menu. But I have to ask myself, 'Is the availability and delivery going to be there when I need it? And if the price is more expensive than another item, is the difference worth the price to my customers?'"

The Recipes

Dark Cove Farms Goat Cheese and Spinach Salad
Serves 4

Balsamic vinaigrette
 ¼ cup sugar
 ¼ cup honey
 ½ tablespoon dry mustard
 1 teaspoon salt
 ⅔ cup balsamic vinegar
 2 tablespoons raspberry vinegar
 1 cup plus 1 tablespoon olive oil

Salad
 ¾ pound fresh baby spinach
 2 cups fresh seasonal berries (blueberries, strawberries, or raspberries, or sliced apples if berries are not in season)
 ½ cup julienned red onion
 4 Roma tomatoes, julienned
 1 pound Dark Cove Farms goat cheese, formed into 8 2-ounce disks and frozen

2 eggs
2 cups milk
2 cups Italian breadcrumbs
enough vegetable oil to coat bottom of pan
¾ cup walnuts, toasted

BALSAMIC VINAIGRETTE

Combine first 6 ingredients in a bowl and mix well with a hand mixer while slowly adding olive oil. Mixture should begin to thicken slightly and turn a dark brown.

SALAD

In a large bowl, combine spinach, berries, onions, and tomatoes. Toss with ½ cup balsamic vinaigrette. Remove goat cheese disks from freezer. Combine eggs and milk to make an egg wash. Dip cheese in egg wash, then in breadcrumbs. Shake off excess breadcrumbs and fry cheese in 350-degree vegetable oil for 1 minute; do not overcook or cheese will fall apart.

TO PRESENT

Divide salad mixture evenly on 4 plates. Place 2 goat cheese disks on top of each salad. Drizzle more vinaigrette on top and garnish with walnuts.

Pecan-Fried Trout on Cheese Grits with Honey Dijon Tartar Sauce and Black-Eyed Pea Corn Relish
Serves 4

Honey Dijon Tartar Sauce
    1 cup mayonnaise (preferably Duke's)
    ½ cup spicy brown mustard (preferably Gulden's)
    2 tablespoons honey
    ¼ cup homemade or favorite brand tartar sauce
    2 teaspoons capers
    1 teaspoon chopped parsley
    2 tablespoons white wine

Black-Eyed Pea Corn Relish

- 5 cups canned black-eyed peas, drained and rinsed
- 2½ cups blanched shoepeg corn
- 2 tablespoons diced Vidalia onion
- 2 tablespoons diced roasted red pepper
- 2 tablespoons diced red pepper
- 2 tablespoons diced roasted poblano pepper
- 1½ teaspoons chopped garlic
- ½ teaspoon salt
- ½ teaspoon pepper
- 2 tablespoons Tabasco sauce
- ¼ cup red wine vinegar
- ½ cup canola oil

Grits

- 2 cups vegetable stock
- 2 cups half-and-half
- 2 teaspoons kosher salt
- ½ teaspoon pepper
- 4 tablespoons unsalted butter
- 1 cup Anson Mills quick yellow grits
- ¾ cup shredded cheddar cheese

Trout

- ½ cup shelled pecans
- 2 cups seafood breader (preferably from House of Autry)
- ½ cup self-rising flour
- 2 eggs
- 2 cups milk
- 4 4- to 6-ounce rainbow trout fillets (preferably "Carolina Cut" from Carolina Mountain Trout Farm)
- 1 gallon peanut oil or vegetable oil for frying
- 1 cup fresh spinach

HONEY DIJON TARTAR SAUCE

Mix all ingredients well.

BLACK-EYED PEA CORN RELISH

Mix all ingredients well.

Pecan-Fried Trout
Photo by Wayan Photography

GRITS

Place all ingredients except grits and shredded cheddar in a heavy-bottomed pot over medium-high heat. Bring to a boil and gradually add grits while stirring with a whisk. Continue stirring until grits begin to bubble and are suspended in boiling water. Decrease heat to low. Cook for 25 to 30 minutes, occasionally whisking to keep grits from clumping and sticking to pot. If grits are too thick, add more stock as needed. Stir in cheese.

TROUT

Pulse pecans in a food processor to the size of corn kernels. Mix seafood breader, flour, and pecans together in a bowl. In a separate bowl, combine eggs and milk to make an egg wash. Dredge trout in egg wash, let excess drain off, then press fillets flesh side down into pecan flour so pecan pieces adhere. Turn fillets over and press skin side down into flour mixture. Fry in oil at 350 degrees for 3 minutes or until golden brown. While fillets are frying, wilt spinach in a small amount of boiling water, drain, and keep warm.

TO PRESENT

Spoon grits onto each of 4 plates. Top each with spinach. Place trout on top of spinach. Spoon sauce on top and garnish with relish.

Highlands

Nicholas Figel

Nicholas Figel
*Photo by Clinton O'Brien,
Fonck Films*

Cyprus

470 Dillard Road
Highlands, N.C. 28741
828-526-4429
www.cyprushighlands.com

308

The Chef

Nick Figel grew up working in his father's restaurant, On the Veranda, also in Highlands. "I did all the grunt work like washing dishes, then I set up salads and desserts," he says. "I learned from my dad how onions work. He showed me how onions are thought of as the mother vegetable—how so many sauces, soups, and other flavor bases start with onions. I learned so much just watching my dad make soups."

At Cyprus, he considers his style "peasant food in an international context—traditional, rough aesthetics where you see the beauty in street food and home cooking. I try to get as much soul into it as possible. There are many manifestations. A Belgian mussel dish has four main elements: fat from cream and butter, lemon, salt, and sour from beer. They all have to be balanced. The only way to monitor that is to taste it with an open mind and an open heart. That's the way you give it soul. My hand prints are on everything I cook. At the end of the day, it has to have soul—my soul.

"Many chefs have a focused style—Italian or French, for example. I stray from those traditions. My style is more playful and more energetic, sometimes loose. I strive for a relationship among elements—sweetness/saltiness, crispness/smoothness, color contrasts. So I'm always hunting for interesting relationships between foods and flavors. From the outside, you can't see how motivated I am. If a sauce separates unexpectedly, or if I or one of the other chefs overcooks something by accident, those things are catastrophic to us. That creates a constant fear of failure. It's always in the background.

"The best aspect of being a chef is the connection you make with customers. At one point, I was looking for recognition for particular recipes, attention for particular dishes. But now, it's more about pleasure, maybe communicating ideas the way an artist or a dancer communicates ideas. The other thing is how you have your hands and your mind involved in interplay with ingredients. Food is extraordinarily complex. Meats, lettuces, for example, are different from one day to the next. The opportunity to have my hands in these ingredients is just a great way to make a living. I used to regret having burns on my hands, olive oil on my sleeves. Now, I consider those things a blessing. It's part of how you become tied to nature and interact with the real world."

Outside the restaurant, Nick considers his options limited. "As cooks, we run on adrenaline," he says. "We can't really eat during service. If I'm at the restaurant after work, I like spinach and tofu. We make great ramen noodles by hand here, and I really like those with hot peppers. I eat those at least twice a week. At home, it's usually peanut butter and jelly sandwiches."

The Restaurant

The restaurant takes its name from the island of Cyprus. Many cultures have settled on the island over the centuries, so the food there reflects myriad influences, including European, Asian, and African. The island's main export is copper. The interior of the restaurant features copper in the décor—the bar is copper, for example. Walls painted in rich green and orange are illuminated by basket-style lanterns overhead.

Chef Figel likes the way different cuisines come together in the diverse dishes he prepares. He has interned in Milan and Venice, experiences that help him combine flavors.

Highlands has a history of second homes and a relatively older crowd. Many residents have been to a variety of restaurants, often in big cities, frequently some of the best in the country or even in the world. Chef Figel seeks to capitalize on their knowledge by creating a menu that provides novelty as well as value. "In other restaurants where I have worked, the mind-set is more closed, the creativity more limited, but the prices are higher," he says. "I tried to reverse that concept, to make an open scenario ensuring that customers can see everything we do. We have a vibrant kitchen. The ambience is a little loud. The music is energetic. The food is a little spicy. Nothing is stuffy here. Even our trash cans are out in the open."

Cyprus has been open since 2002. Kitchen personnel collaborate with Marker Mountain Farms to grow and harvest organic vegetables. Fish is usually an off-menu special rather than a set menu item, since the kitchen buys almost daily in its constant search for whatever is freshest. Staff members seldom know before early afternoon what kind of fish they will be preparing for the evening meal.

Recognition has come from *Garden & Gun* and *WNC* magazines and *The Laurel* newspaper. Cyprus is an Open Table Diner's Choice award winner, based on customer reviews. TripAdvisor users voted the restaurant the number-one destination in Highlands.

The Recipes

Marrow Bones
Serves 2

6 2-inch veal marrow bones, divided
1 cup beef scraps
1 cup odds and ends of onions, celery, and carrots
3 bay leaves
1 plum tomato, chopped
2 tablespoons Madeira wine
1 shallot
2 cloves garlic, chopped
½ cup milk
¼ cup cognac
lettuce leaves
4 figs
4 wedges orange
2 tablespoons horseradish
French bread, toasted

Preheat oven to 400 degrees. Place 4 of the marrow bones in a roasting pan with the scraps, veggie ends, and bay leaves. Roast uncovered for 40 minutes. Remove to a stockpot and cover with water. Gently simmer about 2 hours to reduce by ½. Strain soup so only stock remains. Add tomato and Madeira and reduce again until a dark syrup is simmering in the pan. This is the glacé. In a covered roasting pan, combine 2 remaining bones, shallot, garlic, milk, and cognac. Roast 20 minutes. Place the 2 bones from

Marrow Bones
Photo by Clinton O'Brien, Fonck Films

second step in center of plates. Dress with glacé and surround with lettuce leaves, figs, orange wedges, and a little bit of horseradish. Serve with
toasted French bread.

Lobster Ramen

Serves 4

> 7½ cups water, divided
> 2¼ cups unbleached King Arthur flour
> 1 lobster
> 1½ tablespoons dashi (bonito or mackerel flakes)
> 1½ tablespoons dry seaweed
> 6 large shiitake mushroom caps, cut into strips
> 2 cups rice flour
> 1 tablespoons red miso
> 4 scallions, sliced diagonally
> pepper to taste
> finely shredded cabbage
> hot sauce or hot chili oil
> soy sauce, if desired

Lobster Ramen
Photo by Clinton O'Brien, Fonck Films

Bring ½ cup of the water to a boil. Mix unbleached flour and hot water. Knead mixture on a wooden surface for about 15 minutes. Roll out to ¼-inch thickness and cut carefully into ⅛-inch strips using a straightedge. Set aside. Boil lobster in 4 cups of the water for 6 minutes. Remove lobster from water and remove claws and tail. Pull meat from claws and tail and chop coarse. Rinse out body to remove undesirable flavors and set it in a saucepan with remaining 3 cups water. Add dashi and seaweed. Simmer 10 minutes. In a separate pot, boil noodles for 90 seconds. Toss mushrooms in rice flour and sauté about 1 minute until tender. When lobster broth has reduced to about 2 cups, strain. Add miso, scallions, noodles, and lobster meat. Lightly season with pepper. Top with cabbage, mushrooms, and a few dashes of hot sauce or hot chili oil. A few drops of soy sauce go great with this dish, too.

Johannes Klapdohr

Johannes
Klapdohr
Photo provided by
Old Edwards Inn

Old Edwards Inn

445 Main Street
Highlands, N.C. 28741
828-526-8008
www.oldedwardsinn.com

314

The Chef

Johannes Klapdohr was born in Bad Kreuznach, Germany, located 45 miles west of Frankfurt. He moved to the North Carolina mountains in 2009. "This area of North Carolina reminds me of the Black Forest," he says. "This area provides the connections with nature and the seasons which are so important to a chef. I love the culture of the Appalachian people, and the hotel is a unique property. It has wonderful owners and managers and a lot of growth potential in the future."

Johannes hails from four generations of hoteliers. He started his apprenticeship and hotel school—which are combined in Germany—at the age of 15. After graduation, he spent the next 14 years gaining experience working for some of Europe's best hotels and chefs.

When asked who most influenced his professional career, Johannes cites three people. His father, his earliest mentor, prepared a classical, regional, seasonal style of cuisine. Karl Ederer at Restaurant Ederer in Munich was one of the first German chefs to gain fame for enhancing Bavarian regional cuisine and promoting sustainability. He focused on products that originated nearby and consistently worked on reinventing fine dining. And Eckard Witzigman, one of only four chefs in the world to be named "Chef of the Century" by *Gault & Millau*, was widely regarded as the best chef in Germany at the time. In Johannes's words, "It was 100 percent perfection that made his restaurant [Restaurant Aubergine] so different from everyplace else."

In 1996, Johannes moved to the United States to take the position of *chef de cuisine* at the famed Nikolai's Roof in Atlanta. In 2004, he became executive chef at The Lodge at St. Simons Island on the coast of Georgia, a Mobil Five Star, AAA Five Diamond resort. During Chef Klapdohr's time there, The Lodge was named Zagat's number-one small hotel in the United States, and *Golf Digest* rated it one of the top golf hotels in the world.

After that, he worked with The Chef's Garden in Ohio to help develop programs to provide chefs with sustainable-agriculture products such as micro greens, micro herbs, heirloom vegetables, specialty lettuces, and edible flowers. He brought farmers, chefs, and the public together to learn about healthy eating habits and to implement sustainable practices into daily life.

In April 2009, Chef Klapdohr rejoined Richard Delany, former general manager at The Lodge at St. Simons Island, to oversee culinary operations of the Old Edwards Inn. During his first three years at the North Carolina mountain resort, he transformed the kitchen operations, culinary program, and culinary staff to focus on producing and preparing clean, sustainable food for the restaurants and catering operations. In 2010, he started the first organic chef's garden in the area.

Chef Klapdohr's home cooking centers on vegetables, salads, and ingredients such as amaranth, couscous, and barley. "No refined carbohydrates, only organic meats and produce, only cold-pressed oils—simple food, not junk!" he says. "The world of vegetables is so versatile, it never gets boring." But when eating in restaurants, "I can enjoy opulent meals, because I eat healthy all week."

The Restaurant

Old Edwards Inn has several dining venues. Madison's, the main restaurant, receives consistent honors from *Wine Spectator* and boasts a Four Diamond rating from AAA. *Condé Nast Traveler* named Old Edwards Inn the number-one hotel spa in North America for 2010; in fact, the inn received the first-ever perfect score in the 20-year history of the readers' survey.

Dining at Old Edwards Inn combines Southern elegance, a strong commitment to the highest-quality sustainable ingredients, and a focus on health and nutritional value. "We want to show that we really care for our guests, and that it is entirely possible to eat healthy food that tastes great!" says Chef Klapdohr.

He maintains a philosophy that "respects nature. At Madison's, we want to let nature shine on the plate, to be creative while carefully manipulating ingredients, and to focus on preservation of flavor and nutritional value through the use of modern culinary techniques—*'cuisine naturel,'* if you will!"

According to Chef Klapdohr, kitchen personnel work with area growers "the old-fashioned way," visiting and talking several times a week, person to person. "We are also researching on the Internet to find out who is doing what. Before we decide who makes it onto our regular list of providers, we visit, find out about their commitment, and ensure that they share our ideas of caring. We are not fixated, however, on just local. I always believe that trade is part of human culture, and to me quality comes first! If I don't get the right quality locally, I will go further. Truffles, white asparagus, and olive oil are some examples of ingredients we just have to get from farther away." The menu pays respect to specific local suppliers and sustainable farms. "Madison's supports local farmers and uses sustainable ingredients wherever possible, many from our own organic garden," Chef Klapdohr says. "We appreciate the contributions of Dave Taylor Farms, Painted Hills Farms Beef, Sunburst Trout [see page 291], Ashley Farms, Jolley Farms, Eden Farms, Springer Mountain Farm, Chef's Garden, and Sweet Grass Dairy."

The Recipes

Fennel Pollen Sautéed Trout on Parsnip Purée with Fennel Coleslaw
Serves 4

Chef's note

"I prefer trout with the skin, but you could use skinless if you like that better. The Parsnip Purée as well as the coleslaw can be prepared in advance, but the trout should be served straight out of the pan onto the plate!"

Parsnip Purée

1 tablespoon butter
1 shallot, peeled and diced small
2 parsnips, peeled and diced ½ inch (not more than 2 cups)
salt and pepper to taste
2 cups chicken stock
½ cup heavy cream

Fennel Coleslaw

1 tablespoon mayonnaise
2 tablespoons crème fraiche (sour cream may be substituted if
    absolutely necessary)
1 tablespoon sunflower or grapeseed oil
½ teaspoon Dijon mustard
½ teaspoon horseradish
½ teaspoon lemon juice
½ teaspoon Worcestershire sauce
salt and pepper to taste
1 bulb fennel, quartered and sliced very thin (including greens,
    cut very fine)
1 small carrot, peeled and grated fine
1 teaspoon finely cut parsley

Trout

4 4- to 6-ounce trout fillets, skin on, boned
salt and pepper to taste
½ teaspoon fennel pollen (ground fennel seeds may be substituted if
    necessary)
¼ cup oil

fennel sprigs for garnish

Parsnip Purée

Heat a medium-sized pot over medium heat and melt butter. Add shallots and stir until translucent. Add parsnips and sauté about 2 minutes. Season with salt and pepper. Add stock to cover parsnips and bring to a boil. Turn down heat and cover pot. Simmer about 20 minutes until soft. Add cream and bring to a boil again. Purée mixture in a blender until consistency is smooth. Taste and season again.

Fennel Pollen Sautéed Trout
Photo provided by Old Edwards Inn

Fennel Coleslaw

In a medium-sized bowl, combine first 7 ingredients and season with salt and pepper. Add shaved fennel, fennel greens, carrots, and parsley and toss well. Set aside.

Trout

Season trout evenly on both sides with salt and pepper and fennel pollen. Heat oil over high heat in a large pan. Carefully place trout in pan skin side down; it is important that skin is dry. Turn heat to medium and sear trout about 2 minutes on skin side. Turn trout over and sear again for 2 minutes.

To present

Use a tablespoon to spread purée to create circles in the middle of 10-inch plates. Place trout on top of purée. Arrange Fennel Coleslaw on top of trout and garnish with green fennel sprigs.

Pecan- and Tupelo-Honey-Crusted Chicken on Wilted Mountain Greens

Serves 4

Chicken

¼ cup oil or clarified butter
4 8-ounce chicken breasts
salt and pepper to taste
1 teaspoon Tupelo honey
½ cup pecan flour
½ cup fine breadcrumbs

Wilted greens

1 tablespoon butter
2 shallots, peeled and sliced small
4 slices prosciutto, cut into fine strips
1 bunch chard, stems removed, leaves washed and cut into 1-inch widths
1 bunch kale, stems removed, leaves washed and cut into 1-inch widths
1 bunch collards, stems removed, leaves washed and cut into 1-inch widths
1 bunch turnip greens, stems removed, leaves washed and cut into 1-inch widths
sprinkle of nutmeg
salt and pepper to taste
¼ cup chicken stock

toasted pecans or crisp-fried prosciutto slices, if desired

CHICKEN

Heat a large pan over medium heat and add oil. Season chicken on both sides with salt and pepper. Place chicken skin side down into pan and sear about 2 to 3 minutes until skin is golden brown and crisp. Turn chicken over and sear 1 more minute. Remove chicken from pan and place on a rack. While chicken is still hot, brush skin side with honey. Mix pecan flour and breadcrumbs and sprinkle on top of honey so it covers all of the skin. The honey will make the crust stick to the chicken. Preheat oven to 400 degrees. Place rack with chicken in oven and bake about 10 minutes. Remove chicken from oven and let rest 4 minutes.

Pecan- and Tupelo-Honey-Crusted Chicken
Photo provided by Old Edwards Inn

Wilted greens

Heat a large pot over high heat and melt butter. Add shallots and prosciutto and stir until brown. Quickly add greens so shallots do not get too brown. Sauté for 2 minutes, constantly stirring with a wooden spoon. Season with nutmeg and salt and pepper. Add chicken stock so greens steam and wilt.

To present

Serve greens with liquid in bowls. Cut chicken into 6 quarter-inch slices and fan out over greens. Garnish with toasted pecans or crisp pieces of prosciutto, if desired.

Wolfgang Green

Wolfgang Green
*Photo provided by
Mindy Green*

Wolfgang's Restaurant & Wine Bistro

474 Main Street
Highlands, N.C. 28741
828-526-3807
www.wolfgangs.net

The Chef

He heard the boot steps of the police. He knew that if they caught him, he would spend the rest of his life in prison, in most unpleasant conditions. He had a contact in Hamburg who would take him in if he could get out. He knew the government was building a wall that would make escape much more difficult.

Wolfgang Green made it into West Germany on August 6, 1961. He remembers the date precisely. The Berlin Wall went up on August 13, sealing off East Germany from West Germany for another generation.

Born in Chemnitz, Saxony, in what was then East Germany, Wolfgang trained through the apprenticeship system. He subsequently applied to a large hotel that received 102 applications for 18 positions—six for each of three years, three male and three female. Wolfgang remains convinced he was awarded one of the slots because his father was among the three top soccer referees in East Germany.

The family in Hamburg gave him a home. But after about a year there, Wolfgang began seeking life outside Germany. He posted an advertisement in a restaurant-hotel magazine and received a response from the Sheraton Corporation about a new hotel it was opening in Jamaica. He spoke Russian and German but no English. Fortunately, the executive chef was German, so Wolfgang moved to Jamaica in 1962. He found life in the tropics "really strange" after East Germany. And he had to learn two languages—English and the local Jamaican dialect. He cooked in Jamaica for two years, the duration of his contract, then returned to Germany, where he worked another season. But he realized he didn't want to stay.

A new search led back to a tropical climate. Wolfgang became sous chef at the Mid Ocean Club in Bermuda. He stayed there about two years, then received a chance to return to Jamaica at a proverbial "hot new place," the Playboy Club. That slot lasted only a few months, as Wolfgang learned that the executive chef at the Sheraton where he had worked before was leaving. Although only about 24 years old, he applied and became the youngest executive chef on the island. He held the position at the

Sheraton for about six years. Then he got an offer to move to the Holiday Inn Resort, the largest property in Jamaica. He also married during that time. Wolfgang's newfound stability and the prospects of a family eventually led to concerns about crime in Jamaica. He applied for a transfer within the Holiday Inn group and was moved to the Rivermont in Memphis, Tennessee, one of the chain's flagship properties. A subsequent move took him to Louisiana as executive chef at the Baton Rouge Hilton. While there, he met Ella Brennan of the famous New Orleans restaurant family. That acquaintance led to executive chef positions at the illustrious Commander's Palace in New Orleans and Brennan's in Dallas, Texas.

He held several subsequent positions in Dallas and became involved with the Texas Chef's Association. The Texas Culinary Team, of which he was a member, won several competitions, including a silver medal in the largest international culinary competition, held every four years in Frankfurt, Germany. But corporate life eventually burned him out. In the late 1980s, he began looking for another position in the kitchen. He also married a second time. Wolfgang and his new wife traveled the eastern United States and landed in Highlands during Oktoberfest. The mountains reminded him of the more pleasant aspects of home.

But another job offer took him to Los Angeles. Awhile later, he heard about something that triggered a longtime dream. A cruise ship company was looking for a corporate food and beverage director. He mailed in a résumé and shortly thereafter found himself living in Hawaii and working for American Hawaii Cruises. He later returned to Dallas, where he was in charge of menu and product development for American Italian Foods, his first experience with a test kitchen. The company developed foods for airlines and other large operations. Yet he yearned for a smaller, hands-on role.

When some family members visited from Germany, Wolfgang vacationed with them in Highlands. Over the Fourth of July weekend in 1994, he decided to open his own restaurant. His wife was able to sell their house in Dallas, and they used the money to make a down payment on the restaurant. Wolfgang's thus opened in September 1994. The property had been in operation under former owners for 18 years.

The first two years were tough. Workers with professional kitchen experience were in short supply, so Chef Green contacted Johnson & Wales University in Charleston. The school subsequently made Wolfgang's part of its externship program. The restaurant is now an approved training site for both Johnson & Wales and the Culinary Institute of America in New York. Chef Green thus had access to good personnel but found he had to buy a double-wide mobile home to house four or five students at a time, since affordable lodging was not available for them in Highlands. Business steadily grew. Wolfgang's is now the largest independent restaurant in the area.

Chef Green confesses that he doesn't eat much at home. He is in the restaurant kitchen every night. His wife, Mindy, usually picks up something to take home. She handles all marketing and promotions.

The population of Highlands drops about 90 percent after Thanksgiving, so the restaurant is closed from January through mid-March. Wolfgang and his wife travel extensively during that time, often visiting the restaurant's clients at their primary homes in Florida. Wolfgang's love for the beach from his years in Jamaica remains intact, so they sometimes spend a couple of weeks in St. Kitts to enjoy the restaurant scene.

The Restaurant

Wolfgang's was originally known for German food. Although Chef Green is trying to overcome that reputation, two German items remain on the menu—Wiener Schnitzel and the Bavarian Platter. Otherwise, the restaurant is known for fresh seafoods and steaks. While vacationing in Key Largo, Chef Green made a connection with a seafood supplier he still uses.

In big cities, chefs can find a niche and draw a clientele on that basis. But in small towns like Highlands, customers have a wide range of interests, so a restaurant's menu must be eclectic and not confined to a particular genre. Chef Green tries to let customers guide what he serves, but he also picks up ideas from his travels. For example, he and his wife saw a great bar menu while visiting Germany. When they returned to North Carolina, they installed parts of that concept in their Wine Bistro—the casual section adjacent to the main dining area. Their facility is well suited to weddings, receptions, and other large parties.

Chef Green has been elected a member of the Academy of Chefs and holds a certified executive chef's degree from the American Culinary Federation. Wolfgang's has received numerous accolades. *Southern Living* rates it the best dinner spot in Highlands and a "perennial favorite." Feature articles have appeared in *Southern Accents, WNC, Our State, Outside,* and *Talk Greenville*. Chaines des Rotisseurs has held meals at the restaurant. And *Wine Spectator* has recognized Wolfgang's for its wine list every year for over a decade.

The Recipes

Veal Wolfgang
Serves 4

Chef's Note

"This dish, one of our bestsellers, evolved while trying to pay tribute to my time with the Brennan family. It doesn't use any dish that was actually on their menu but somehow reflects their philosophy."

Béarnaise sauce

2 shallots, minced
¼ cup champagne vinegar
¼ cup dry white wine
3 egg yolks
1 stick clarified butter, melted
salt and pepper to taste

Veal

12 2-ounce veal cutlets, pounded thin
2 tablespoons flour

Veal Wolfgang
Photo provided by Mindy Green

meat seasoning to taste (Paul Prudhomme brand recommended)
4 tablespoons olive oil
4 tablespoons butter
½ medium onion, diced
8 ounces fresh crawfish tails, peeled

4 large stalks rosemary

BÉARNAISE SAUCE

Combine shallots, vinegar, and wine in a small saucepan. Simmer over medium-high heat until reduced by ½. Remove from heat and set aside to cool. When liquid has cooled to warm, pour in blender and slowly blend in egg yolks. With blender running, add ⅓ of the butter in a slow, steady stream. Once mixture emulsifies, increase blender speed to high and add remaining butter. Season with salt and pepper and set aside. Keep warm.

Lightly dredge veal in flour and meat seasoning. Flash-sear on each side in hot olive oil. Remove veal from pan and drain oil. Let cool a little, then add butter and onions. Sauté until glazed. Add crawfish tails and heat thoroughly.

To present

Assemble veal and crawfish in layers on plates. Secure through middle with rosemary stalks. Top with Béarnaise sauce.

Strawberries Romanoff

Serves 4

Chef's Note

"This is a traditional recipe, simple and easy to prepare but stunning, and one of our most popular desserts, next to Bananas Foster," Chef Green says.

Romanoff sauce

  2 tablespoons blackberry jam
    or jelly
  2 tablespoons Cabernet Sauvignon

Strawberry mixture

  12 ounces fresh local strawberries,
    cleaned and sliced
  1 tablespoon brown sugar
  ⅓ teaspoon ground cinnamon
  ½ ounce Grand Marnier
  1 cup whipped cream
  ½ cup sour cream

  4 scoops premium-quality vanilla ice cream
  2 large strawberries, halved
  1 bunch fresh mint

Strawberries Romanoff
Photo provided by Mindy Green

ROMANOFF SAUCE

Bring jam or jelly and Cabernet Sauvignon to a quick boil. Chill.

STRAWBERRY MIXTURE

Place strawberries in a bowl. Add brown sugar and cinnamon and mix well. Add Grand Marnier. Add whipped cream and sour cream. Mix well with a wooden spoon.

TO PRESENT

Ladle Romanoff sauce into the bottom of 4 large wineglasses. Add 1 scoop ice cream, then top with strawberry mixture. Garnish with rest of Romanoff sauce, plus ½ strawberry and several mint leaves.

Index of Recipes

330

Index of Names